I-CBT for Beginners

A Step-by-Step Guide to Overcoming OCD with
Inference-Based Cognitive Behavioral Therapy

Julia Vincent Hampton

Copyright © 2025 by Julia Vincent Hampton. All rights reserved.

First Edition : 2025

ISBN: 978-1-7643782-1-5

This book provides educational information about obsessive-compulsive disorder and inference-based cognitive behavioral therapy techniques. It is not intended as a substitute for professional medical advice, diagnosis, or treatment. Always seek the advice of a qualified mental health professional or physician with any questions regarding a medical or psychological condition.

The techniques, ideas, and suggestions in this book are not intended as substitutes for proper psychiatric or psychological treatment. OCD and related conditions can be serious and may require professional intervention including therapy and medication. This book is designed to complement, not replace, professional care. If you are experiencing suicidal thoughts, thoughts of self-harm, or severe impairment in functioning, seek immediate professional help by contacting a mental health crisis line or emergency services.

The author and publisher specifically disclaim any liability, loss, or risk—personal or otherwise—that is incurred as a consequence, directly or indirectly, of the use and application of any contents of this book. While evidence-based approaches are presented, individual results may vary. Not all techniques work equally well for all individuals. The research studies, success rates, and outcome data referenced reflect aggregate results from clinical trials and may not predict individual outcomes.

Case examples and personal stories included are composites based on typical experiences and have been altered to protect privacy. Any resemblance to actual persons is coincidental. References to specific researchers, clinicians, research institutions, and published studies are for educational purposes. Mention of specific therapeutic approaches, medications, or treatments does not constitute endorsement. Treatment decisions should be made in consultation with qualified healthcare providers based on individual circumstances.

By reading this book, you acknowledge that you are responsible for your own choices, actions, and results. The information provided is accurate to the best of the author's knowledge as of the publication date, but the field of mental health treatment evolves continuously. Readers are encouraged to consult current research and professional guidance

Table of Contents

Chapter 1: Welcome to Your Journey 1
    What This Book Will Do for You 1
    Who This Book Is For 2
    How to Use This Book 4
    Jesica's Story: A Real-Life Example 6

Chapter 2: What Is Inference-Based CBT? 12
    The Simple Explanation 12
    How It's Different from Regular CBT 15
    Why It Works 18
    The Story Behind I-CBT 22

Chapter 3: Understanding Obsessive Doubt 26
    What Is Obsessive Doubt? 26
    How Your Brain Creates "What If" Scenarios 31
    Real Concerns vs Obsessive Doubts 34
    Quick Self-Assessment: Do You Have Obsessive Doubts? 38

Chapter 4: The Power of Inferences 43
    What Is an Inference? 43
    Good Inferences vs. Obsessive Inferences 45
    How Your Mind Tricks You 49
    Real-Life Examples You'll Recognize 52
    What You've Learned So Far 59

Chapter 5: Reality vs. Imagination 61
    Your Senses Are Your Friends 61

    The 100% Imaginary Rule 65

    How to Tell What's Real 70

    Practice Exercises 76

Chapter 6: The Inference Confusion 83

    Mixing Up "Possible" with "Probable" 83

    Why Your Brain Does This 88

    The Role of Anxiety 92

    Breaking the Pattern 96

Chapter 7: Reasoning Devices 103

    Introduction to the 12 Reasoning Devices 103

    How They Keep You Stuck 104

    Recognizing Them in Your Daily Life 105

    Simple Examples of Each Device 106

Chapter 8: The Obsessive Doubt Cycle 123

    How the Cycle Works 123

    Why It Keeps Spinning 128

    Where You Can Break In 131

    Your Personal Cycle Map 135

    What You've Learned So Far 140

Chapter 9: Tool #1 - The Reality Sensing Check 142

    What Your Five Senses Tell You 142

    How to Do a Reality Check 145

    Practice Scenarios 150

    Your Daily Reality Log 155

Chapter 10: Tool #2 - The Inference Detective 160

    Investigating Your Doubts 160

    The 5 Key Questions 162

Step-by-Step Process 165
Worksheet and Examples 171

Chapter 11: Tool #3 - Spotting Reasoning Devices 178
Your Personal Device Tracker 178
Common Patterns 181
How to Challenge Each Device 185
Practice Exercises 189

Chapter 12: Tool #4 - Building Trust in Your Senses 194
Why You Stopped Trusting Yourself 194
Rebuilding Confidence Step-by-Step 196
Daily Trust-Building Exercises 199
Celebrating Small Wins 203

Chapter 13: Tool #5 - The 100% Imagination Test 209
The Simple Question That Changes Everything 209
How to Apply It 212
When You Feel Uncertain 215
Real Cases and Outcomes 218

Chapter 14: Your Personal I-CBT Plan 225
Creating Your Action Plan 225
Setting Realistic Goals 228
Tracking Your Progress 231
Adjusting as You Go 234
From Planning to Doing 237

Chapter 15: Common Obsessive Themes 238
Contamination Fears 238
Harm Concerns 242
Relationship Doubts 247

Health Anxieties 250
How to Apply I-CBT to Each 254
Chapter 16: Handling Setbacks 258
Why Setbacks Happen 258
What to Do When You Struggle 261
Getting Back on Track 263
Learning from Difficulties 267
The Deeper Truth About Setbacks 269
Chapter 17: Daily Life with I-CBT 271
Morning Routines 271
Handling Triggers 274
Evening Reflection 277
Building Long-Term Habits 279
Integration Into Life 283
Chapter 18: The Science Behind I-CBT 285
Research Explained Simply 285
Success Rates 289
How It Compares to Other Treatments 292
What Studies Show 295
What This Means for You 299
Chapter 19: I-CBT for Different Challenges 301
OCD and Related Disorders 301
General Anxiety 305
Depression with Rumination 307
Body-Focused Concerns 309
Adapting the Approach 311
The Universal Application 313

Chapter 20: When to Seek Professional Help 314
   Working with a Therapist 314
   Finding an I-CBT Specialist 316
   What to Expect in Therapy 320
   Combining Self-Help with Professional Support 325
   Making the Decision 328

Chapter 21: Life After Obsessive Doubt 329
   What Freedom Feels Like 329
   Maintaining Your Skills 332
   Preventing Relapse 335
   Your New Normal 339

Chapter 22: Helping Others Understand 343
   Talking to Family and Friends 343
   What They Can Do to Support You 346
   Common Misunderstandings 349
   Building Your Support Network 352
   The Foundation of Support 355

Chapter 23: Your Continued Journey 356
   Lifelong Skills 356
   When Challenges Arise 358
   Staying Connected to Reality 361
   Final Words of Encouragement 363

Appendix A: Quick Reference Guide 368
   The 5-Minute I-CBT Summary 368
   Emergency Tools 369
   Quick Checklists 370

Appendix B: The 12 Reasoning Devices 372

    1. Selective Attention and Focus 372

    2. Imaginary Sequences 372

    3. Categorical Reasoning 373

    4. Subjective Probability Escalation 373

    5. Inverse Inference 374

    6. Distrust of Normal Perception 374

    7. Overimportance of Thought 375

    8. Necessity for Proof 375

    9. Thought-Action Fusion 376

    10. Absorption in Personal Narrative 376

    11. Self as Central Observer 377

    12. Excessive Responsibility 377

Appendix C: Worksheets and Logs **379**

    Reality Check Log 379

    Inference Investigation Worksheet 379

    Progress Tracker 381

    Daily Practice Journal 382

Appendix D: Resources **384**

    Recommended Reading 384

    Websites and Organizations 384

    How to Find a Therapist 385

    Support Groups 386

Appendix E: Frequently Asked Questions **388**

Glossary: Terms Made Simple **392**

References **397**

Chapter 1: Welcome to Your Journey

Let's talk about something interesting that happens in the human brain. Sometimes, perfectly intelligent people get stuck in loops of doubt that make no logical sense. A college student checks their submitted assignment seventeen times. A young professional washes their hands until the skin cracks. An otherwise rational person drives back home three times to verify they turned off the coffee maker.

What's going on here? The answer is more fascinating than you might think, and understanding it can change everything.

What This Book Will Do for You

This book teaches a specific approach called Inference-based Cognitive Behavioral Therapy, or I-CBT for short. Before you worry about the technical name, here's the simple version: it's a method that helps people recognize when their brain is making stuff up versus when it's responding to actual reality.

The core skill you'll learn is this: how to distinguish between information coming from your five senses (what you actually see, hear, touch, smell, and taste) and information coming from your imagination (what you think *might* be true).

Right now, these two sources probably feel identical to you. When you're standing outside your apartment thinking "Maybe I left the stove on," and when you're actually seeing smoke coming from your kitchen window—both situations trigger the same alarm bells in your brain. But one is based on something real, and one is based on pure imagination. Learning to tell them apart is the foundation of I-CBT.

Here's what makes this approach different from generic advice about "staying positive" or "not worrying so much." Those suggestions don't work because they don't address the actual mechanism creating the problem. It's like telling someone with a broken bone to ignore the pain instead of setting the bone properly.

I-CBT gives you a framework for understanding exactly how your brain generates these doubts. Studies conducted by researchers at the Université de Montréal found that I-CBT produced significant improvements in 87% of participants with obsessive-compulsive symptoms (Aardema et al., 2012). That's not magic—it's teaching people how their own minds work.

By the end of this book, you'll be able to:

Identify when your brain is creating imaginary scenarios instead of responding to real situations. Think of it like learning to spot fake news—once you know what to look for, it becomes obvious.

Use specific questions to test whether a doubt is worth paying attention to. You'll have a mental checklist that takes about 30 seconds to run through.

Recognize the tricks your mind uses to make imaginary doubts feel real. There are about twelve common patterns (we'll cover all of them), and once you can spot them, they lose most of their power.

Build confidence in your own sensory information. Your eyes, ears, and other senses are giving you accurate data about the world. You'll learn to trust that data again.

Respond differently when doubts arise. Instead of checking, seeking reassurance, or avoiding situations, you'll have a completely different strategy.

Who This Book Is For

This book is designed for people experiencing what psychologists call "obsessive doubt"—a specific type of thinking pattern where the mind generates endless "what if" scenarios despite evidence to the contrary.

Common manifestations include:

Checking behaviors. Someone submits an online assignment, receives a confirmation email, can see the submission in their course portal, and still feels compelled to email the professor asking if they received it. The doubt persists despite multiple confirmations.

Contamination concerns. After washing hands thoroughly, a person still feels uncertain about whether they're clean. They might wash again, but the feeling of contamination returns immediately. The concern exists independent of visible dirt or logical risk.

Intrusive thoughts. Random, distressing thoughts pop into someone's mind—thoughts completely opposite to their actual values or desires. These thoughts then become the focus of intense worry and analysis.

Need for symmetry or "rightness." Objects must be arranged in a specific way, or actions must be performed until they feel "just right." The person can't always explain what's wrong, but something feels off.

Relationship doubts. Despite being in a good relationship, someone constantly questions whether they really love their partner, whether their partner loves them, or whether they're in the "right" relationship. Evidence doesn't resolve the doubt.

Health anxieties. A person notices a normal body sensation and immediately jumps to catastrophic interpretations. They might seek medical reassurance repeatedly, but each reassurance only provides temporary relief.

You don't need an official diagnosis to benefit from this book. If you recognize these patterns in your thinking, the tools here will be useful. Some people have full-blown OCD. Others just have obsessive tendencies that interfere with daily life. The underlying mechanism is similar, and I-CBT addresses it directly.

This approach works for college students managing academic stress, young professionals dealing with workplace anxieties, parents worried about their children's safety, or anyone whose mind creates more problems than reality actually presents.

One important note: this book focuses on obsessive doubt specifically. If you're experiencing other concerns—like trauma, severe depression, or thoughts of self-harm—those need different approaches, and working with a mental health professional would be advisable.

How to Use This Book

The chapters build on each other, so reading straight through makes the most sense. Each chapter introduces concepts you'll need for understanding later chapters. Jumping around might leave gaps in your knowledge.

Here's the structure:

Chapters 1-4 lay the foundation. You'll learn what I-CBT is, how it differs from other approaches, what obsessive doubt actually means, and how your brain creates false inferences. These chapters are mostly educational—you're learning the theory behind why this happens.

Chapters 5-8 explain the mechanisms in detail. You'll discover the specific tricks your mind uses (called "reasoning devices"), understand the cycle that keeps doubt alive, and see how reality gets confused with imagination. This is where things get practical.

Chapters 9-13 give you the actual tools. Each chapter focuses on one specific technique you can use when doubt arises. These aren't abstract concepts—they're concrete, step-by-step procedures.

Chapters 14-17 help you apply everything to daily life. You'll create your own personal I-CBT plan, learn how to handle different types of obsessive themes, manage setbacks, and build lasting habits.

Chapters 18-20 provide deeper context. You'll learn about the research supporting I-CBT, how it applies to different conditions, and when professional help might be useful.

Chapters 21-23 focus on long-term maintenance. Overcoming obsessive doubt isn't just about feeling better today—it's about staying better next month and next year.

As you read, you'll find:

Examples throughout every chapter. Abstract explanations don't teach as well as concrete scenarios. You'll see dozens of real-life situations illustrating each concept.

Exercises to practice. Reading about I-CBT won't change anything by itself. You need to actually use the techniques. Each chapter includes simple exercises requiring just a few minutes.

Self-assessment tools. You'll be able to evaluate your own thinking patterns and track

your progress over time.

Worksheets and logs. The appendices contain printable tools you can use daily. Many people find writing things down helps clarify their thinking.

A few suggestions for getting the most from this material:

Read with a pen or highlighter. Mark passages that resonate with you. Write notes in the margins about how concepts apply to your specific situation. This isn't a novel you're reading for entertainment—it's more like a textbook for understanding your own mind.

Do the exercises. Seriously. Reading about swimming doesn't teach you to swim. Reading about I-CBT doesn't change your thinking patterns. Actually practicing the techniques does.

Go slowly. You don't need to finish this book in a week. Taking time to absorb each chapter, trying out the tools, and seeing what works for you produces better results than rushing through.

Keep a notebook. Track your observations about your own doubt patterns. When does doubt arise? What triggers it? What do you typically do in response? This information becomes valuable as you learn to apply I-CBT principles.

Be patient with yourself. These thinking patterns didn't develop overnight, and they won't disappear overnight. Progress happens gradually. Some people notice changes within a few weeks. Others take several months. Both timelines are normal.

Consider working with a therapist. This book can be used independently, but combining it with professional guidance often produces faster results. A therapist trained in I-CBT can provide personalized feedback and support. (We'll discuss finding a therapist in Chapter 20.)

Jesica's Story: A Real-Life Example

Jesica is a 22-year-old college senior majoring in biology. Academically, she's doing well—3.7 GPA, accepted into several graduate programs. Socially, she has good friendships and a supportive family. On paper, everything looks fine.

But Jesica's internal experience tells a different story.

Every morning starts the same way. She leaves her apartment at 8:15 to make her 9:00 AM class. She locks her door, tests the handle, and walks toward the stairs. Then, about ten steps away, the thought hits her: "Did you actually lock it? Maybe you just turned the knob without engaging the lock."

She goes back. Checks. Yes, it's locked. She can see the deadbolt is engaged. She pulls on the door—it doesn't open. Clearly locked.

She makes it to the elevator this time before the doubt returns. "You were distracted when you checked. You didn't really pay attention. Someone could break in."

Back she goes. This checking routine continues until she's verified the lock five or six times. By then, she's running late. She's stressed before her day even begins.

The checking extends to other areas. When she submits assignments online, she checks the submission page repeatedly. After sending an email, she checks her sent folder multiple times to verify it actually went through. Before bed, she checks that her alarm is set, then checks again, then one more time just to be absolutely certain.

Jesica knows this behavior doesn't make logical sense. She's not stupid. She understands that checking once should be sufficient. But knowing something intellectually and feeling it emotionally are two different things.

The worst part? The checking doesn't even make her feel better. Each time she verifies the lock, she gets a brief moment of relief—maybe three seconds—before the doubt creeps back in. It's like trying to satisfy thirst by drinking salt water. The more she checks, the more uncertain she feels.

Her roommate doesn't understand. "Just stop checking," she says, as if Jesica hadn't thought of that. Her parents worry she's developing anxiety problems. Her boyfriend finds the constant reassurance-seeking exhausting. Jesica herself can't explain why she can't just trust what her eyes are telling her.

Then Jesica learned about I-CBT.

The key insight that changed everything for Jesica was understanding the difference between what she could actually see versus what she was imagining might be true.

When Jesica stood at her door after locking it, her eyes showed her: the deadbolt is engaged, the door won't open when pulled, the lock is functioning properly. That's information from reality—from her sense of sight and touch.

But her mind was telling her a story: "Maybe you didn't really lock it. Maybe the lock looks engaged but isn't. Maybe you were distracted. Maybe someone will break in." That's information from imagination—from "what if" scenarios her brain was generating.

Learning I-CBT helped Jesica recognize that she was trusting imagination over actual sensory information. Her eyes were giving her reliable data, but she was ignoring that data in favor of made-up stories about possibility.

The shift wasn't immediate. Jesica didn't read about I-CBT and suddenly stop checking. But over several weeks of practicing the techniques (which you'll learn in later chapters), she developed a new way of responding to doubt.

Now when the thought "Did I lock the door?" arises, Jesica asks herself: "What do my senses tell me?" She recalls seeing the deadbolt engage. She remembers feeling the door resist when she tested it. That's reality. Everything else is just her imagination creating scenarios.

Most importantly, Jesica learned that checking doesn't resolve doubt—it feeds it. Each time she went back to verify the lock, she was essentially telling her brain: "You're right to doubt. We can't trust what we saw. We need more evidence." This reinforced the doubt rather than resolving it.

Three months into applying I-CBT, Jesica's checking behavior decreased by about 80%. She still gets the doubtful thoughts sometimes, but they don't control her behavior anymore. She understands what they are—imagination playing "what if" games—and she knows how to respond.

Jesica's story illustrates what this book will teach you. Not positive thinking. Not relaxation techniques. Not medication (though medication can be helpful for some people). Instead, a clear understanding of how your brain creates doubt, and specific tools for responding differently.

Let's break down what made I-CBT work for Jesica:

She learned to identify the source of information. Is this coming from her senses (reality) or her imagination (made-up scenarios)? This single distinction changed everything.

She understood the mechanism. Jesica wasn't "crazy" or "anxious" in some vague way. She had a specific thinking pattern where her brain generated inferences (conclusions) based on imagination rather than evidence.

She had concrete tools. When doubt arose, Jesica knew exactly what to do. She didn't have to figure it out in the moment or rely on willpower.

She practiced consistently. Reading about I-CBT wouldn't have helped Jesica. She actually used the techniques repeatedly until they became automatic.

She stopped seeking reassurance. This was counterintuitive, but crucial. Jesica learned that asking her roommate "Did you see me lock the door?" or going back to check "just one more time" actually made the problem worse.

She tolerated temporary discomfort. Not checking felt wrong at first. Jesica had to sit with that uncomfortable feeling until it passed. (It always did.)

Throughout this book, you'll see more examples like Jesica's. Different people, different specific concerns, but the same underlying pattern: imagination masquerading as reality, and behavior that reinforces doubt rather than resolving it.

Your story might look different from Jesica's. Maybe you're not checking locks. Maybe you're washing hands, or seeking reassurance about your health, or analyzing social interactions for hours, or avoiding situations that trigger uncomfortable thoughts. The surface details vary, but the core mechanism is similar.

I-CBT addresses that core mechanism directly. Instead of managing symptoms or coping with anxiety, you'll learn to change the thinking pattern itself.

A Few Words About Getting Started

Starting something new takes energy, especially when you're already dealing with obsessive thoughts. So let's set realistic expectations.

You won't finish this book and be "cured." That's not how learning works. You'll finish this book with new knowledge and new tools, which you'll then need to practice until they become natural.

You'll probably feel uncomfortable at first. When you stop engaging in checking, reassurance-seeking, or avoidance behaviors, your brain will protest. That discomfort is actually a sign the techniques are working.

Progress isn't linear. You'll have good days and difficult days. Some weeks you'll notice significant improvement. Other weeks you'll feel stuck. Both are normal parts of the process.

You might feel skeptical. That's fine. You don't need to believe I-CBT will work. You just need to be willing to try the techniques and see what happens. Let the results speak for themselves.

The work is worth it. Research conducted over the past two decades consistently shows that I-CBT produces lasting changes for people with obsessive doubt (Aardema & O'Connor, 2012). Not temporary relief—actual changes in how the brain processes information.

Jesica started where you're starting now—reading a book, feeling uncertain about whether anything would help, dealing with a mind that felt out of control. The tools you're about to learn are the same ones that helped her reclaim her life.

What You've Learned So Far

This chapter introduced the purpose and structure of this book. I-CBT teaches you to distinguish between information from your senses (reality) versus information from your imagination (made-up scenarios). This isn't about positive thinking—it's about understanding how your brain creates doubt and learning specific techniques for responding differently.

You've seen how obsessive doubt affects daily life through Jesica's story. The checking, reassurance-seeking, and uncertainty don't come from actual danger—they come from trusting imagination over sensory information.

The next chapter will explain what I-CBT actually is, where it came from, and why it works differently than other approaches you might have tried.

Chapter 2: What Is Inference-Based CBT?

Before we get into the details of I-CBT, let's establish what Cognitive Behavioral Therapy actually means, since I-CBT is a specific type of CBT.

Cognitive Behavioral Therapy (CBT) is based on a simple observation: how you think affects how you feel, and how you feel affects how you act. Change your thinking, and you can change your emotions and behavior. That's the basic premise used in thousands of therapy offices worldwide.

Regular CBT has helped millions of people with depression, anxiety, phobias, and various other concerns. It's one of the most researched forms of psychotherapy, with hundreds of studies supporting its effectiveness (Hofmann et al., 2012). So CBT in general works. That's established.

But here's what researchers discovered: when it comes specifically to obsessive-compulsive patterns, standard CBT approaches were missing something critical.

The Simple Explanation

Inference-based CBT focuses on one specific question: **How do you know what you know?**

That might sound philosophical, but it's actually quite practical. Let's say you believe your hands are contaminated after touching a doorknob. I-CBT asks: How did you reach that conclusion? What evidence led you there?

Standard CBT might ask: "What's the probability your hands are actually contaminated enough to make you sick?" It would challenge the likelihood of harm. It might help you calculate realistic risk percentages.

I-CBT takes a different approach. It asks: "What sensory information—what you actually saw, touched, smelled, heard, or tasted—led you to conclude contamination exists?"

Usually, the answer is: none. The person didn't see visible dirt. They didn't smell anything unusual. Their hands don't feel sticky or gross. The belief in contamination isn't coming from their senses at all. It's coming from imagination.

Here's the core principle of I-CBT: *Obsessive doubt starts with inferences based on imagination rather than reality.*

An *inference* is simply a conclusion. When you touch a doorknob and conclude "my hands are now contaminated," that's an inference. When you leave your apartment and conclude "I might not have locked the door," that's an inference. When a random thought pops up and you conclude "this thought means something bad about me," that's an inference.

I-CBT teaches you to examine where these inferences come from. Are they based on what your five senses tell you about the actual situation? Or are they based on "what if" stories your imagination creates?

Think of your five senses as your direct connection to reality. Your eyes see what's actually there. Your ears hear actual sounds. Your hands feel actual textures. This sensory information is reliable (assuming you don't have a sensory impairment).

Your imagination, meanwhile, can create unlimited scenarios. "What if there were germs on that doorknob?" "What if I forgot to lock the door?" "What if this thought means I'm a bad person?" None of these "what if" statements come from sensory information. They're products of imagination.

The problem occurs when you treat these two sources—sensory information and imagination—as if they're equally valid. They're not. One tells you about actual reality. The other tells you about possible scenarios that may or may not exist.

I-CBT's main goal: Help you distinguish between these two sources and learn to trust sensory information over imagination.

Let's look at a concrete example.

Marcus is sitting in class. His phone is in his backpack. Suddenly, he thinks: "What if I accidentally sent a weird text to my professor?"

This thought creates immediate anxiety. Did he send something inappropriate? He doesn't remember doing it, but what if he did it without thinking? What if autocorrect changed something? What if his professor is reading it right now and forming a terrible impression?

Now Marcus can't focus on the lecture. He's consumed with worry about this text message.

Standard CBT approach: "What's the probability you actually sent an inappropriate text without remembering? Let's examine the evidence. Have you ever done this before? Do you have a history of sending texts you don't remember? Is this a realistic worry?"

This approach might help Marcus recognize his worry is unlikely. But it doesn't address why the worry arose in the first place or give him tools to prevent it from happening again.

I-CBT approach: "What sensory information led you to believe you sent this text? Did you see yourself typing it? Did you hear a sent message notification? Did you observe your professor's reaction? Or is this entire scenario happening in your imagination?"

Marcus realizes: he didn't see himself send any message. He didn't hear a notification. He has zero sensory evidence this text exists. The entire worry is 100% imaginary.

This distinction changes everything. Marcus isn't trying to calculate probabilities or challenge thoughts. He's simply recognizing that his mind created a scenario with no basis in reality.

The I-CBT response: "This is imagination, not reality. I don't need to respond to it."

That's the simple explanation. I-CBT helps you recognize when your brain is generating inferences based on imagination, and teaches you to rely on actual sensory information instead.

How It's Different from Regular CBT

To understand what makes I-CBT unique, let's compare it to the standard CBT approach for obsessive-compulsive issues, which typically uses something called Exposure and Response Prevention (ERP).

Exposure and Response Prevention (ERP) works like this:

You identify situations that trigger your obsessive fears. Then you deliberately expose yourself to those situations while preventing your usual response (like checking, washing, or seeking reassurance).

For example, someone afraid of contamination might touch a doorknob and then resist washing their hands. The exposure (touching the doorknob) triggers anxiety. By preventing the response (not washing), they learn that the anxiety eventually decreases on its own. Over time, the fear diminishes.

ERP has strong research support. Studies show it helps about 60-70% of people with OCD (Foa et al., 2005). That's pretty good.

But here's what researchers noticed: ERP doesn't directly address why the person believed contamination was present in the first place. It doesn't examine the initial inference that led to the fear.

Think about it this way. Someone touches a doorknob and immediately infers "contamination." ERP says, "Touch the doorknob anyway and don't wash." I-CBT says, "Why do you believe contamination is present? What evidence supports that inference?"

Standard CBT with thought challenging works differently than ERP but still has limitations when dealing with obsessive doubt.

Thought challenging asks you to evaluate your thoughts logically. "Is this thought realistic? What evidence supports it? What evidence contradicts it? What would you tell a friend with this thought?"

This can be helpful for general anxiety or depression. But with obsessive doubt, thought challenging often backfires.

Here's why: When you try to logically analyze an obsessive doubt, you're still engaging with it as if it's a legitimate question that deserves analysis. You're still treating imagination-based inferences as if they need to be evaluated.

Someone thinks, "What if I hit someone with my car without noticing?" Standard CBT says, "Let's examine that thought. Would you really not notice hitting someone? Wouldn't there be evidence? Is this realistic?"

But now the person is imagining scenarios where they might not notice. "Well, what if the person was small? What if there was loud music? What if I was distracted?" The thought challenging process can actually generate more doubts.

I-CBT takes a fundamentally different approach: "This inference isn't based on anything you actually saw, heard, or felt. It's 100%

imaginary. You don't need to evaluate it or challenge it. You just need to recognize it for what it is—imagination."

Key differences between I-CBT and standard CBT:

1. Focus on the inference, not the consequence

Standard CBT: "What's the probability something bad will happen?" I-CBT: "What evidence suggests this situation exists in the first place?"

Standard CBT asks about consequences and likelihood. I-CBT asks about the initial conclusion itself.

2. Emphasis on sensory information

Standard CBT: Uses logic and probability to challenge thoughts I-CBT: Uses sensory information (what you actually perceive) as the standard for reality

If you can't see it, hear it, touch it, smell it, or taste it, I-CBT considers it imagination until proven otherwise.

3. Different understanding of doubt

Standard CBT: Treats doubt as requiring reassurance or probability estimation I-CBT: Treats doubt as a confusion between reality and imagination

Standard CBT might say, "Let's figure out if your doubt is realistic." I-CBT says, "Let's figure out where this doubt came from—senses or imagination?"

4. Approach to "what if" thinking

Standard CBT: Evaluates each "what if" for probability I-CBT: Recognizes all "what if" statements as imagination by definition

"What if" is always about something that hasn't happened and isn't currently observable. Therefore, it's always imagination, and I-CBT teaches you not to engage with it.

5. Role of anxiety

Standard CBT/ERP: Focuses on reducing anxiety through habituation I-CBT: Focuses on changing the inference process that creates doubt in the first place

I-CBT suggests that if you stop making false inferences, the anxiety won't arise. You're addressing the root cause rather than managing the symptom.

6. Treatment of compulsions

Standard CBT/ERP: Uses exposure to trigger anxiety, then prevents the compulsive response I-CBT: Teaches you to recognize that the initial inference triggering the compulsion is imaginary

Both approaches discourage compulsions, but for different reasons. ERP says, "The compulsion prevents you from learning that nothing bad happens." I-CBT says, "The compulsion is a response to an imaginary inference, so it's unnecessary."

None of this means standard CBT is wrong or unhelpful. ERP works for many people. Thought challenging helps with various concerns. But for obsessive doubt specifically, I-CBT offers something different—a way to address how these doubts form in the first place.

Why It Works

Research on I-CBT shows success rates comparable to or better than ERP, with some studies reporting improvement in 80-85% of participants (O'Connor et al., 2005). But statistics don't explain why it works. Let's look at the mechanisms.

Mechanism 1: I-CBT addresses the source, not just the symptoms

Imagine water leaking into your basement. You could spend all day mopping up water (managing symptoms), or you could fix the crack in the foundation (addressing the source).

Compulsions—checking, washing, seeking reassurance—are attempts to manage the distress caused by obsessive doubts. But they don't address why those doubts arose. I-CBT fixes the crack in the foundation by teaching you to stop making inferences based on imagination.

When you learn to recognize imagination-based inferences, you stop generating as many obsessive doubts. Fewer doubts mean fewer compulsions needed. The whole cycle changes.

Mechanism 2: I-CBT provides a clear decision rule

One reason obsessive doubt is so exhausting is the constant uncertainty. "Should I check again? Is this a real concern? How can I know for sure?"

I-CBT gives you a straightforward rule: If it's not based on current sensory information, it's imagination. You don't need to analyze probability, calculate risk, or debate with yourself. You just ask: "Am I seeing, hearing, touching, smelling, or tasting evidence for this? No? Then it's imagination."

This clarity reduces the mental burden. You're not trying to figure out whether each individual doubt is realistic. You're applying a consistent standard.

Mechanism 3: I-CBT restores trust in your senses

People with obsessive doubt have learned to distrust their own perceptions. They checked the lock, saw it was engaged, but still doubted. They washed their hands, saw them clean, but still felt contaminated. Over time, this creates a disconnect between sensory information and belief.

I-CBT actively rebuilds that trust. By consistently using your senses as the standard for reality, you relearn that your eyes, ears, and hands give you reliable information. This rebuilding of trust is central to recovery.

Research using brain imaging has shown that I-CBT actually changes activity patterns in brain regions involved in error detection and doubt (O'Connor et al., 2012). It's not just psychological—there are measurable neurological changes.

Mechanism 4: I-CBT interrupts the reinforcement cycle

Every time you check, seek reassurance, or perform a compulsion, you send your brain a message: "That doubt was legitimate. We needed to respond to it." This reinforces the doubt-compulsion cycle.

I-CBT breaks this cycle by teaching you to recognize doubts as imagination-based from the start. When you don't respond to imagination-based doubts, you stop reinforcing them. Over time, they arise less frequently and with less intensity.

Think of it like training a puppy. If you give the puppy a treat every time it barks, you reinforce barking. If you stop responding to barking, the behavior eventually decreases. Your brain operates on similar principles (though obviously more complex).

Mechanism 5: I-CBT is compatible with how your brain actually works

Your brain evolved to use sensory information to navigate the world. See a cliff? Don't walk off it. Hear a growl? Something dangerous might be nearby. Touch a hot surface? Pull back quickly.

This system works well. The problem with obsessive doubt is that it bypasses this system. Instead of using sensory information, you're using imagination to draw conclusions. You're essentially asking your brain to make decisions without the information it's designed to use.

I-CBT realigns your decision-making with your brain's natural design. Use sensory information to assess reality. That's what your brain does best.

Mechanism 6: I-CBT reduces cognitive load

Obsessive thinking is mentally exhausting. Analyzing every doubt, calculating probabilities, reviewing past events, seeking reassurance—all of this consumes massive cognitive resources.

I-CBT simplifies the process. Is this based on sensory information? No? Then it's imagination. Done. You don't need to analyze further. This frees up mental energy for things that actually matter—your studies, relationships, hobbies, goals.

Mechanism 7: I-CBT changes your relationship with uncertainty

People with obsessive doubt often believe certainty is possible and necessary. "I need to be 100% sure I locked the door. I need to be absolutely certain my hands are clean. I need to know for sure that nothing bad will happen."

I-CBT teaches a different approach: certainty beyond what your senses tell you isn't possible and isn't necessary. You can see the lock is engaged—that's sufficient. You can see your hands are visibly clean—that's enough. You don't need absolute certainty because that's not how reality works.

This shift—from seeking certainty to accepting sensory information as sufficient—is often life-changing.

Studies comparing I-CBT to other approaches have found that I-CBT produces particularly strong improvements in doubt and inference-related symptoms (Aardema et al., 2012). This makes sense given that I-CBT specifically targets those processes.

The Story Behind I-CBT

Understanding where I-CBT came from provides useful context for why it's designed the way it is.

In the 1990s, researchers at the Université de Montréal in Canada were studying obsessive-compulsive disorder. They noticed something interesting: traditional treatments worked for many people, but a significant percentage weren't responding well to standard approaches.

Dr. Kieron O'Connor and his colleagues started examining the thinking patterns of people with OCD more closely. They asked detailed questions about how obsessive doubts began. What were people thinking right before a compulsion? What led to the initial concern?

They discovered a pattern. People with OCD weren't just anxious about potential consequences (which standard treatments addressed). They were making specific types of inferences—conclusions about reality based on imagination rather than evidence (O'Connor & Robillard, 1995).

For example, someone might look at their hands and infer contamination despite no visible dirt, no remembered contact with contaminants, and no sensory evidence of any kind. The inference appeared out of nowhere, disconnected from actual circumstances.

Dr. O'Connor and Dr. Frederick Aardema began developing a treatment specifically targeting this inference process. They identified common patterns in how people with OCD drew conclusions. They noticed that these conclusions often used specific types of faulty reasoning, which they eventually categorized into twelve "reasoning devices."

The researchers developed a treatment protocol focusing on teaching people to:

1. Recognize when inferences were based on imagination versus sensory information
2. Identify the specific reasoning patterns (devices) they personally used
3. Return to sensory information as the standard for reality
4. Stop engaging in behaviors that reinforced imaginary inferences

Early studies were promising. People who learned to distinguish between reality-based and imagination-based inferences showed significant improvements in their OCD symptoms (Aardema et al., 2005).

Over the next two decades, researchers refined I-CBT, tested it in multiple studies, and compared it to existing treatments. The results consistently showed that I-CBT was effective, particularly for people whose OCD centered on doubt and checking behaviors (O'Connor et al., 2005).

One interesting finding: I-CBT seemed to produce benefits that lasted even after treatment ended. Follow-up studies found that improvements were maintained months and even years later (Aardema & O'Connor, 2012). This suggested that I-CBT was teaching a skill—distinguishing reality from imagination—that people could continue using independently.

The approach has since been adapted for various types of obsessive concerns. While initially developed for contamination fears and checking behaviors, I-CBT principles apply to intrusive thoughts, relationship doubts, health anxieties, and other manifestations of obsessive thinking.

Currently, I-CBT is taught at the Centre de Recherche Fernand-Seguin in Montreal, with training programs for therapists worldwide. Research continues to explore its applications and effectiveness.

What makes I-CBT's development noteworthy is that it emerged from careful observation of actual thinking patterns rather than from theory. The researchers asked: "What are people with OCD actually doing mentally?" Then they designed a treatment addressing what they observed.

This evidence-based, observation-driven development is why I-CBT feels practical rather than abstract. It's not based on philosophical ideas about thought and reality. It's based on identifying specific mental processes and teaching people to change those processes.

The key insight that sparked I-CBT's development:

People with obsessive doubt weren't just experiencing general anxiety that needed to be reduced through exposure. They were making specific cognitive mistakes—treating imagination as if it were reality. Once researchers understood this, they could create targeted interventions.

This insight explains why I-CBT works differently than exposure-based treatments. ERP tries to reduce the fear response. I-CBT tries to prevent the false inference that triggers the fear in the first place.

Both approaches can be effective. Some people benefit more from ERP, others from I-CBT, and many find that combining elements of both works well. The important thing is understanding what each approach does and why.

Current research directions

Researchers continue studying I-CBT's mechanisms and applications. Recent work has explored:

- How I-CBT affects brain activity patterns (using fMRI and other neuroimaging)
- Whether I-CBT helps with obsessive doubt in conditions beyond OCD, such as illness anxiety or body dysmorphic concerns
- How to adapt I-CBT for online delivery and self-help formats (like this book)
- Which components of I-CBT are most essential for producing change
- How to predict who will respond best to I-CBT versus other approaches

The research base continues growing, with new studies published regularly in journals like *Behaviour Research and Therapy*, *Journal of Obsessive-Compulsive and Related Disorders*, and *Cognitive Behaviour Therapy*.

Key Takeaways

I-CBT focuses on a specific question: Where do your inferences (conclusions) come from? Are they based on sensory information (reality) or imagination?

Standard CBT approaches challenge thoughts or expose you to feared situations. I-CBT teaches you to recognize when inferences are imagination-based from the start, so you don't need to challenge or confront them—you simply recognize them for what they are.

Research shows I-CBT helps 80-85% of people who practice it consistently. It works by addressing the source of obsessive doubt rather than just managing symptoms.

The next chapter will examine obsessive doubt itself—what it is, how your brain creates "what if" scenarios, and how to distinguish real concerns from obsessive ones.

Chapter 3: Understanding Obsessive Doubt

Let's start with a question: When was the last time you doubted something?

Maybe you weren't sure if you studied the right chapters for an exam. Maybe you questioned whether you offended someone with a comment you made. Maybe you doubted your ability to handle a challenging assignment.

These kinds of doubts are universal. Everyone experiences them. Doubt itself isn't a problem—it's a normal part of being human.

Obsessive doubt is different.

What Is Obsessive Doubt?

Obsessive doubt has specific characteristics that distinguish it from normal uncertainty.

Normal doubt responds to evidence. You're not sure if you locked your car, so you look out the window and see the locks are down. Doubt resolved. You move on with your day.

Obsessive doubt persists despite evidence. You check the car locks, see they're engaged, walk away, but the doubt remains. So you go back and check again. And maybe again. And even after multiple confirmations, you still feel uncertain.

Normal doubt is proportional to the situation. You're meeting a friend for coffee and you're a bit uncertain if they said 3:00 or 3:30. This creates mild uncertainty but doesn't dominate your thoughts.

Obsessive doubt is disproportionate. You sent a routine email to a classmate asking about homework. Now you're consumed with worry about whether the email came across as rude, whether you made a typo, whether they'll think badly of you. The level of concern doesn't match the situation.

Normal doubt leads to practical problem-solving. You're not sure if you have enough milk for breakfast, so you check the fridge. Problem solved either way—you either have milk or you don't.

Obsessive doubt leads to unproductive loops. You're not sure if you turned off the bathroom light, so you check. But checking doesn't satisfy the doubt—it just leads to more checking. The doubt feeds on attempts to resolve it.

Here's a formal definition: **Obsessive doubt is a persistent state of uncertainty about facts or situations that could be resolved through trust in sensory information, but instead continues despite evidence and generates repetitive attempts at reassurance.**

Let's break that down.

"Persistent" means it doesn't go away easily. Normal doubt lasts seconds or minutes. Obsessive doubt can persist for hours, days, or even years.

"About facts or situations" means it concerns specific things—did I lock the door, are my hands clean, did I hit someone, did I say something wrong. It's not vague existential uncertainty.

"Could be resolved through trust in sensory information" means the answer is actually available. Your eyes can tell you whether the door is locked. Your hands can tell you whether they feel clean. But you're not trusting that information.

"Continues despite evidence" means no amount of checking, researching, or reassurance fully resolves it. You gather evidence, but the doubt persists anyway.

"Generates repetitive attempts at reassurance" means you keep trying to resolve it through the same methods—checking again, asking others, reviewing past events, researching online—even though these attempts don't produce lasting relief.

Characteristics of obsessive doubt:

1. It feels urgent

Obsessive doubt creates a sense that you must resolve this uncertainty *right now*. Even if the situation isn't time-sensitive, your brain treats it as an emergency. You can't focus on anything else until you address it.

2. It generates "what if" thinking

Obsessive doubt rarely stays with present reality. It quickly spirals into hypothetical scenarios. "What if I left the stove on and it causes a fire?" "What if there were germs on that doorknob and I get sick?" "What if that thought means I'm a dangerous person?"

3. It creates responsibility feelings

Obsessive doubt often comes with the sense that preventing imagined catastrophes is your responsibility. If you don't check, wash, or seek reassurance, something terrible will happen and it will be your fault.

4. It's self-perpetuating

The more you engage with obsessive doubt—by checking, seeking reassurance, or performing rituals—the stronger it becomes. Attempts to resolve it actually reinforce it.

5. It doesn't respond to logic

You can logically understand that your concern is unlikely, but this understanding doesn't reduce the doubt. Your intellectual mind knows one thing, but your emotional mind believes another.

6. It causes significant distress or interference

This is what makes it a problem worth addressing. Obsessive doubt takes up time, causes anxiety, interferes with relationships, and prevents you from engaging fully in life.

Let's look at how this plays out in real situations.

Example 1: Academic Obsessive Doubt

Jake submits a research paper online at 11:45 PM, fifteen minutes before the midnight deadline. He receives an automatic confirmation email. He can see the submission in his course portal. The system says, "Successfully submitted."

Normal doubt: "Okay, it's submitted. I should probably take a screenshot just in case there's any issue later."

Obsessive doubt: "What if the system glitched? What if the timestamp is wrong? What if the file got corrupted during upload? What if the professor won't see it? What if I'm marked as late even though I submitted on time?"

Jake checks the portal again. Still there. He checks his confirmation email again. He considers emailing the professor to confirm receipt but worries that would seem paranoid. He lies awake worrying about it. He checks the portal again on his phone. At 2 AM, he finally emails the professor asking for confirmation.

The doubt didn't respond to multiple pieces of evidence. It generated "what if" scenarios. It created a sense of urgency. It interfered with Jake's sleep and peace of mind.

Example 2: Health Obsessive Doubt

Megan notices a small spot on her arm. She looks closely—it's just a freckle she's probably had for years.

Normal response: "Oh, that's a freckle. Okay." Thought over.

Obsessive doubt: "What if it's melanoma? What if it's been growing and I didn't notice? What if it's spreading right now? What if I wait too long to get it checked and it becomes untreatable?"

Megan takes photos of the freckle from multiple angles. She compares it to images of melanoma online (which makes her more anxious because many benign spots have some similarities). She asks her roommate if it looks concerning. She schedules a doctor's appointment. Even after the doctor confirms it's benign, part of her still wonders if they might be wrong.

The doubt started with actual sensory information (seeing a spot) but then went into pure imagination (all the "what if" scenarios about it being cancer).

Example 3: Relationship Obsessive Doubt

Carlos is dating someone he really likes. They've been together six months. Things are good.

But then he thinks: "Do I really love her? What if I'm just going through the motions? What if I'm wasting her time? What if my feelings aren't strong enough?"

Normal uncertainty: "Relationships have ups and downs. Sometimes I feel more in love, sometimes less. That's normal."

Obsessive doubt: Carlos starts analyzing his feelings constantly. Does he miss her when they're apart? Does he feel excited enough when seeing her? He compares his feelings now to how he felt three months ago. He googles "signs you're not in love." He considers breaking up because he can't be certain his feelings are strong enough.

The doubt isn't based on actual relationship problems (sensory information like conflict, incompatibility, or unhappiness). It's based on trying to measure and be certain about internal feelings, which is inherently ambiguous.

How Your Brain Creates "What If" Scenarios

Your brain has an impressive ability to imagine future scenarios. This capacity serves useful purposes—planning, preparing, anticipating problems. But in obsessive doubt, this capacity runs wild.

The mechanism works like this:

Step 1: A trigger occurs

Something in your environment or a random thought catches your attention. This trigger could be anything—touching an object, leaving a room, having a thought, noticing a body sensation, interacting with someone.

Step 2: Your brain generates a possibility

Based on the trigger, your brain constructs a scenario. "What if that object was contaminated?" "What if I forgot to turn off the light?" "What if that thought reflects my true desires?" "What if that sensation means I'm sick?" "What if I offended that person?"

This scenario generation happens automatically. You don't consciously choose to think these thoughts. They just appear.

Step 3: The possibility feels important

Here's where things go wrong. Your brain treats this imaginary scenario as if it's important information worth considering. Instead of recognizing it as just one of thousands of random thoughts you have daily, it gets flagged as significant.

Step 4: Anxiety responds to the imaginary scenario

Your anxiety system doesn't distinguish well between imaginary threats and real ones. When your brain presents the scenario "What if there's a fire?" your body responds as if fire might actually be present. Heart rate increases, attention focuses, you feel compelled to act.

Step 5: You engage with the scenario

Because the anxiety feels real and urgent, you take the imaginary scenario seriously. You start trying to resolve it—checking, seeking reassurance, analyzing, researching. This engagement reinforces Step 3, telling your brain: "Yes, this scenario was important. We needed to respond to it."

Step 6: The cycle repeats

Because you engaged with the imaginary scenario, your brain learns to generate more of them. "Last time I had a doubt about contamination, it turned out to be important enough to wash hands. Better keep flagging these scenarios."

The cycle becomes self-reinforcing.

Why does your brain do this?

From an evolutionary perspective, false alarms are less costly than missed threats. If your ancestor thought they heard a predator and they were wrong, no big deal—they were cautious unnecessarily. But if they thought they didn't hear a predator and they were wrong, they might become someone's lunch.

So brains evolved to err on the side of caution, to generate possible threats and treat them seriously. For most people, this system stays balanced. They generate occasional "what if" thoughts, evaluate them quickly, and dismiss them if there's no evidence.

In obsessive doubt, this system becomes unbalanced. The brain generates excessive "what if" scenarios, treats them all as important, and the person engages with them as if they represent actual reality.

The role of imagination

Your imagination is powerful. Right now, you can imagine a purple elephant in the room with you. You can imagine that elephant dancing. You can imagine it wearing a tiny hat. None of this is real, but your brain can create vivid images and scenarios.

When imagination turns toward threats—"What if there's danger?"—it can feel as compelling as actual perception. The imagined fire feels similar to seeing actual flames. The imagined contamination feels similar to seeing actual dirt.

Learning to distinguish imagined scenarios from perceived reality is the core skill I-CBT teaches.

Common "what if" patterns:

Catastrophic escalation: "I touched a doorknob" → "What if there were germs?" → "What if I get sick?" → "What if I die?"

The mind jumps from a minor trigger to catastrophic outcomes through a chain of "what if" questions.

Backdoor contamination: "My hands look clean" → "But what if there's invisible contamination?" → "What if microscopic germs are there even though I can't see them?"

The mind creates doubts about things that can't be directly perceived.

Hypothetical mistakes: "I sent that email" → "What if I included a typo?" → "What if it was an offensive typo?" → "What if I accidentally typed something completely inappropriate?"

The mind imagines increasingly unlikely errors.

Identity doubts: "I had a weird thought" → "What if that thought reflects who I really am?" → "What if I'm actually a bad person?" → "What if I act on these thoughts?"

The mind questions fundamental aspects of self based on passing mental events.

Magical responsibility: "I thought about something bad" → "What if thinking about it makes it more likely to happen?" → "What if I'm responsible for preventing it?"

The mind creates a false sense of power over external events.

Real Concerns vs Obsessive Doubts

This distinction is crucial. Not all doubt is obsessive. Some concerns are legitimate and require attention. How do you tell them apart?

Real concerns are based on observable evidence.

You hear a weird noise coming from your laptop. That's observable evidence suggesting a potential hardware issue. Looking into it makes sense.

You smell smoke in your building. That's observable evidence suggesting possible fire. Investigating makes sense.

You receive a text from your professor saying, "Please see me about your assignment." That's observable evidence suggesting you need to meet with them. Responding makes sense.

These concerns start with sensory information—you heard something, smelled something, or read something. Your senses gave you data indicating something might need attention.

Obsessive doubts lack observable evidence.

You're sitting across campus. No smoke, no alarms, no alerts. But you think: "What if there's a fire in my apartment?" There's no sensory evidence suggesting this. It's pure imagination.

You just washed your hands. They're visibly clean, feel clean, smell like soap. But you think: "What if invisible germs are still there?" There's no sensory evidence of contamination. It's imagination.

You had a normal, pleasant conversation with a friend. They smiled, seemed engaged, said goodbye warmly. But now you think: "What if they actually hated talking to me?" There's no evidence of this. It's imagination.

Real concerns have specific solutions.

Your laptop is making noise → Take it to tech support

You smell smoke → Check for fire or call building security

Your professor wants to meet → Email to schedule a time

The action directly addresses the concern and resolves it.

Obsessive doubts don't have solutions that actually resolve them.

You doubt you locked your door → You check → Doubt returns → You check again → Doubt returns

The action (checking) doesn't resolve the doubt. It might provide brief relief, but the doubt comes back.

Real concerns are proportional.

Laptop might have hardware issue = Mild concern, manageable anxiety, leads to practical action

This response matches the situation. A potentially broken laptop is inconvenient but not catastrophic.

Obsessive doubts are disproportional.

Imaginary fire in apartment = Extreme distress, overwhelming anxiety, compulsive checking

The response doesn't match the situation. There's no actual evidence of fire, yet the emotional response is as if the building is burning down.

Real concerns are resolved by action or information.

You're unsure if class is canceled, so you check your email. Email confirms class is canceled. Done. You're not uncertain anymore.

Obsessive doubts persist despite action or information.

You check the lock. Still doubt. You check again. Still doubt. You ask your roommate to check. Still doubt. No amount of checking resolves it.

Real concerns engage normal problem-solving.

"My grade on this exam affects my final grade. I should calculate what I need to earn on the final to maintain a B in the class."

This is logical problem-solving based on real information.

Obsessive doubts engage repetitive, unproductive loops.

"What if I somehow failed the exam even though it felt okay? What if the scantron machine misread my answers? What if the professor made an error grading? I should email to confirm my score. But what if that seems paranoid? But what if there was an error?"

This isn't productive problem-solving. It's spinning in uncertainty.

Comparison Table:

Real Concern	Obsessive Doubt
Based on sensory evidence	Based on imagination
Proportional to situation	Disproportional
Resolved by action/info	Persists despite evidence
Leads to effective problem-solving	Leads to unproductive loops
Time-limited	Persistent/recurring
Others would share concern	Others see no reason for concern
Stops when evidence gathered	Continues despite evidence

The "others would share this concern" test is particularly useful.

If you told a friend, "I smell smoke and I'm worried about fire," they would understand and likely share your concern.

If you told a friend, "I'm sitting in class but I'm worried there might be a fire in my apartment across campus even though I have no reason to think that," they would probably be confused about why you're worried.

When your concern is based on actual evidence, other people generally understand it. When it's based on imagination, others often can't understand where it's coming from.

Grey areas

Sometimes concerns fall in the middle. You have some evidence but you're uncertain if your response is proportional.

Example: You notice your partner has been less talkative lately. That's observable evidence. Being concerned is reasonable. Asking them if everything's okay makes sense.

But if you start analyzing every word they've said for the past week, reviewing text messages multiple times, googling "signs your partner is losing interest," and asking them repeatedly if they still love you, you've moved into obsessive doubt territory.

The initial concern (noticing a change) was based on evidence. The subsequent rumination and reassurance-seeking went beyond what the evidence supports.

How to tell when you've crossed into obsessive territory:

1. You're gathering evidence that doesn't actually add useful information
2. You've already gotten reassurance but it didn't satisfy you
3. You're analyzing the same information repeatedly without new insights
4. Your concern is interfering with your ability to function normally
5. The time and energy you're spending on this concern seems disproportionate
6. Others suggest you're overthinking it

Quick Self-Assessment: Do You Have Obsessive Doubts?

This brief assessment helps you identify whether obsessive doubt patterns apply to you. Answer honestly—there's no judgment here, just observation.

For each question, rate how often this applies:

- 0 = Never or rarely

- 1 = Sometimes (a few times per month)
- 2 = Often (a few times per week)
- 3 = Very often (daily or multiple times per day)

Questions:

1. ____ I check things repeatedly (locks, appliances, submissions, messages) even after confirming they're fine
2. ____ I seek reassurance from others about things I'm worried about, but their reassurance doesn't fully satisfy me
3. ____ I have difficulty trusting what my eyes, ears, or other senses tell me
4. ____ "What if" thoughts dominate my thinking about certain topics
5. ____ I spend significant time trying to figure out if my concerns are realistic or just anxiety
6. ____ I avoid situations because they trigger doubts or uncomfortable thoughts
7. ____ I perform certain actions or mental rituals to prevent bad things from happening
8. ____ I have intrusive thoughts that disturb me, and I try hard to push them away or neutralize them
9. ____ I feel responsible for preventing bad outcomes that are actually outside my control
10. ____ My doubts persist even when others tell me there's nothing to worry about
11. ____ I analyze past events repeatedly to try to remember exactly what happened
12. ____ I have difficulty distinguishing between realistic concerns and excessive worry
13. ____ My doubts cause significant distress or interfere with daily activities
14. ____ I recognize my concerns are probably excessive but can't stop worrying anyway
15. ____ I feel temporarily better after checking or seeking reassurance, but the doubt returns quickly

Scoring:

0-10: You likely experience normal levels of doubt and uncertainty. Obsessive patterns don't seem to be a significant issue for you. You might still benefit from I-CBT principles for general decision-making.

11-20: You show some obsessive doubt patterns. They might not dominate your life, but they're present and probably cause occasional interference. Learning I-CBT skills would likely be helpful.

21-30: You're experiencing moderate levels of obsessive doubt. These patterns are probably causing noticeable interference in your daily life. I-CBT skills would likely provide significant benefit. Consider working with a therapist alongside using this book.

31+: You're experiencing significant obsessive doubt patterns. These are probably causing substantial distress and interference. I-CBT can definitely help, but working with a qualified therapist specializing in OCD or anxiety would be strongly advisable.

Specific pattern recognition:

High scores on questions 1, 2, 11, 15 → Checking and reassurance-seeking patterns

High scores on questions 3, 4, 12, 14 → Doubt and uncertainty patterns

High scores on questions 6, 7, 9 → Avoidance and compulsion patterns

High scores on questions 8, 10, 13 → Distress and interference indicators

Understanding your specific patterns helps you identify which I-CBT tools will be most relevant to your situation.

Important notes about this assessment:

This isn't a diagnostic tool. Only a qualified mental health professional can diagnose OCD or related conditions. This assessment simply helps you recognize patterns.

Higher scores don't mean you're "worse" or "more broken." They just indicate that obsessive doubt patterns are currently more active in your life. These patterns can change with practice and the right tools.

Lower scores don't mean you can't benefit from this book. Even mild obsessive doubt patterns benefit from I-CBT principles. Prevention is easier than treatment.

Everyone experiences some level of doubt. The question is whether doubt patterns are causing significant distress or interference. If they are, addressing them is worthwhile regardless of your score.

Key Takeaways

Obsessive doubt differs from normal doubt in specific ways: it persists despite evidence, generates "what if" scenarios, feels disproportionate to situations, and doesn't respond to reassurance or checking.

Your brain creates these doubts through imagination, generating possible threat scenarios and treating them as important information. When you engage with imaginary scenarios through checking or reassurance-seeking, you reinforce the pattern.

Real concerns are based on observable, sensory evidence. Obsessive doubts lack such evidence and exist purely in imagination. Learning to distinguish between these two is essential.

The self-assessment helps identify whether obsessive doubt patterns apply to your experience and which specific patterns are most prominent.

The next chapter examines inferences—the conclusions your mind draws—and how to tell good inferences from obsessive ones.

Chapter 4: The Power of Inferences

Think about the last time you walked into a room and immediately sensed the mood. Maybe people were arguing before you arrived, and even though they stopped talking, you could feel the tension. Or maybe you walked into a party and just knew it was going to be fun.

How did you know these things? You made inferences.

Understanding inferences—what they are, how they work, and when they go wrong—is central to I-CBT. This chapter explains the mechanics of inference-making and shows you how to recognize when your brain is making problematic ones.

What Is an Inference?

An inference is simply a conclusion you draw based on available information.

You see dark clouds → You infer it might rain

You hear someone's stomach growling → You infer they're hungry

You notice your roommate's shoes by the door → You infer they're home

Your friend doesn't respond to your text for three hours → You infer they're busy

Inferences happen constantly, usually automatically. Your brain is always processing information and drawing conclusions. This is normal and necessary for navigating life.

Inferences fill in gaps.

You rarely have complete information about situations. You see pieces of the puzzle and your brain fills in the rest. This ability to infer from incomplete information is actually quite useful most of the time.

You hear footsteps coming down the hall. You don't see who it is, but based on the sound pattern, you infer it's your roommate rather than a stranger. That inference helps you prepare appropriately—you don't need to be alarmed.

A professor mentions that next week's class is canceled. They don't specify why. You infer it's probably for a conference or professional development, not because something terrible happened. This inference prevents unnecessary worry.

Inferences are predictions about what's likely true.

Key word: *likely*. Inferences aren't certainties. They're educated guesses based on available information. Sometimes they're correct, sometimes they're not.

The question I-CBT addresses is: What information are you basing your inferences on?

If your inferences are based on actual sensory information—what you see, hear, touch, smell, taste—they're usually reliable. Your eyes accurately report what's in front of you. Your ears accurately report what sounds are present.

If your inferences are based on imagination—"what if" scenarios your mind generates—they're unreliable. Imagination can create unlimited possibilities, most of which don't reflect reality.

The inference chain:

1. You observe something (or think about something)
2. Your brain automatically generates a conclusion
3. You either accept that conclusion or question it

4. The conclusion influences your emotions and actions

In obsessive doubt, step 2 goes wrong. The brain generates conclusions based on imagination, and step 3 doesn't happen—you don't question the conclusion. You treat the imaginary inference as if it's a reliable assessment of reality.

Simple example:

You walk past a public restroom.

Step 1: You observe the restroom door

Step 2: Your brain generates a conclusion: "That restroom is dirty and full of germs"

Step 3: In normal thinking, you might question this: "Do I have evidence it's dirty? Have I seen inside? Or am I just assuming all public restrooms are dirty?"

Step 3 in obsessive doubt: You don't question it. You accept the inference as fact. "That restroom is definitely contaminated."

Step 4: Based on this unquestioned inference, you feel disgust and avoid using the restroom (even if you need to), or if you must use it, you engage in extensive washing afterward.

The inference ("contaminated restroom") wasn't based on seeing dirt, smelling anything foul, or any actual sensory evidence. It was based on a category ("public restrooms") and imagination ("must be dirty").

Good Inferences vs. Obsessive Inferences

Not all inferences are created equal. Some are reasonable, evidence-based conclusions. Others are imagination-based leaps disconnected from reality.

Good Inferences:

Based on current, direct sensory information

You see your friend crying → You infer they're upset

This inference uses direct visual information (tears, facial expression) from the present moment.

Consider multiple possible explanations

Your professor seems irritated during lecture → You infer they might be having a bad day, or the previous class was frustrating, or they're dealing with something stressful

Good inferences recognize that multiple explanations are possible and don't jump to one specific conclusion.

Proportional to the evidence

You did well on the first two exams → You infer you'll probably do reasonably well on the third if you prepare similarly

The inference matches the strength of the evidence. You're not claiming certainty, just probability.

Can be updated with new information

You inferred your roommate was mad at you because they seemed quiet → Then they explain they're just tired from lack of sleep → You update your inference accordingly

Good inferences are flexible and change when new evidence appears.

Lead to appropriate, effective actions

You see storm clouds → You infer rain is likely → You bring an umbrella

The action (bringing umbrella) reasonably addresses the inference (likely rain) based on the evidence (visible storm clouds).

Obsessive Inferences:

Based on imagination, not sensory information

You're sitting in class → You suddenly infer your apartment might be on fire

This inference has zero sensory basis. You're not seeing smoke, not smelling anything, not receiving any alerts. Pure imagination.

Jump to one specific, usually catastrophic conclusion

You have a headache → You infer it must be a brain tumor

Obsessive inferences skip over numerous more likely explanations (stress, dehydration, eye strain, normal headache) and jump to the worst possibility.

Disproportionate to any actual evidence

You sent a normal email → You infer you definitely offended the recipient and ruined the relationship

The inference is far stronger than any evidence would support. Nothing about sending a routine email suggests relationship destruction.

Resistant to new information

You check the stove (it's off) → Your inference doesn't change → You still believe it might be on → You check again

New information (seeing that the stove is off) doesn't update the inference. This rigidity is a hallmark of obsessive inferences.

Lead to repetitive, ineffective actions

You infer contamination → You wash hands → Inference persists → You wash again → Inference still persists → You wash again

The action doesn't resolve the inference. You're stuck in a loop.

Comparison:

Good Inference	Obsessive Inference
"I studied hard, so I'll probably do okay on this exam"	"I studied, but what if I studied the wrong material?"
"My friend seems distracted—maybe they're stressed about something"	"My friend was quiet—they must hate me now"
"I see the lock is engaged"	"I see the lock is engaged but what if it's not really locked?"
"My hands look clean after washing"	"My hands look clean but what if there are invisible germs?"
"That was an awkward moment in conversation, but these things happen"	"I said something awkward—they definitely think I'm weird now and our friendship is ruined"

Notice the pattern? Good inferences stay close to observable evidence. Obsessive inferences leap into imagination.

The "100% imaginary" test:

Here's a quick way to identify obsessive inferences. Ask yourself: "If I subtract everything based on what I actually saw, heard, touched, smelled, or tasted, what's left?"

If the answer is "nothing"—if the entire inference disappears when you remove imagination—it's an obsessive inference.

Example: "My hands are contaminated"

What do you see? Hands that look clean What do you feel? Hands that feel normal What do you smell? Soap or nothing unusual

Remove imagination from "contaminated hands" and nothing remains. The contamination exists only in imagination, not in any sensory evidence.

Example: "I might have hit someone with my car"

What did you see? Normal driving, no impacts What did you hear? Normal traffic sounds, no crashes What did you feel? Normal vehicle operation, no bumps

Remove imagination and nothing suggests any impact occurred. The entire inference is imaginary.

How Your Mind Tricks You

Your brain uses specific patterns to make obsessive inferences feel real. These patterns (which I-CBT calls "reasoning devices") create an illusion that imagination-based conclusions are actually grounded in reality.

We'll explore all twelve reasoning devices in detail in later chapters. For now, let's look at a few common ones to understand how the tricks work.

Trick #1: Category-Based Inference

Your brain takes a category ("public restrooms") and applies general properties to specific instances without checking if they actually apply.

"Public restrooms are dirty" (general category belief) → "This specific public restroom is definitely dirty" (inference about specific instance) → You've never looked inside this particular restroom

The inference skips the step of gathering actual information about *this* restroom. You're responding to the category, not to reality.

Real-life example: Jamie avoids all public restrooms. When asked why a specific restroom is dirty, Jamie can't point to evidence. "It's a public restroom. Everyone knows they're disgusting." The inference is based on category membership, not observation.

Trick #2: "Possibility Equals Probability"

Your brain treats the mere possibility of something as evidence that it's likely.

"It's possible someone broke into my apartment" → Your brain treats this as "It's likely someone broke into my apartment" → You feel compelled to check

The problem: countless things are *possible* that aren't *probable*. It's possible a meteor will hit your building today. Possible doesn't mean worth worrying about.

Real-life example: Nicole reads a news story about identity theft. Now every time she makes an online purchase, she thinks: "What if this site is stealing my information?" The mere possibility (yes, some sites are fraudulent) becomes treated as a probability (this specific site is probably stealing from her), despite no evidence.

Trick #3: Absence of Proof Treated as Proof of Danger

Your brain interprets lack of evidence for safety as evidence of danger.

"I can't prove nothing bad will happen" → Your brain concludes "Therefore something bad probably will happen"

This reverses normal logic. Normally, you need evidence that danger exists before treating something as dangerous. Obsessive thinking flips this: you need evidence that danger *doesn't* exist, or you assume danger is present.

Real-life example: Derek sends an email to his professor. He doesn't receive a response within three hours. His brain infers: "They're probably offended. I must have said something wrong." He has no evidence of offense—no angry reply, no indication of a problem. But the absence of proof everything is fine gets interpreted as proof something is wrong.

Trick #4: Emotional Reasoning

Your brain uses feelings as evidence for facts.

"I feel contaminated" → Your brain concludes "I am contaminated"

"I feel like I forgot something important" → Your brain concludes "I definitely forgot something"

Feelings are real—you genuinely feel them. But feelings aren't always accurate reporters of external reality. You can feel afraid when no danger exists. You can feel guilty when you've done nothing wrong.

Real-life example: After attending a party, Alicia feels like she said something embarrassing, even though she can't remember any specific awkward moment. The feeling is strong, so her brain concludes it must be based on something real. She spends hours reviewing the evening in her mind, trying to figure out what she said wrong.

Trick #5: Inverse Inference

Your brain takes a true statement and reverses it illogically.

True statement: "If there's visible dirt, then contamination exists"
Reversed: "If I can't see cleanliness, then contamination probably exists"

True statement: "If I smell gas, there might be a leak" Reversed: "If I don't trust my sense of smell, there might be a leak I can't detect"

The reversal sounds logical but isn't. Just because A implies B doesn't mean not-A implies B.

Real-life example: Taylor knows that if their door were unlocked, someone could enter. Their brain reverses this: "If I can't be certain the door is locked, someone can probably enter." The reversal creates doubt where evidence shows the door is locked.

Why these tricks work:

These patterns feel convincing because they use structures that resemble actual reasoning. They sound logical. Your brain is doing something that looks like problem-solving.

But they're not genuine reasoning—they're counterfeit versions. They create conclusions that feel solid but aren't actually connected to evidence.

Think of it like fool's gold. Looks like gold at first glance. Might even feel heavy like gold. But it's not actually gold—it's iron pyrite. Similarly, obsessive inferences look like genuine conclusions but they're actually imagination dressed up to look like reasoning.

Learning to spot these tricks is crucial. Once you recognize them, they lose their power. It's like watching a magic show after someone explained how the trick works—you can still see the illusion, but you're not fooled anymore.

Real-Life Examples You'll Recognize

Let's look at common scenarios where obsessive inferences appear. You might recognize yourself in some of these.

Academic/Work Examples:

Example 1: Email Checking

Situation: You sent a work email at 9 AM. It's now 11 AM with no response.

Obsessive inference: "They're probably angry about something I said. Or they think my idea is stupid. Or they're ignoring me."

Sensory evidence: You received no response. That's all.

Reality-based inference: "They haven't responded yet. Could be busy, could be thinking about it, could check email once a day. I'll hear back eventually."

The obsessive inference added multiple layers of imagination (anger, judgment, intentional ignoring) to the simple fact of no response yet.

Example 2: Assignment Submission

Situation: You submitted an assignment online and received a confirmation.

Obsessive inference: "What if the file was corrupted? What if it didn't actually go through? What if the professor never sees it? I should check the portal again. And again. And maybe email to confirm."

Sensory evidence: You see the confirmation. You can see the submission in your portal.

Reality-based inference: "It's submitted. The confirmation and portal visibility indicate successful submission. Done."

The obsessive inference creates hypothetical problems (corruption, failure) despite evidence of successful submission.

Health/Body Examples:

Example 3: Body Sensations

Situation: You notice your heart beating faster than usual.

Obsessive inference: "Something's wrong with my heart. This could be a heart attack. What if I have a serious condition? I should go to the emergency room."

Sensory evidence: Heart beating faster. No chest pain, no shortness of breath, no other symptoms.

Reality-based inference: "My heart is beating faster. Could be from the coffee I just had, could be from anxiety, could be from climbing stairs. If other concerning symptoms develop, I'll assess then."

The obsessive inference jumps to catastrophic medical explanations for a normal variation in heart rate.

Example 4: Minor Symptoms

Situation: You have a mild headache.

Obsessive inference: "This could be something serious. What if it's a brain tumor? What if it's an aneurysm about to rupture? I need to look up these symptoms online."

Sensory evidence: Mild head discomfort. Nothing else unusual.

Reality-based inference: "I have a headache. Probably tension, dehydration, or eye strain. I'll drink water and rest. If it worsens or persists unusually long, I'll consider seeing a doctor."

The obsessive inference immediately jumps to rare, severe conditions rather than common causes.

Social/Relationship Examples:

Example 5: Text Response Timing

Situation: Your friend usually responds to texts within an hour. It's been three hours with no response.

Obsessive inference: "They're mad at me. I must have done something wrong. They're probably deciding how to end our friendship. What did I say in our last conversation that offended them?"

Sensory evidence: No response for three hours. That's the only fact.

Reality-based inference: "They haven't responded yet. Could be busy, could have their phone on silent, could be in a meeting. I'll hear from them when they're available."

The obsessive inference creates an entire negative narrative from delayed response timing.

Example 6: Social Interaction Analysis

Situation: During a conversation, you mentioned something about your weekend plans and your friend's response was brief.

Obsessive inference: "They didn't seem interested. They probably think my plans are boring. They probably think I'm boring. What if they only hang out with me out of pity?"

Sensory evidence: Friend gave a brief response to one comment during a longer conversation.

Reality-based inference: "They gave a short response to that particular comment. Could mean lots of things—distracted, thinking about something else, no strong opinion on that topic. The overall conversation was fine."

The obsessive inference extracts one brief moment and builds an entire negative interpretation about the relationship.

Safety/Checking Examples:

Example 7: Door Lock

Situation: You locked your door and left.

Obsessive inference: "But did I really lock it? Maybe I just turned the knob without actually locking it. Maybe I was distracted and didn't do it properly. Someone could break in. I need to go back and check."

Sensory evidence: You remember the action of locking. You felt the key turn or saw the deadbolt engage.

Reality-based inference: "I locked the door. I do this every day and know how it feels. It's locked."

The obsessive inference questions reliable memory and sensory experience.

Example 8: Appliance Safety

Situation: You turned off the stove and left the kitchen.

Obsessive inference: "What if I didn't actually turn it off? What if I only thought I did but didn't? What if there's gas leaking right now? What if the house burns down?"

Sensory evidence: You saw yourself turn the knob. You saw the flame go out or the heating element turn off.

Reality-based inference: "I turned off the stove. I saw it go off. It's off."

The obsessive inference creates catastrophic scenarios despite sensory confirmation.

Contamination Examples:

Example 9: Public Spaces

Situation: You touched a handrail on public stairs.

Obsessive inference: "That handrail definitely has germs. Probably really disgusting germs. What if someone who was sick touched it? What if I get infected? I need to wash my hands immediately and thoroughly."

Sensory evidence: You touched a metal rail. It felt like metal. No visible dirt.

Reality-based inference: "I touched a handrail. Lots of people touch handrails. I'll wash my hands when I get to a bathroom, like normal. Done."

The obsessive inference assumes contamination based on category (public handrail) rather than observable evidence.

Example 10: Food Safety

Situation: You're eating at a restaurant.

Obsessive inference: "What if the kitchen isn't clean? What if the food is contaminated? What if I get food poisoning? Should I ask to see the kitchen? Should I leave?"

Sensory evidence: Food looks normal, smells normal, tastes normal. Restaurant appears clean.

Reality-based inference: "This restaurant looks fine. The food seems normal. No reason for concern."

The obsessive inference creates imaginary contamination scenarios despite no sensory evidence of problems.

Intrusive Thought Examples:

Example 11: Random Violent Thought

Situation: You're standing near a window and have a fleeting thought about jumping.

Obsessive inference: "Why did I think that? What if that means I'm suicidal? What if I actually want to do it? What if I lose control and do it? What does this say about me?"

Sensory evidence: A thought occurred. That's all.

Reality-based inference: "A random thought popped up, as thoughts do. Humans have thousands of random thoughts daily, including weird ones. This doesn't mean anything about my intentions or mental state."

The obsessive inference treats a mental event (a thought) as if it's evidence of desires, intentions, or future actions.

Example 12: Inappropriate Thought

Situation: You're at a serious event (funeral, important meeting) and have an inappropriate thought about laughing or saying something wrong.

Obsessive inference: "What if I actually do that? What if I lose control? What does it mean that I thought this? Am I a bad person? What's wrong with me?"

Sensory evidence: You had a thought. You're sitting quietly and behaving appropriately.

Reality-based inference: "Minds generate random thoughts, especially taboo ones in serious situations. Having a thought doesn't mean acting on it. My behavior is fine."

The obsessive inference confuses thought content with identity or likely actions.

Pattern Recognition:

Notice how obsessive inferences always add layers beyond what sensory evidence supports:

- Adding catastrophic outcomes ("What if..." scenarios)
- Adding judgments ("They think..." statements)
- Adding doubt to clear evidence ("But what if I didn't really...")
- Adding meaning to random mental events ("This thought means...")
- Adding hidden dangers to normal situations ("There might be...")

Good inferences stay close to observable facts. Obsessive inferences pile imagination on top of those facts.

The next chapters will give you tools to catch these obsessive inferences in action and replace them with evidence-based thinking.

What You've Learned So Far

Inferences are conclusions your brain draws based on available information. They happen automatically and constantly. The key question is: What information are your inferences based on?

Good inferences use current sensory information, consider multiple explanations, remain proportional to evidence, and update with new information. Obsessive inferences are based on imagination, jump to catastrophic conclusions, ignore contradictory evidence, and lead to repetitive behaviors.

Your mind uses specific tricks (reasoning devices) to make imagination-based inferences feel real. Recognizing these patterns helps you spot obsessive inferences.

Real-life examples show how obsessive inferences appear in academic, health, social, safety, contamination, and thought-related situations. In each case, the inference adds layers of imagination beyond what sensory evidence supports.

The upcoming chapters will teach you specific tools for working with these inferences and returning to reality-based thinking.

Chapter 5: Reality vs. Imagination

Here's a simple experiment. Right now, imagine there's a purple elephant standing next to you. Picture it clearly—trunk, tusks, purple skin, maybe wearing a hat.

Got it? Good.

Now, is there actually a purple elephant next to you?

Of course not. You just imagined it. You can tell the difference between the elephant you imagined and actual reality. That distinction seems obvious.

But here's what happens with obsessive doubt: that clear distinction gets blurred. Your brain generates an imaginary scenario—"What if there's contamination?"—and suddenly you're not sure if contamination is real or imaginary. The made-up elephant starts feeling as real as the chair you're sitting in.

This chapter teaches you to restore that distinction. You'll learn to recognize what's actually real (based on your senses) versus what's imaginary (generated by your mind).

Your Senses Are Your Friends

Your five senses—sight, hearing, touch, smell, and taste—are your direct connection to reality. They tell you what's actually happening right now, in the physical world around you.

Sight shows you what objects are present, their colors, their positions, their movements. Your eyes are remarkably accurate. When you look at a locked door, you can see whether the deadbolt is engaged.

Hearing tells you what sounds exist in your environment. You can hear traffic, voices, music, appliances running, or silence. Your ears reliably report these sounds.

Touch provides information about textures, temperatures, pressure, and physical contact. When you touch a surface, your hands accurately report whether it's smooth, rough, hot, cold, wet, or dry.

Smell detects odors and chemicals in the air. If something is burning, your nose will tell you. If food is spoiled, you'll smell it. If there's no odor, your nose reports that absence.

Taste identifies flavors and tells you about what's in your mouth. Bitter, sweet, salty, sour, savory—your tongue distinguishes these accurately.

These senses evolved over millions of years to give organisms accurate information about their environment. They work. They're trustworthy.

The problem in obsessive doubt: You've learned to distrust your senses.

You look at your hands and see they're clean, but you don't trust what you see. You check the lock and see it's engaged, but you don't trust what you see. You taste food that's perfectly fine, but you don't trust what you taste.

Instead of trusting sensory information, you trust imagination. "What if there are invisible germs?" "What if the lock looks engaged but isn't?" "What if the food is contaminated even though it tastes normal?"

Imagination can generate unlimited doubts about anything. Your senses, meanwhile, give you straightforward facts about the current situation.

I-CBT's fundamental principle: When your senses and your imagination give you different information, trust your senses.

If you see your hands are clean but imagine they might be contaminated—trust what you see.

If you hear silence but imagine you might have left an appliance running—trust what you hear.

If you feel the door is locked but imagine it might not be—trust what you feel.

This might sound overly simplistic. "Just trust your senses" seems like it can't be the whole solution. But research consistently shows that returning to sensory-based reality is one of the most effective interventions for obsessive doubt (O'Connor et al., 2005).

Why your senses are more reliable than your thoughts:

Your senses report present, observable facts. Right now, what do you see in front of you? That's what's actually there. Your eyes aren't making it up.

Your thoughts, meanwhile, can generate any scenario. You can think about things that happened in the past, things that might happen in the future, things that could possibly happen but probably won't, or things that are completely impossible. Thoughts have unlimited range.

This unlimited range is useful for planning, creativity, and problem-solving. But it becomes a liability when thoughts masquerade as sensory information.

Example: The Clean Hands Test

Alex washes their hands thoroughly. Soap, warm water, 20 seconds of scrubbing, rinse, dry with a clean towel.

Sensory information:

- **Sight:** Hands look clean. No visible dirt, no discoloration.
- **Touch:** Hands feel smooth and clean. Skin texture is normal.
- **Smell:** Hands smell like soap or have no particular odor.

Imaginative information:

- "But what if there are microscopic germs I can't see?"
- "What if the soap wasn't effective enough?"
- "What if the towel had germs on it?"
- "What if I didn't scrub every spot properly?"

Notice: All the imaginative information uses "what if"—the hallmark of imagination. None of it comes from actual observation.

I-CBT's approach: The sensory information (hands look, feel, and smell clean) represents reality. The imaginative information (what if germs remain) represents possibility but not actuality. Trust the senses.

Example: The Locked Door

Maria locks her apartment door before leaving. She turns the deadbolt, hears the click, tests the handle.

Sensory information:

- **Sight:** She sees the deadbolt in the locked position. She sees the door stays closed when she pulls the handle.
- **Hearing:** She heard the click of the lock engaging.
- **Touch:** She felt the key turn fully. She felt the door resist when she tested the handle.

Imaginative information:

- "What if I was distracted and didn't actually turn it all the way?"

- "What if the lock looks engaged but there's a mechanical problem?"
- "What if I only imagined locking it?"
- "What if someone breaks in and it's my fault for not checking more carefully?"

I-CBT's approach: Three separate senses (sight, hearing, touch) all confirm the door is locked. That's reality. The "what if" scenarios are imagination. Trust the senses.

Building trust in your senses:

If you've spent months or years questioning your sensory information, rebuilding trust takes practice. You can't just decide "I'll trust my senses now" and have it work instantly. The doubt patterns are habitual.

But you can start deliberately noticing when your senses give you clear information:

When you look at something, acknowledge: "My eyes are showing me this clearly."

When you hear something, note: "My ears are detecting this sound."

When you touch something, recognize: "My hands are feeling this texture accurately."

This conscious acknowledgment, repeated consistently, begins rebuilding the connection between sensory data and confidence.

Research on sensory discrimination training shows that people with OCD can improve their ability to trust sensory information through deliberate practice (Radomsky & Alcolado, 2010).

The 100% Imaginary Rule

Here's a powerful tool for identifying obsessive inferences. Ask yourself this question:

"If I remove everything based on imagination—all the 'what if' thinking—is there any sensory evidence left supporting this concern?"

If the answer is no—if the concern is 100% imaginary—then you're dealing with an obsessive inference that doesn't deserve your attention or behavioral response.

How to apply the 100% Imaginary Rule:

Step 1: Identify the concern

What are you worried about? What doubt is present?

"My hands might be contaminated." "I might have left the stove on." "That person probably thinks I'm weird." "This thought means something bad about me."

Step 2: List the sensory evidence

What do your five senses actually tell you about this situation right now?

Hands concern:

- Sight: Hands look clean
- Touch: Hands feel normal
- Smell: No unusual odor

Stove concern:

- Sight: You're not home, can't see the stove
- Hearing: No fire alarms
- Smell: No smoke

Social concern:

- Sight: Person smiled and engaged normally
- Hearing: Their tone was friendly
- (No actual indication of negative judgment)

Thought concern:

- Only sensory fact: You had a thought
- No other sensory information

Step 3: List the imagination-based elements

What parts of the concern rely on "what if" thinking, assumptions, or scenarios you're generating mentally?

Hands: "What if there are invisible germs? What if the soap wasn't strong enough?"

Stove: "What if I forgot to turn it off? What if there's a fire right now?"

Social: "What if they thought my comment was weird? What if they're judging me?"

Thought: "What if this thought reflects my true desires? What if it means I'll act on it?"

Step 4: Apply the rule

Remove all imagination-based elements. What remains?

Hands: You washed your hands. They look and feel clean. No evidence of contamination.

Stove: You're away from home. No evidence of fire.

Social: You had a normal interaction. No evidence of negative judgment.

Thought: You experienced a mental event. No evidence about your character or future actions.

Step 5: Make the determination

If nothing (or almost nothing) remains after removing imagination—if the concern is 100% or nearly 100% imaginary—then it's an obsessive inference.

Obsessive inferences don't require action, checking, or reassurance. They require recognition: "This is imagination, not reality."

Examples of 100% Imaginary Concerns:

"What if I accidentally sent an embarrassing text to my professor?"

- Sensory evidence: Zero. You don't see the text in your sent folder, don't remember sending it, received no response about it.
- Imagination: 100%. The entire scenario exists in "what if" thinking.

"What if I hit someone with my car and didn't notice?"

- Sensory evidence: You didn't see any impact, hear any crash, feel any bump.
- Imagination: 100%. Generated by "what if" thinking with no supporting evidence.

"What if there's deadly mold growing inside my walls?"

- Sensory evidence: None. You don't see mold, don't smell anything unusual, have no symptoms of mold exposure.
- Imagination: 100%. Based on possibility, not observable fact.

Examples of NOT 100% Imaginary (these contain real concerns):

"I smell gas in my apartment"

- Sensory evidence: You're smelling something unusual
- This is NOT 100% imaginary. Your sense of smell is giving you information. Appropriate action: Investigate, call utility company if needed.

"My professor sent an email asking to meet about my paper"

- Sensory evidence: You received an email with specific content
- This is NOT 100% imaginary. Something real occurred that warrants response.

"I see smoke coming from my apartment window"

- Sensory evidence: Visual observation of smoke
- This is NOT 100% imaginary. This is actual sensory data indicating a real situation.

The distinction is critical. The 100% Imaginary Rule doesn't tell you to ignore all concerns. It helps you distinguish between:

- Concerns based on actual sensory information (pay attention, take appropriate action)
- Concerns based purely on imagination (recognize as obsessive inference, don't engage)

Common challenges applying this rule:

"But it's possible germs are there even if I can't see them!"

Yes, it's possible. Many things are possible. Possibility isn't the same as sensory evidence. If you can't detect it with any of your five senses, it's imagination, not reality.

"But what if my senses are wrong? What if I'm missing something?"

Your senses can occasionally make errors under unusual circumstances (optical illusions, very dark environments, very loud backgrounds). But under normal conditions, with clear observation, your senses are highly accurate. Doubting your senses "just in case" means never trusting reality.

"But some real dangers are invisible!"

True. Carbon monoxide is odorless. Radiation can't be detected by unaided senses. This is why we have detectors for these specific dangers. If you're concerned about specific invisible threats, get appropriate detection equipment. But don't use "some dangers are invisible" as justification to doubt everything.

"But I feel so uncertain!"

Feeling uncertain is not the same as having evidence for danger. Feelings can be powerful, but they're not sensory observations of the external world. The 100% Imaginary Rule asks: Do your senses detect the concern, or only your imagination?

How to Tell What's Real

This section provides a practical, step-by-step process for determining whether something is real (sensory-based) or imaginary.

The Reality Check Process:

Question 1: "What am I currently seeing?"

Look at your actual environment. What do your eyes show you right now?

If you're worried about contamination, what do your eyes show? Clean surfaces? Visible dirt?

If you're worried about an unlocked door, what do your eyes show? The lock position?

If you're worried about social judgment, what do your eyes show? The person's facial expression and body language?

Be specific. Don't add interpretation. Just report what your eyes detect.

Question 2: "What am I currently hearing?"

What sounds are present right now?

If you're worried about a fire, what do your ears detect? Fire alarms? Normal silence?

If you're worried about having offended someone, what did you hear? Their actual words and tone?

Again, be specific about actual sounds, not interpretations of sounds.

Question 3: "What am I currently touching or feeling physically?"

What physical sensations are present?

If you're worried about contamination, what do your hands feel? Clean skin? Soapy residue? Actual dirt?

If you're worried about safety, what do you feel? A locked door that won't open when pulled?

Physical sensation, not emotional feeling. What is your sense of touch telling you?

Question 4: "What am I currently smelling?"

What odors are present?

If you're worried about gas leaks, spoiled food, or smoke, what does your nose detect?

Most concerns involve no smell at all, which is itself information.

Question 5: "What am I currently tasting?" (less commonly relevant)

This applies mainly to food-related concerns. What does your tongue tell you?

Question 6: "Is my concern based on any of these five senses, or is it based on 'what if' thinking?"

This is the crucial question. After checking what your senses actually tell you, determine: Is your concern supported by sensory data, or is it imagination?

Reality Check Example 1: Contamination Concern

Jordan touches a doorknob in a campus building and feels contaminated.

Q1 (Sight): "What do I see?" My hand looks normal. No visible dirt on the doorknob or my hand.

Q2 (Hearing): Not applicable to this concern.

Q3 (Touch): "What do I feel?" Normal skin texture. The doorknob felt like metal.

Q4 (Smell): "What do I smell?" Nothing unusual. No odor.

Q5 (Taste): Not applicable.

Q6 (Real or imaginary?): My senses show a normal hand and a normal doorknob. The contamination concern is 100% imaginary—based on "what if there were germs" not on seeing, feeling, or smelling anything concerning.

Conclusion: This is imagination, not reality.

Reality Check Example 2: Unlocked Door

Taylor left their dorm room and now worries the door might be unlocked.

Q1 (Sight): "What did I see?" I saw the lock engage when I turned the key. I saw the door stay shut when I pulled the handle.

Q2 (Hearing): "What did I hear?" I heard the lock click.

Q3 (Touch): "What did I feel?" I felt the key turn fully. I felt resistance when I tested the handle.

Q4 (Smell): Not applicable.

Q5 (Taste): Not applicable.

Q6 (Real or imaginary?): Three senses (sight, hearing, touch) all confirmed locking. The doubt about whether it's really locked is 100% imaginary—based on "what if I didn't really lock it" not on sensory information suggesting it's unlocked.

Conclusion: This is imagination, not reality.

Reality Check Example 3: Academic Submission

Sam submitted an assignment online and worries it didn't actually go through.

Q1 (Sight): "What do I see?" I see a confirmation email. I see the assignment listed in the course portal with a submission timestamp.

Q2 (Hearing): Not applicable.

Q3 (Touch): Not applicable.

Q4 (Smell): Not applicable.

Q5 (Taste): Not applicable.

Q6 (Real or imaginary?): My sense of sight shows two forms of confirmation. The worry about whether it "really" went through is 100% imaginary—based on "what if the system glitched" not on any sensory evidence of problems.

Conclusion: This is imagination, not reality.

Reality Check Example 4: Social Interaction

Casey had a conversation with a classmate and now worries they came across badly.

Q1 (Sight): "What did I see?" The person smiled, made eye contact, seemed engaged in the conversation.

Q2 (Hearing): "What did I hear?" They responded to my comments. Their tone was normal/friendly. They laughed at a joke I made.

Q3 (Touch): Not applicable.

Q4 (Smell): Not applicable.

Q5 (Taste): Not applicable.

Q6 (Real or imaginary?): My senses (sight and hearing) showed normal, positive social interaction. The worry that they thought badly of me is 100% imaginary—based on "what if they were just being polite" or "what if they're judging me" not on any sensory evidence of negative reaction.

Conclusion: This is imagination, not reality.

Reality Check Example 5: Actual Problem (for contrast)

Devon smells something burning in their apartment.

Q1 (Sight): Looking around, don't see flames yet but seems hazy.

Q2 (Hearing): Might hear a crackling sound.

Q3 (Touch): Not currently relevant.

Q4 (Smell): "What do I smell?" Definitely smell smoke. Strong burning odor.

Q5 (Taste): Might taste smoke in the air.

Q6 (Real or imaginary?): Multiple senses (smell, possibly sight and hearing) are detecting actual evidence of smoke/burning. This is NOT imaginary.

Conclusion: This is real sensory information requiring appropriate action (investigate, call fire department if needed, evacuate if necessary).

The difference should now be clear. When your concern is based on actual sensory input, it's real and deserves response. When it's based on "what if" thinking without sensory support, it's imagination.

Making this automatic:

Initially, running through these questions might feel mechanical or time-consuming. That's normal when learning a new skill.

With practice, the reality check becomes faster and more automatic. Eventually, you can assess "sensory evidence or imagination?" in just a few seconds.

The goal isn't to spend five minutes analyzing every concern. The goal is to develop the habit of automatically checking: "Is this based on what I'm actually seeing/hearing/feeling, or on what I'm imagining?"

Practice Exercises

These exercises help you build the skill of distinguishing reality from imagination. Start with the easier ones and work up to applying this in real-time with your actual concerns.

Exercise 1: Basic Sensory Observation

Purpose: Practice paying attention to sensory information without adding interpretation.

Instructions:

1. Pick an object near you (a cup, book, phone, etc.)
2. Describe what you SEE about it in pure sensory terms
    - Colors, shapes, size, position
    - No interpretation, just observation
3. If you can, describe what you HEAR from it (or silence)
4. Pick it up and describe what you FEEL
    - Temperature, texture, weight
5. If applicable, describe smell or taste

The point: Practice separating sensory observation from interpretation. "I see a red cup" is sensory. "I see a dirty cup" adds interpretation about cleanliness.

Exercise 2: Reality vs. Imagination Sorting

Purpose: Practice categorizing information as sensory or imaginary.

Instructions: For each statement below, determine if it's based on sensory information or imagination.

1. "The door is closed." (What sense tells you this?)
2. "The door might not be locked properly." (Sensory or imagination?)
3. "I hear my neighbor's TV." (What sense?)
4. "My neighbor probably thinks I'm too quiet." (Sensory or imagination?)
5. "My hands feel dry." (What sense?)
6. "My hands might have germs on them." (Sensory or imagination?)
7. "I see a confirmation email." (What sense?)
8. "The email might not have actually sent." (Sensory or imagination?)
9. "I smell coffee." (What sense?)
10. "The coffee might have been contaminated." (Sensory or imagination?)

Answers:

1. Sensory (sight)
2. Imagination (no sensory data about lock quality)
3. Sensory (hearing)
4. Imagination (no sensory data about neighbor's thoughts)
5. Sensory (touch)
6. Imagination (no sensory detection of germs)
7. Sensory (sight)
8. Imagination (speculation despite sensory evidence)
9. Sensory (smell)

10. Imagination (no sensory evidence of contamination)

Exercise 3: The 100% Imaginary Test Practice

Purpose: Practice applying the 100% Imaginary Rule to common concerns.

Instructions: For each concern, identify what sensory evidence exists versus what's imaginary. Then determine what percentage is imaginary.

Concern 1: "I might have left my straightener/curling iron plugged in."

Sensory evidence:

- (Think: What did you see, hear, or feel about the straightener?)

Imaginary elements:

- (List all the "what if" components)

Percentage imaginary: ____%

Concern 2: "That person I just walked past might think I look weird."

Sensory evidence:

Imaginary elements:

Percentage imaginary: ____%

Concern 3: "I might be getting sick because I have a slight headache."

Sensory evidence:

Imaginary elements:

Percentage imaginary: ____%

Do this analysis with several concerns. You'll notice that obsessive concerns are typically 90-100% imaginary, while real concerns have substantial sensory evidence.

Exercise 4: Real-Time Reality Checks

Purpose: Apply the reality check process to your actual concerns as they arise.

Instructions:

1. When a doubt or concern arises, pause
2. Run through the five senses questions:
    - What do I see?
    - What do I hear?
    - What do I feel (physically)?
    - What do I smell?
    - What do I taste?
3. Ask: Is my concern based on these senses or on "what if" thinking?
4. Make a note of the result

Keep a log for one week:

Date/Time	Concern	Sensory Evidence	Imaginary Elements	Conclusion

This log helps you recognize patterns in when and how obsessive inferences arise.

Exercise 5: Sensory Trust Building

Purpose: Practice trusting sensory information even when doubt arises.

Instructions:

1. Choose a simple checking behavior you do (lock, appliance, submission, etc.)
2. Do the action once while paying full attention
3. Deliberately notice all sensory confirmation:
    - "I SEE the lock engage"
    - "I HEAR the click"
    - "I FEEL the resistance when I test the handle"
4. When doubt arises later, remind yourself of the sensory information
5. Resist the urge to check again
6. Notice that despite not checking, nothing bad happens

This builds trust through direct experience that sensory information is reliable.

Exercise 6: Imagination Labels

Purpose: Practice identifying imagination-based thinking in the moment.

Instructions: Throughout your day, when "what if" thoughts arise, simply label them:

"That's imagination" (not as a criticism, just as a factual observation)

Don't argue with the thoughts. Don't try to make them go away. Just identify them accurately.

"What if I said something wrong?" → "That's imagination" "What if the door isn't really locked?" → "That's imagination" "What if there are germs?" → "That's imagination"

This creates separation between you and the imagination-based thoughts. They're just mental events, not reality reports.

Exercise 7: Comparing Past Predictions to Reality

Purpose: Build evidence that imagination-based concerns don't match reality.

Instructions:

1. Review the past week
2. List times you had strong concerns or checked/sought reassurance
3. For each, note:
    o What you worried would happen
    o What actually happened
4. Calculate how often imagination matched reality

Most people discover their imaginative concerns almost never match what actually occurs. This data helps you trust sensory reality over imagination.

Exercise 8: Sensory Grounding

Purpose: Practice returning to present sensory reality when imagination takes over.

Instructions: When you notice obsessive doubt arising:

1. Name 5 things you can see right now
2. Name 4 things you can hear right now
3. Name 3 things you can physically feel right now
4. Name 2 things you can smell right now
5. Name 1 thing you can taste right now

This simple exercise pulls your attention out of imagination and back into sensory reality. It's a quick reset.

Progress indicators:

You'll know these exercises are working when:

- You catch yourself generating imaginary concerns more quickly
- The distinction between sensory and imaginary becomes clearer
- You feel less compelled to check or seek reassurance
- You can stay with sensory information despite feeling uncomfortable
- You notice fewer obsessive doubts arising overall

Be patient. These skills develop with consistent practice, typically over several weeks.

What You've Learned So Far

Your five senses provide accurate information about reality. They're trustworthy. Obsessive doubt develops when you stop trusting sensory information and instead trust imagination.

The 100% Imaginary Rule helps identify obsessive inferences: if a concern has no sensory evidence supporting it—if it's entirely based on "what if" thinking—it's imagination, not reality.

The Reality Check Process systematically examines what each sense tells you, then determines whether a concern is sensory-based or imagination-based. Real concerns have sensory support. Imaginary concerns don't.

Practice exercises build the skill of distinguishing reality from imagination, making this assessment automatic over time.

The next chapter examines a specific error that maintains obsessive doubt: confusing what's possible with what's probable.

Chapter 6: The Inference Confusion

Let's start with a thought experiment.

It's possible that a meteor will hit your building tomorrow. Actually possible—meteors do hit Earth occasionally. It could happen.

Should you evacuate immediately? Should you spend today preparing emergency plans? Should you worry about this?

Most people would say no. Yes, it's possible, but it's so improbable that treating it as a realistic concern would be irrational.

Now consider: You touched a doorknob in a public building. It's possible that doorknob had dangerous pathogens on it. That's actually true—surfaces do sometimes carry germs.

Should you scrub your hands raw? Should you worry intensely about infection? Should you avoid all doorknobs?

If you have obsessive doubt, you might answer yes to these questions. But logically, this situation is similar to the meteor. Yes, possible. But probable? No.

This chapter explores a critical error that maintains obsessive thinking: treating possibility as if it equals probability.

Mixing Up "Possible" with "Probable"

Possible means something could conceivably happen. The category includes everything from common occurrences to incredibly rare events to things that have never happened but technically could.

Probable means something is likely to happen based on evidence, frequency, or reasonable expectation.

The number of possible things is essentially infinite. The number of probable things in any given situation is quite small.

Examples of possible but improbable events:

- You could choke on your food at dinner tonight (possible—it happens to some people sometimes)
- Your professor could be an alien in disguise (possible—we can't prove they're not)
- The chair you're sitting on could collapse (possible—furniture does occasionally break)
- You could develop a rare disease tomorrow (possible—rare diseases exist)
- Someone could rob your apartment tonight (possible—crime exists)

All of these are technically possible. If we measured probability:

- Choking: roughly 1 in 2,700 per year (National Safety Council, 2020)
- Professor being alien: essentially 0% (no evidence aliens exist or can disguise as humans)
- Chair collapse: depends on chair quality, but generally very low
- Rare disease: by definition, very low
- Apartment robbery: depends on area, but generally low (most people don't experience this)

When functioning normally, your brain automatically distinguishes possible from probable. You don't evacuate for meteors despite the possibility. You sit in chairs despite the possibility of collapse. You eat food despite the possibility of choking.

In obsessive doubt, this distinction breaks down.

Possibility gets treated as probability. If something could happen, your brain acts as if it's likely to happen.

"It's possible there are germs on this doorknob" becomes "There are probably dangerous germs on this doorknob."

"It's possible I forgot to lock the door" becomes "I probably forgot to lock the door."

"It's possible I offended that person" becomes "I probably offended that person."

The word "possible" doesn't appear in your conscious thought, so you might not notice this substitution happening. But behaviorally, you're responding to possibility as if it's probability.

How to recognize this error in your thinking:

Ask yourself: "Am I responding to what's likely, or to what's merely possible?"

If you're washing hands excessively after touching normal objects, you're responding to possibility (germs could be present) not probability (germs are likely to cause harm in this situation).

If you're checking locks repeatedly despite confirming they're engaged, you're responding to possibility (the lock could fail) not probability (the lock is likely fine given what you observed).

If you're seeking reassurance about social interactions that seemed fine, you're responding to possibility (the person could have been offended) not probability (they likely weren't, given their friendly behavior).

The probability question:

For any concern, ask: "What's the actual likelihood of this?"

Not "Could this happen?" but "What are the realistic odds?"

Sometimes you can find actual statistics. Other times you use reasonable estimation based on experience and observation.

"What are the odds I left the straightener plugged in when I specifically remember unplugging it and seeing it cool down?" Very low. Has it ever happened when you've had clear memory of unplugging it? Probably not.

"What are the odds this normal-looking, normal-smelling food from a licensed restaurant will cause serious illness?" Very low. The health department regulates this. Millions of restaurant meals are served safely daily.

"What are the odds I somehow hit a pedestrian while driving home when I didn't see, hear, or feel any impact?" Essentially zero. Hitting a person creates obvious sensory feedback.

The base rate fallacy:

Your brain might focus on "Yes, it's possible" while ignoring how rarely that possibility actually occurs.

Car accidents do happen (possible). But most trips are completed safely. If you've driven or ridden in cars hundreds or thousands of times without incident, the base rate suggests your next trip will also be safe.

Food poisoning does happen (possible). But most meals don't cause it. If you've eaten thousands of meals without serious illness, the base rate suggests your next meal will be fine.

Locks do occasionally fail (possible). But most locks function properly for years. If your lock has worked correctly hundreds of times, the base rate suggests it's working now.

Obsessive thinking focuses on the possibility while ignoring the base rate—the actual frequency of occurrence.

Example: The Email Anxiety

Devon sends an email to their study group suggesting meeting times.

Possible concerns (things that could happen):

- They could misinterpret the tone as demanding
- They could think the suggested times are inconvenient and blame Devon
- They could be annoyed at receiving another email
- Devon could have made a typo that changes the meaning
- Devon could have accidentally included someone not in the group
- The email could get lost or filtered to spam

All technically possible. Anything could happen.

Probable reality:

- They'll read a straightforward message about meeting times
- They'll respond with their availability
- This is normal group coordination
- The email will function as intended

Base rate: Devon has sent hundreds of similar emails. How many have resulted in the imagined catastrophes? Probably zero or very few. How many have functioned normally? Nearly all of them.

If Devon treats possibility as probability, they'll spend hours worrying, re-reading the sent email, maybe sending follow-up clarifications, maybe apologizing preemptively. They're responding as if email disaster is likely.

If Devon distinguishes possible from probable, they'll recognize: "Yes, technically many things could go wrong. But realistically, this is a routine email that will be received normally like the hundreds before it."

The "anything could happen" trap:

When anxious, you might think "But anything could happen! You never know!" This is technically true but functionally useless.

Yes, technically anything within the laws of physics could happen. You could win the lottery tomorrow. You could discover you're royalty. A famous director could randomly decide to make you a movie star.

Do you plan your life around these possibilities? No. Because possibility isn't the same as probability.

The "anything could happen" defense of obsessive worry treats all possibilities as equally worth considering. They're not. Some possibilities are so unlikely they don't merit behavioral response.

Why Your Brain Does This

If confusing possibility with probability is irrational, why does your brain do it? Several mechanisms contribute.

Mechanism 1: Evolutionary bias toward false alarms

Your brain evolved in an environment where false alarms were less costly than missed threats.

Ancient human hears rustling in bushes. Two possibilities:

- It's just wind (no threat)
- It's a predator (serious threat)

Treating every rustle as a possible predator (false alarm) costs energy and causes unnecessary fear. But treating a predator rustle as just wind (missed threat) could cost your life.

Over evolutionary time, brains that erred toward false alarms survived better. Better to run from wind than to ignore a predator.

This same mechanism operates today. Your brain treats possibilities as probabilities because false alarm (unnecessary caution) seems safer than missed threat (potential danger).

The problem: This mechanism doesn't distinguish between genuine survival threats (predators) and modern obsessive concerns (germs on doorknobs, unlocked doors, social judgment). It applies the same "better safe than sorry" logic to everything.

Research shows that people with OCD have particularly active threat detection systems, generating more false alarms than necessary (Cisler & Koster, 2010).

Mechanism 2: Difficulty assessing actual probability

Your brain isn't naturally good at statistical thinking. Probability assessment requires mathematical reasoning that doesn't come automatically.

Quick: What's more likely, dying in a plane crash or dying in a car accident?

Most people guess plane crash because plane crashes are dramatic and memorable. Actually, car accidents are far more likely. The U.S. National Safety Council estimates you're about 200 times more likely to die in a car crash than a plane crash (National Safety Council, 2020).

Your brain uses mental shortcuts (heuristics) that often overestimate risk:

Availability heuristic: Things that come to mind easily seem more likely. If you recently read about food poisoning, all food seems riskier.

Salience bias: Dramatic, emotional events seem more probable than they are. Terrorist attacks get more mental weight than heart disease, though heart disease kills far more people.

Confirmation bias: You notice things that confirm your concerns. If you're worried about germs, you notice every news story about disease outbreaks while missing all the non-events.

These mental shortcuts make everything feel riskier than it is, contributing to possibility-probability confusion.

Mechanism 3: Anxiety amplification

Anxiety doesn't feel like other emotions. It feels like information about danger.

When you feel afraid, your brain interprets that feeling as evidence: "I'm feeling afraid, so there must be danger."

But anxiety can be triggered by imagination. You imagine a possible threat ("What if there are germs?") and your anxiety system responds to the imagined scenario as if it's real. Then you feel anxious.

Then comes the error: You interpret the anxiety as confirmation of danger. "I'm feeling anxious about these germs, so there must really be germs worth worrying about."

This creates a loop:

1. Imagine possibility
2. Feel anxiety in response to imagined possibility
3. Interpret anxiety as evidence the possibility is probable
4. Imagine more possibilities
5. Feel more anxiety

The anxiety itself becomes treated as probability data. "If the concern weren't realistic, why would I feel so anxious?"

Answer: Because you imagined it vividly enough to trigger your threat response. The anxiety is real, but it's responding to imagination, not reality.

Mechanism 4: "Better safe than sorry" reasoning

This internal logic sounds sensible on the surface:

"Yes, it's unlikely there are dangerous germs on my hands. But what if there are? It won't hurt to wash them again. Better safe than sorry."

"Yes, I probably locked the door. But what if I didn't? It only takes a minute to check. Better safe than sorry."

The problem: "Better safe than sorry" reasoning doesn't account for costs.

Cost of checking: Time, energy, reinforcement of doubt, increased anxiety over time, interference with daily functioning.

Cost of not checking when genuine danger exists: Depends on the actual probability and severity.

If probability of real danger is essentially zero (locked door that you clearly remember locking), the cost of checking (reinforcing obsessive patterns) outweighs any benefit.

"Better safe than sorry" only makes sense when:

- There's reasonable probability of actual danger
- The cost of caution is low
- The cost of not being cautious is high

Obsessive doubt inverts this. It applies maximum caution to minimum probability threats at high cost to your functioning.

Mechanism 5: Loss of confidence in memory and perception

Each time you check despite sensory confirmation, you tell your brain: "Don't trust what you saw. Don't trust what you remember. We need more verification."

This erodes confidence in your own memory and perception over time (Radomsky et al., 2001).

Once confidence is damaged, everything becomes uncertain. You can't trust that you locked the door because you no longer trust your memory of locking it. You can't trust that your hands are clean because you no longer trust your perception of cleanliness.

When you don't trust your perception, you can't accurately assess probability. Every possibility feels equally plausible because you have no confidence in your ability to determine what actually occurred.

Research shows that repeated checking actually decreases memory confidence and increases uncertainty, creating a vicious cycle (van den Hout & Kindt, 2003).

The Role of Anxiety

Anxiety plays a central role in maintaining the confusion between possible and probable. Understanding this relationship helps you break the pattern.

How anxiety responds to imagination:

Your anxiety system is designed to respond to threats. It doesn't distinguish well between actual threats and imagined ones.

When you imagine "What if there's a fire in my apartment right now?" your brain processes this similarly to "There is a fire in my apartment right now."

The amygdala (brain's threat detection center) activates. Stress hormones release. Heart rate increases. You feel urgency.

This physiological response feels exactly like the response to actual danger. You can't tell the difference internally between:

- Anxiety from imagining a fire
- Anxiety from seeing actual flames

This is why anxiety feels like such compelling evidence. The physical sensations are real and intense, so the threat must be real too, right?

Wrong. The sensations are real. The threat might not be.

Anxiety creates a sense of urgency:

When anxious, you feel like you must act immediately. This urgency overrides rational probability assessment.

"I need to check the stove right now." "I need to wash my hands immediately." "I need to know for certain that I didn't offend anyone."

The urgency makes the possibility feel probable. If it weren't a real concern, why would you feel such strong urgency?

But urgency is a feature of anxiety, not a feature of probability. You can feel urgent about something very unlikely. The intensity of the feeling doesn't correlate with the likelihood of the feared outcome.

Anxiety intolerance:

People with obsessive doubt often have low tolerance for anxiety. The uncomfortable feeling itself seems unacceptable or dangerous.

"I can't stand feeling this anxious" leads to "I must do something to reduce this feeling right now" which leads to checking, washing, or reassurance-seeking.

But here's what research shows: Anxiety, while uncomfortable, isn't dangerous. It's temporary. It peaks and then naturally decreases (Craske et al., 2014).

When you engage in compulsions to reduce anxiety, two things happen:

1. You get temporary relief (anxiety decreases)
2. You reinforce the behavior (your brain learns: "When anxious about X, doing Y brings relief")

This reinforcement strengthens the obsessive pattern. You're essentially training your brain that the imagined threat was real enough to require action.

Anxiety as the real problem:

Many people with obsessive doubt believe the content of their obsessions is the problem:

- "If only I could be certain my hands are clean..."
- "If only I could know for sure the door is locked..."
- "If only I could verify I didn't offend anyone..."

But the actual problem is: "I can't tolerate the anxiety that arises when I imagine these scenarios."

The content varies. The inability to tolerate uncertainty and anxiety is the constant.

I-CBT addresses this by:

1. Helping you recognize that anxiety is a response to imagination, not to reality
2. Teaching you to tolerate anxiety without engaging in compulsions
3. Showing you that anxiety decreases naturally when you don't respond to it

The anxiety paradox:

Trying to eliminate anxiety through checking or reassurance-seeking actually increases anxiety long-term.

Short-term: Check → Feel better Long-term: Check more → Doubt increases → Need to check more often → Anxiety increases

The behavior that temporarily reduces anxiety is the same behavior that creates more anxiety overall.

Alternatively: Short-term: Don't check → Feel anxious temporarily Long-term: Don't check → Doubt decreases → Less need to check → Anxiety decreases

The behavior that temporarily increases anxiety is the same behavior that reduces anxiety overall.

Anxiety is information about your thoughts, not about reality:

When you feel anxious about contamination, the anxiety tells you: "I'm thinking about contamination."

It doesn't tell you: "Contamination is present."

When you feel anxious about the unlocked door, the anxiety tells you: "I'm imagining the door might be unlocked."

It doesn't tell you: "The door is actually unlocked."

Anxiety is a response to your thoughts, not a report about external reality.

This distinction is crucial. You can't use anxiety as evidence for probability. Anxiety tells you what you're thinking about, not what's actually likely.

Breaking the Pattern

Now that you understand how possibility-probability confusion works and why anxiety maintains it, here are specific strategies for breaking this pattern.

Strategy 1: Ask the probability question explicitly

When a concern arises, ask: "What's the actual likelihood of this happening?"

Force yourself to give a percentage or odds.

"What are the odds I left the stove on when I remember turning it off and seeing the burner go dark?" Maybe 0.1%. One in a thousand.

"What are the odds I hit someone with my car when I didn't see, hear, or feel any impact?" Maybe 0.01%. One in ten thousand.

"What are the odds this interaction will ruin the relationship when the person seemed friendly and engaged?" Maybe 1%. One in a hundred.

Once you've assigned a probability, ask: "Do I respond to other 0.1% probability events with this level of concern and action?"

Probably not. You do thousands of things daily with similar or higher risk and don't worry about them.

Strategy 2: The "everyone vs. me" test

Ask: "If everyone responded to this level of possibility with this level of caution, what would happen?"

If everyone washed their hands for 15 minutes after touching normal objects, productivity would collapse.

If everyone turned around to re-check their locked doors 6 times, nobody would get anywhere on time.

If everyone sought reassurance about every normal email they sent, communication would be paralyzed.

Normal functioning requires accepting tiny possibilities without behavioral response. If your standard is different from what allows normal human functioning, you're treating possibility as probability.

Strategy 3: Distinguish internal feelings from external facts

Create two mental categories:

Internal (feelings, thoughts):

- "I feel anxious"
- "I'm imagining contamination"
- "I'm uncertain whether I locked the door"

External (observable facts):

- "I see the lock is engaged"
- "I see my hands are clean"
- "I received a confirmation email"

Remind yourself: Internal feelings don't determine external facts.

"I feel uncertain" doesn't mean "Therefore the door is probably unlocked."

"I feel contaminated" doesn't mean "Therefore contamination is probably present."

Feelings are real. The conclusions you draw from feelings might not be.

Strategy 4: Calculate cost-benefit accurately

"Better safe than sorry" sounds wise, but only when costs and benefits are accurately assessed.

Cost of checking/compulsion:

- Time spent (could be hours daily)
- Reinforcement of doubt pattern (makes problem worse long-term)
- Interference with activities
- Relationship strain
- Reduced quality of life
- Increased anxiety over time

Benefit of checking/compulsion:

- Brief anxiety reduction (minutes)
- Protection against very low probability threat

Cost of not checking:

- Temporary anxiety (typically peaks in 15-30 minutes, then decreases)

Benefit of not checking:

- Breaking the reinforcement cycle
- Building tolerance for uncertainty
- Reducing doubt over time
- Regaining normal functioning
- Decreased anxiety long-term

When calculated accurately, not checking is almost always the better choice when probability is low and you already have sensory confirmation.

Strategy 5: Use evidence from your history

Review past instances where you worried about something.

How many times did your worst-case scenario actually occur? Probably rarely or never.

How many times did things turn out fine despite your worry? Probably the vast majority.

This historical data is more reliable than your current anxious feeling for assessing probability.

"I've worried about sending weird emails hundreds of times. How many times have I actually sent a weird email that ruined a relationship? Zero. How many times have my emails been fine? Hundreds."

Your track record is strong evidence that the current possibility is improbable.

Strategy 6: Accept uncertainty as normal

You cannot achieve 100% certainty about anything except direct sensory observation of the present moment.

You're never 100% certain what will happen in the future. You can't be 100% certain about things you can't currently observe. You can't be 100% certain about other people's thoughts.

Normal functioning requires accepting "certain enough" rather than demanding "absolutely certain."

"Certain enough" is when sensory information supports a conclusion. That's the standard I-CBT recommends.

You saw the lock engage—that's certain enough. You washed your hands and they look clean—that's certain enough. You received confirmation—that's certain enough.

Demanding more certainty than sensory information provides means demanding the impossible.

Strategy 7: Respond to probability, not possibility

Make a rule for yourself: "I respond behaviorally to what's probable, not to what's merely possible."

Probable concerns get action. Improbable concerns (even if possible) don't.

If you smell smoke (probable concern) → Investigate If you imagine there might be fire with no sensory evidence (improbable concern) → No action

If your professor emails asking to meet (probable concern) → Respond If you imagine they might be mad even though they were friendly (improbable concern) → No action

If you see actual dirt on your hands (probable concern) → Wash If you imagine invisible contamination despite clean appearance (improbable concern) → No action

This creates a clear decision rule that doesn't depend on how you feel, only on evidence.

Strategy 8: Practice anxiety tolerance

Since anxiety maintains the pattern, building tolerance for anxiety breaks it.

When anxiety arises from imagination-based concerns:

1. Recognize it as anxiety in response to imagination
2. Label it: "This is anxiety, not danger"
3. Don't engage in compulsions
4. Observe the anxiety without trying to eliminate it
5. Notice that it peaks and decreases naturally

This practice teaches your brain that anxiety isn't dangerous and doesn't require action.

Initially uncomfortable, but crucial for long-term improvement. Research shows that anxiety tolerance is one of the strongest predictors of treatment success (Wheaton et al., 2016).

Strategy 9: Time-delay technique

When feeling compelled to check or seek reassurance, tell yourself: "I'll wait 15 minutes first."

Often, the urge decreases during those 15 minutes. If it doesn't, try another 15 minutes.

This technique:

- Prevents automatic response to urges
- Allows time for anxiety to decrease naturally
- Helps you realize that checking isn't actually necessary
- Builds tolerance gradually

Strategy 10: Reality testing through behavioral experiments

Systematically test your probability estimates against reality.

Prediction: "If I don't check the lock again, I'll worry about it all day and won't be able to focus."

Experiment: Don't check. Observe what actually happens.

Result: Usually, you can focus reasonably well. The worry decreases over time. Nothing bad happens.

Running these experiments repeatedly builds evidence that your probability estimates are inaccurate and that not engaging in compulsions is safe.

Takeaways

Possibility and probability are different. Something can be technically possible while being highly improbable. Obsessive doubt treats possibility as probability, responding to what could happen as if it's what's likely to happen.

Your brain makes this error due to evolutionary bias, difficulty assessing probability, anxiety amplification, "better safe than sorry" reasoning, and loss of confidence in perception.

Anxiety responds to imagination as if it's reality, creating physical sensations that feel like evidence of danger. But anxiety tells you what you're thinking about, not what's actually probable.

Breaking the pattern requires: asking explicit probability questions, distinguishing feelings from facts, calculating costs accurately, using historical evidence, accepting uncertainty, responding only to probable concerns, and building anxiety tolerance.

The next chapter examines the twelve specific reasoning patterns (reasoning devices) that create and maintain obsessive inferences.

Chapter 7: Reasoning Devices

You're probably familiar with optical illusions—images that trick your eyes into seeing something that isn't there. The lines look different lengths but they're actually the same. The squares look different shades but they're identical.

Your brain has cognitive illusions too—reasoning patterns that trick your mind into believing something that isn't true. I-CBT researchers identified twelve specific patterns commonly used in obsessive thinking. They call these "reasoning devices."

Understanding these devices is like learning how a magic trick works. Once you see the technique, you can't be fooled by it anymore. This chapter explains all twelve devices with clear examples, so you can spot them in your own thinking.

Introduction to the 12 Reasoning Devices

Reasoning devices are flawed thinking patterns that make imaginary inferences seem legitimate (O'Connor & Aardema, 2012). They're cognitive shortcuts that bypass evidence and create conclusions from nothing.

Everyone uses these patterns occasionally. But in obsessive doubt, they become dominant modes of thinking, constantly generating false inferences.

The twelve devices are:

1. **Selective attention and focus**
2. **Imaginary sequences**
3. **Categorical reasoning**
4. **Subjective probability escalation**
5. **Inverse inference**

6. **Distrust of normal perception**
7. **Overimportance of thought**
8. **Necessity for proof**
9. **Thought-action fusion**
10. **Absorption in personal narrative**
11. **Self as central observer**
12. **Excessive responsibility**

Don't worry about memorizing the names. What matters is recognizing the patterns when they occur in your thinking.

How They Keep You Stuck

Before examining each device individually, let's understand their collective function in maintaining obsessive doubt.

Devices create inferences from nothing:

Normal inference: Observe evidence → Draw conclusion Reasoning device: Imagine scenario → Treat it as conclusion

The device substitutes imagination for evidence, making you believe something is true without sensory support.

Devices resist counter-evidence:

Once a reasoning device generates an inference, contradictory evidence doesn't dispel it.

You check the lock (counter-evidence that doubt is unfounded) → The device generates a new doubt ("What if I didn't check properly?") → You're back to uncertainty.

Devices are automatic and feel compelling:

These aren't deliberate choices. The patterns happen automatically, below conscious awareness. By the time you notice, you already believe the false inference.

And they feel logical in the moment. The reasoning seems to make sense, even though it's actually flawed.

Devices work together:

Often, multiple devices combine to create a single obsessive inference.

"What if I hit someone with my car?" might involve:

- Imaginary sequence (creating a story about impact)
- Subjective probability escalation (treating tiny possibility as likely)
- Necessity for proof (needing absolute certainty nothing happened)
- Excessive responsibility (believing you must verify)

Understanding individual devices helps you untangle these combinations.

Devices bypass reality:

The fundamental problem with all reasoning devices: they generate conclusions without checking reality.

Instead of looking at the door to see if it's locked, you imagine it might be unlocked.

Instead of observing whether your hands look clean, you imagine they might have invisible contamination.

The device replaces observation with imagination.

Recognizing Them in Your Daily Life

Each device has characteristic features. Learning these features helps you identify which devices you personally use most often.

Most people with obsessive doubt rely heavily on 3-5 of these devices. You might not use all twelve regularly. The point isn't to find every device in every thought—it's to recognize the patterns you personally default to.

As we go through each device, notice which ones feel familiar. Those are probably your primary reasoning devices.

Simple Examples of Each Device

Now let's examine each reasoning device in detail with clear examples.

Device 1: Selective Attention and Focus

Pattern: Focusing exclusively on one possible danger while ignoring all evidence of safety or other explanations.

Your attention narrows to a single concern, and everything else fades from awareness. You fixate on "What if there's contamination?" while ignoring all sensory evidence that no contamination exists.

How it works:

Your brain has limited attention capacity. What you focus on becomes your experienced reality. The device directs focus exclusively toward imagined danger, making it feel real and pressing while the broader context disappears.

Examples:

You touched a doorknob. Your attention immediately fixates on "germs on doorknob." You don't notice: the doorknob looked clean, your hands look clean, you've touched thousands of doorknobs without getting sick, most people touch doorknobs daily without problems. Your entire awareness narrows to contamination possibility.

You send an email. Your attention fixates on one sentence that might be misinterpreted. You don't notice: the overall message was clear, the tone was appropriate, you included context, the recipient has always responded reasonably before. Your awareness narrows to the single sentence.

You're driving home. A thought pops up: "What if I hit someone?" Your attention fixates on this possibility. You don't notice: you didn't see, hear, or feel any impact, you were paying attention to the road, other cars are driving normally behind you, you've driven this route hundreds of times without incident.

Counter to this device:

Deliberately broaden your attention. Ask: "What am I not noticing while focusing on this concern?" Usually, you're ignoring extensive evidence that everything is fine.

Device 2: Imaginary Sequences

Pattern: Creating detailed stories about how something bad might have happened or could happen, treating these stories as if they're based on fact.

You construct a narrative—a sequence of events—entirely in your imagination, then respond to this narrative as if it's reality or likely reality.

How it works:

Your brain is good at storytelling. It can take a tiny seed of possibility and build an entire scenario around it. The scenario feels concrete and real because you can visualize it clearly.

The device substitutes this imaginary sequence for actual observation of what happened or is happening.

Examples:

You're in class. You think: "What if I left my straightener plugged in?" Then your brain generates: "It's still on. It's heating up. It's touching the curtains. The curtains are catching fire. The fire is spreading. My whole apartment building is burning down. It's my fault."

None of this is based on observation—it's an imaginary sequence. But because you can picture it so vividly, it feels real.

You touched a shopping cart handle. Your brain generates: "Someone who was sick touched this yesterday. They coughed on their hand. Then they touched the cart. The virus is still on the handle. Now it's on my hand. It's going to enter my body. I'm going to get sick. I might die."

This entire story is imagined. No part of it is based on seeing germs, knowing someone sick touched it, or any sensory information.

You're at a social gathering. You said something that might have sounded weird. Your brain generates: "They thought that was strange. Now they're questioning whether I'm normal. They're probably talking about me when I'm not around. They're going to exclude me from future events. I'm going to lose all my friends."

A complete narrative constructed from one possibly-awkward moment, with no evidence any of it is happening.

Counter to this device:

Recognize storytelling. Ask: "Am I observing reality or narrating a story?" Stories feel real when you're absorbed in them, but they're still fiction.

Device 3: Categorical Reasoning

Pattern: Applying general characteristics of a category to specific instances without checking if they actually apply.

You place something in a mental category, then assume it has all the properties you associate with that category, without verifying through observation.

How it works:

Categories are useful cognitive shortcuts. If you know something is a "chair," you don't need to analyze it from scratch—you already know chairs are for sitting.

But categories can lead to errors when you assume all category members share all properties, or when you apply category properties without checking the specific instance.

Examples:

"Public restrooms are dirty" → You walk past a public restroom → You assume this specific restroom is dirty → You avoid it or feel contaminated after using it → You never actually looked to see if this particular restroom was clean or dirty.

"Unattended packages could be dangerous" → You see an unattended backpack in the library → You assume this specific backpack is dangerous → You feel anxious and consider reporting it → You don't consider that students leave belongings in libraries constantly and 99.99% are just normal backpacks.

"Raw meat carries bacteria" → You cooked chicken thoroughly → You assume this specific chicken might still have bacteria → You worry about food poisoning → You ignore that proper cooking kills bacteria and you can't smell or taste anything wrong.

"Relationships are hard" → You have a minor disagreement with your partner → You assume this specific disagreement means the relationship is failing → You catastrophize → You ignore that all relationships have minor conflicts and this is normal.

Counter to this device:

Check the specific instance. Don't assume category properties apply without observation. Ask: "What do I actually observe about this specific situation?"

Device 4: Subjective Probability Escalation

Pattern: Treating low-probability events as if they're likely, based on how they feel rather than actual odds.

Your subjective feeling of probability doesn't match objective probability. Something that's 0.01% likely feels like it's 50% likely because of anxiety.

How it works:

When anxious, your brain overestimates risk. The more vividly you imagine something, the more probable it seems. The more anxious you feel, the more likely the threat appears.

This device escalates tiny probabilities into seemingly major ones based purely on internal feelings.

Examples:

Objective probability of food poisoning from a normal meal at a licensed restaurant: < 0.1%

Subjective feeling: "I'm probably going to get sick from this. It's likely."

You treat < 0.1% as if it's 50%+, purely because you can imagine getting sick and feel anxious about it.

Objective probability of leaving an appliance on when you remember turning it off and seeing it go off: < 0.01%

Subjective feeling: "I probably forgot. It's likely still on."

You treat < 0.01% as if it's significant, purely because the thought generates anxiety.

Objective probability of hitting a pedestrian without any sensory feedback (no sight, sound, or feeling of impact): Essentially 0%

Subjective feeling: "It's possible I hit someone. It could have happened."

You treat 0% as if it's worth considering, purely because you can imagine it.

Counter to this device:

Ask explicitly: "What's the actual statistical probability?" Separate how something feels from how likely it actually is. Feelings aren't probability data.

Device 5: Inverse Inference

Pattern: Reversing logical relationships, treating the absence of something as evidence of its opposite.

You take a true conditional statement (if A, then B) and incorrectly reverse it (if not A, then not B, or worse, if not clearly B, then A).

How it works:

True: "If there's visible dirt, contamination exists"

Inverse reasoning: "If I can't see absolute cleanliness, contamination probably exists"

This reversal sounds logical but isn't. The absence of visible contamination is actually evidence of no contamination, not evidence of contamination.

Examples:

True statement: "If I definitely didn't lock the door, it's unlocked"

Inverse: "If I'm not 100% certain I locked it, it's probably unlocked"

This reversal is illogical. Uncertainty doesn't equal unlocked. Your observation shows it's locked; your uncertainty is about memory, not about the actual state of the lock.

True statement: "If someone is definitely offended, they'll show signs"

Inverse: "If I can't prove they're definitely not offended, they probably are offended"

Illogical reversal. Absence of proof of not-offended isn't evidence of offended.

True statement: "If I intentionally said something mean, that's wrong"

Inverse: "If I had a mean thought, even unintentionally, I'm probably a bad person"

The reversal equates involuntary thoughts with intentional actions, which is illogical.

Counter to this device:

Check the logic. If A → B doesn't mean not-A → not-B. Absence of evidence isn't evidence of absence, and uncertainty about A doesn't determine B.

Device 6: Distrust of Normal Perception

Pattern: Doubting your senses and memory even when they're functioning normally and giving clear information.

You received clear sensory information, but you question whether you really saw what you saw, really heard what you heard, or really remember what you remember.

How it works:

This device creates a gap between what your senses tell you and what you believe. Your eyes show you the lock is engaged, but the device questions: "Did you really see that? Were you paying attention? Might you have been mistaken?"

The device treats your normal perception as unreliable.

Examples:

You locked the door. You saw the deadbolt engage. You felt the key turn fully. You heard the click. But you think: "Did I really see that? Maybe I only thought I saw it. Maybe I was on autopilot and didn't really pay attention."

Your senses gave clear information. The device makes you doubt it.

You washed your hands. You see they're clean. You feel they're clean. But you think: "Maybe I missed a spot. Maybe there's contamination I can't see. Maybe my perception of clean isn't accurate."

Your senses tell you one thing. The device overrules them.

You had a conversation. You heard positive, friendly responses. But you think: "Maybe I misread their tone. Maybe they were being polite but actually annoyed. Maybe I didn't accurately perceive their reaction."

Your ears gave clear information. The device questions it.

Counter to this device:

Trust your senses when they're functioning normally. Ask: "Do I have any actual reason to doubt my perception, or am I just doubting out of habit?" Usually, you're doubting functional perception.

Device 7: Overimportance of Thought

Pattern: Treating the mere occurrence of a thought as meaningful or significant, rather than recognizing thoughts as random mental events.

Having a thought means the thought is important, carries special meaning, or says something about you or the world.

How it works:

Humans have thousands of thoughts daily. Most are random, meaningless, and quickly forgotten. But this device treats certain thoughts (usually unwanted or disturbing ones) as if they're significant signals requiring attention.

Examples:

You're standing on a balcony. The thought "I could jump" pops into your head. The device makes you think: "Why did I think that? Does this mean I'm suicidal? Is this a warning sign? What does this say about me?"

Reality: Brains generate random thoughts, including weird ones about physical possibilities. The thought means nothing.

You're in a serious meeting. The thought "What if I laughed right now?" occurs. The device makes you think: "That's inappropriate. Why would I think about laughing? Am I going to lose control? What's wrong with me?"

Reality: Brains often generate taboo thoughts in situations where they're inappropriate. It's normal and meaningless.

You have a brief aggressive thought about someone who annoyed you. The device makes you think: "This thought means I'm a violent person. What if I act on it? This reveals my true character."

Reality: Momentary aggressive thoughts are universal and don't predict behavior or reflect character.

Counter to this device:

Recognize that having a thought doesn't make it important. Thoughts are mental events, not meaningful messages. Ask: "Am I treating this thought as significant only because I had it, without any other evidence?"

Device 8: Necessity for Proof

Pattern: Requiring absolute certainty or positive proof that everything is fine, rather than accepting sensory evidence as sufficient.

You can't accept "certain enough"—you demand "absolutely certain." You need proof of safety rather than simply observing absence of danger.

How it works:

This device reverses normal reasoning. Normally, you need evidence that something is wrong before treating it as wrong. This device says you need proof nothing is wrong before you can stop worrying.

But many things can't be proven absolutely. The device therefore creates permanent uncertainty.

Examples:

You washed your hands. They look clean. The device says: "But can you prove there are zero germs? Can you guarantee you're not contaminated?"

You can't prove zero germs exist (you'd need laboratory testing). So the device keeps uncertainty alive despite sensory evidence of cleanliness.

You locked the door. You saw and felt it lock. The device says: "But can you prove with absolute certainty it won't somehow unlock itself? Can you guarantee no mechanical failure?"

You can't prove absolute certainty about future mechanical function. So the device maintains doubt despite sensory confirmation.

You sent a normal email. The device says: "But can you prove the recipient won't misinterpret it? Can you guarantee they're not offended?"

You can't prove someone else's internal reactions. So the device creates anxiety despite a normal interaction.

Counter to this device:

Accept that sensory evidence is sufficient. You don't need absolute proof or guaranteed certainty. You need "certain enough," which is what your senses provide.

Device 9: Thought-Action Fusion

Pattern: Believing that having a thought makes something more likely to happen, or that thinking about something is morally equivalent to doing it.

Your thoughts have magical power to influence reality, or thinking something is as bad as doing it.

How it works:

This device confuses different domains: internal mental events and external actions. It treats them as if they're connected when they're not.

Having a thought about something doesn't make it more likely. Thinking doesn't cause events. But the device makes you feel responsible for your thoughts as if they're actions.

Examples:

You think: "What if my parent gets in a car accident?" The device makes you feel like thinking this increases the probability of an accident. Now you feel responsible for thinking it and try to cancel it out with a counter-thought.

Reality: Your thoughts don't influence whether accidents occur. Thinking about an accident doesn't make one more likely.

You have an unwanted sexual thought about someone. The device makes you feel this thought is as morally wrong as actually doing something inappropriate.

Reality: Thoughts and actions are completely different. Having an unwanted thought has no moral weight—only actions do.

You imagine something bad happening to someone who wronged you. The device makes you feel guilty, as if you actually harmed them or wished them harm.

Reality: Passing thoughts, even negative ones, aren't the same as intentions or actions. You're not responsible for random thoughts.

Counter to this device:

Separate thoughts from actions. Thoughts are internal, private, and morally neutral. Actions are external, public, and morally relevant. Having a thought doesn't cause anything in the world.

Device 10: Absorption in Personal Narrative

Pattern: Creating and believing an elaborate story about yourself, your situation, or your characteristics that's maintained by imagination rather than evidence.

You construct a narrative about who you are or what your situation is, then selectively notice things that fit the narrative while ignoring contradictory evidence.

How it works:

Humans are storytelling creatures. We create narratives to make sense of our experiences. But sometimes these narratives become more powerful than reality, and we filter all new information through the narrative.

Examples:

Narrative: "I'm a contaminated person. I attract germs. I'm always at risk."

You interpret every situation through this narrative. You touch something → "Of course I'm contaminated now, that's just who I am." You ignore all the times you touch things and don't get sick. The narrative persists despite evidence.

Narrative: "I'm socially awkward. People always judge me. I don't fit in."

You interpret every social interaction through this lens. Someone is briefly distant → "See, they don't like me. I'm awkward." Someone is friendly → "They're just being polite." Evidence that contradicts the narrative gets reinterpreted to fit it.

Narrative: "I'm irresponsible. I forget important things. I can't be trusted."

You lock your door and then doubt it → "Of course I doubt it. I'm irresponsible and probably did forget." You ignore all the evidence of being reliable in hundreds of other areas.

Counter to this device:

Question the narrative. Ask: "What evidence actually supports this story about myself? What evidence contradicts it?" Usually, contradictory evidence is abundant but being ignored.

Device 11: Self as Central Observer

Pattern: Believing that your perspective is privileged or that you're being watched/judged by others more than you actually are.

You overestimate how much others notice or care about your actions. You assume everyone is observing you as closely as you observe yourself.

How it works:

This is sometimes called the "spotlight effect." You feel like you're in a spotlight with everyone watching. In reality, most people are focused on their own concerns, not on observing you.

The device makes you interpret neutral situations as if others are paying special attention to you.

Examples:

You trip slightly while walking across campus. The device makes you think: "Everyone saw that. They're all judging me. They think I'm clumsy."

Reality: Most people didn't notice. Those who did will forget in 30 seconds. Nobody is thinking about it except you.

You say something in class that doesn't come out quite right. The device makes you think: "Now everyone thinks I'm stupid. They're going to remember this. My reputation is damaged."

Reality: Others probably didn't notice or thought nothing of it. They're focused on their own concerns about how they're being perceived.

You're at the gym and you're not sure you're using equipment correctly. The device makes you think: "Everyone is watching me and noticing I don't know what I'm doing. They're judging me."

Reality: Everyone else is focused on their own workout. They're not observing you nearly as much as you imagine.

Counter to this device:

Remember that people are generally focused on themselves, not on scrutinizing you. Ask: "Is there evidence people are actually paying this much attention, or am I assuming I'm more central to their awareness than I really am?"

Device 12: Excessive Responsibility

Pattern: Believing you're responsible for preventing bad outcomes that are actually outside your control, or that you must act to prevent very unlikely negative events.

You overestimate your responsibility and power. You feel you must prevent any possible harm, even when it's not realistically your responsibility or when the probability is tiny.

How it works:

The device confuses possibility with obligation. If you can imagine a bad outcome, you feel responsible for preventing it, regardless of whether you have actual control or whether the outcome is likely.

This creates constant pressure to check, verify, and control things beyond your actual sphere of responsibility.

Examples:

You imagine someone might trip on an irregularity in the sidewalk. The device makes you feel responsible for warning everyone or fixing it, even though: it's not your property, thousands of people walk past without incident, you're not responsible for every possible hazard in the world.

You have a thought that something bad might happen to someone. The device makes you feel you must warn them or prevent it, even though: you have no evidence anything will happen, your thought doesn't predict reality, they're responsible for their own safety.

You worry that if you don't check the stove enough times, a fire will occur and it will be your fault, even though: you already confirmed it's off, you've never caused a fire, you're treating a 0.01% possibility as if you're obligated to prevent it with certainty.

You feel responsible for making sure everyone around you is happy and not offended, even though: you can't control others' reactions, people are responsible for their own emotions, trying to prevent any possible upset is impossible.

Counter to this device:

Clarify actual responsibility boundaries. Ask: "What am I actually responsible for vs. what am I imagining I'm responsible for?" Usually, you're taking responsibility for things outside your control or for preventing extremely unlikely events.

Key aways

Reasoning devices are twelve specific cognitive patterns that generate false inferences without evidence. They make imaginary scenarios feel real and legitimate.

The devices work by substituting imagination for observation, creating inferences from nothing, and resisting counter-evidence. They're automatic, feel compelling, and often work in combination.

Understanding which devices you personally use most often helps you recognize when your thinking has shifted from reality-based observation to imagination-based inference.

Each device has a characteristic pattern:

1. Selective attention - focusing only on imagined danger
2. Imaginary sequences - creating detailed stories
3. Categorical reasoning - assuming category properties without checking
4. Subjective probability escalation - treating low probability as high
5. Inverse inference - reversing logical relationships
6. Distrust of normal perception - doubting functional senses
7. Overimportance of thought - treating thoughts as meaningful
8. Necessity for proof - requiring absolute certainty
9. Thought-action fusion - believing thoughts affect reality
10. Absorption in personal narrative - maintaining imaginary self-story
11. Self as central observer - overestimating others' attention
12. Excessive responsibility - feeling obligated to prevent unlikely events

The next chapter examines how these devices, along with the other mechanisms we've discussed, combine to create and maintain the obsessive doubt cycle.

Chapter 8: The Obsessive Doubt Cycle

Picture a hamster wheel. The hamster runs and runs, putting in enormous effort. The wheel spins. But the hamster goes nowhere—it stays in exactly the same place despite all that running.

Obsessive doubt works the same way. You put in enormous mental effort—checking, analyzing, seeking reassurance, researching, reviewing. Things seem to be happening. But you end up right back where you started: uncertain and anxious.

This chapter maps out exactly how the obsessive doubt cycle works, why it keeps spinning despite your efforts, and where you can actually break in to stop it.

How the Cycle Works

The obsessive doubt cycle has six stages that repeat continuously. Understanding each stage helps you recognize where you are in the cycle at any given moment.

Stage 1: Trigger

Something catches your attention. This could be:

- An external event (touching something, leaving a room, sending an email)
- An internal sensation (body feeling, random thought)
- A memory (recalling something from earlier)
- A situation (being in a certain place or around certain people)

The trigger itself is usually neutral—it's just something that happens. But it sets the cycle in motion.

Example triggers:

- You touch a doorknob
- You leave your apartment
- You send a text message
- You have a random intrusive thought
- You notice a physical sensation
- You interact socially
- You remember something from earlier

Stage 2: Inference Generation

Your brain generates an inference (conclusion) about the trigger.

This is where reasoning devices activate. Your mind uses one or more of the twelve devices to create an inference that's not based on sensory evidence.

The inference usually takes the form of: "What if [bad thing]?" or "Maybe [danger exists]."

Examples:

- Trigger: Touch doorknob → Inference: "This is probably contaminated"
- Trigger: Leave apartment → Inference: "I might not have locked the door"
- Trigger: Send text → Inference: "I probably said something wrong"
- Trigger: Random thought → Inference: "This thought means something bad about me"
- Trigger: Physical sensation → Inference: "This could be a serious health problem"

Notice: The inference isn't based on seeing contamination, observing an unlocked door, receiving a negative reply, or having any evidence. It's generated by imagination using reasoning devices.

Stage 3: Anxiety Response

The inference triggers anxiety.

Your threat detection system responds to the imagined scenario as if it's real. Physiologically, your body prepares for danger:

- Heart rate increases
- Breathing quickens
- Muscles tense
- Attention narrows
- Sense of urgency intensifies

This is a real anxiety response to an imaginary situation. The physical feelings are genuine, even though the trigger for them isn't based on reality.

Stage 4: Urge to Neutralize

The anxiety creates a strong urge to do something to reduce it.

This urge feels compelling and urgent. Your brain is essentially saying: "This is a threat. You must do something. Now."

The "something" usually falls into these categories:

- **Checking:** Physically verifying something (re-checking locks, appliances, messages)
- **Washing/cleaning:** Removing perceived contamination
- **Seeking reassurance:** Asking others to confirm everything is okay
- **Researching:** Looking up information online to verify or rule out concerns
- **Mental reviewing:** Replaying events in your mind to analyze them
- **Avoidance:** Staying away from triggering situations
- **Ritualistic behavior:** Performing specific actions that feel like they prevent danger

Stage 5: Compulsive Response

You engage in the compulsion—the checking, washing, reassurance-seeking, or other neutralizing behavior.

This provides temporary relief. For a brief period (seconds to minutes), anxiety decreases. You feel better.

This temporary relief reinforces the behavior. Your brain learns: "When anxious about X, doing Y brings relief."

Stage 6: Return to Doubt

Here's the critical part: The relief is temporary. The doubt returns.

Why? Because the compulsion didn't address the actual problem (the faulty inference process). It only provided temporary anxiety reduction.

Soon, you're back to uncertainty:

- "Did I check thoroughly enough?"
- "What if I wasn't paying close attention when I checked?"
- "What if I need to check one more time to be sure?"
- "What if the situation has changed since I checked?"

And the cycle begins again. Trigger (the recurring doubt) → Inference → Anxiety → Urge → Compulsion → Brief relief → Return to doubt.

Complete Cycle Example: The Door Lock

Stage 1 - Trigger: Maya walks away from her apartment door

Stage 2 - Inference: "Wait, did I actually lock it? Maybe I just looked at it. Maybe I turned the knob but didn't engage the lock." (Reasoning devices active: Distrust of normal perception, Inverse inference)

Stage 3 - Anxiety: Heart rate increases, feels urgent, can't focus on anything else

Stage 4 - Urge: Strong compulsion to go back and check

Stage 5 - Compulsion: Maya goes back, checks the lock (it's locked), tests the handle

Stage 6 - Return to Doubt: Brief relief... then: "But was I paying attention when I just checked? Maybe I need to check once more to really register it."

Cycle repeats. Maya checks again. And possibly again. Each check provides momentary relief but then doubt returns.

Complete Cycle Example: Contamination

Stage 1 - Trigger: Jordan touches a cart handle at the grocery store

Stage 2 - Inference: "That handle is probably covered in germs. Someone sick definitely touched this recently." (Reasoning devices active: Categorical reasoning, Imaginary sequences, Subjective probability escalation)

Stage 3 - Anxiety: Feels contaminated, disgusted, anxious about getting sick

Stage 4 - Urge: Must clean hands immediately

Stage 5 - Compulsion: Jordan uses hand sanitizer twice, then washes hands in the store bathroom for three minutes

Stage 6 - Return to Doubt: Brief relief... then: "But was the water in that bathroom clean? Did I rinse all the soap off? What if I missed a spot?"

Cycle repeats. More sanitizer. More washing. Relief never lasts.

Complete Cycle Example: Social Doubt

Stage 1 - Trigger: Casey makes a comment in class discussion

Stage 2 - Inference: "That sounded weird. Everyone probably thinks I'm strange. The professor is probably judging me." (Reasoning devices active: Self as central observer, Selective attention, Absorption in personal narrative)

Stage 3 - Anxiety: Feels embarrassed, anxious, worried about judgment

Stage 4 - Urge: Need reassurance that the comment was okay

Stage 5 - Compulsion: Casey asks a friend after class: "Did I sound weird when I said that thing?" Friend says no, everything was fine.

Stage 6 - Return to Doubt: Brief relief... then: "But they're just being nice. They probably don't want to hurt my feelings. What if they really did think it was weird?"

Cycle repeats. Asks another friend. Replays the moment mentally. Relief never comes.

Why It Keeps Spinning

If compulsions don't provide lasting relief, why does the cycle continue? Why doesn't your brain learn that checking doesn't work?

Several mechanisms keep the wheel spinning:

Mechanism 1: Short-term reinforcement

Even though relief is temporary, it's immediate. You check → anxiety decreases right away. This immediate reinforcement is powerful.

Your brain prioritizes immediate outcomes over long-term consequences. The instant relief from checking is more salient than the long-term pattern of increased doubt.

This is similar to other reinforcement patterns. Eating junk food provides immediate pleasure despite long-term health consequences. Hitting snooze provides immediate comfort despite making you late. Checking provides immediate relief despite long-term amplification of doubt.

Mechanism 2: Avoiding the test

By engaging in compulsions, you never test whether something bad would actually happen if you didn't check.

If you always check the lock, you never discover: "I didn't check, and nothing bad happened."

If you always wash excessively, you never discover: "I didn't overwash, and I didn't get sick."

If you always seek reassurance, you never discover: "I didn't ask for reassurance, and the relationship was fine."

Without these counter-experiences, your brain never updates its threat assessment. The imagined danger seems to remain real and likely.

Mechanism 3: Checking erodes confidence

Paradoxically, checking makes you less confident about what you checked.

Research shows that repeated checking actually decreases memory confidence and increases uncertainty (van den Hout & Kindt, 2003). Each time you check:

- Your memory of checking becomes fuzzier

- You trust your initial perception less
- You feel more need to check again

The behavior meant to increase certainty actually decreases it.

Mechanism 4: The inference process never gets addressed

Compulsions respond to the anxiety but not to the faulty inference that created the anxiety.

Think of it this way: Your inference process is a factory producing defective products (false inferences). Compulsions are like downstream quality control—you're checking each defective product, but the factory keeps producing more defective ones.

I-CBT focuses on fixing the factory (the inference process itself) rather than just managing the defective products.

Mechanism 5: Standards escalate

Over time, what counts as "certain enough" increases.

Initially, checking once might satisfy you. But as the pattern continues, you need to check twice. Then three times. Then five times. The doubt threshold keeps rising.

The same applies to cleanliness standards, reassurance needs, or any other compulsion. What used to be sufficient becomes insufficient. You're chasing a moving target.

Mechanism 6: Cognitive dissonance

You've invested so much time and effort in checking that admitting it's unnecessary would create uncomfortable dissonance.

"I've checked this door 500 times. If checking isn't necessary, that means I wasted enormous time and energy. That's hard to accept. So checking must be necessary."

This makes it psychologically difficult to stop the pattern even when you recognize it's problematic.

Mechanism 7: Fear of responsibility

You might think: "Yes, the probability is low. But if something did happen and I hadn't checked, I'd feel responsible."

This reasoning keeps the cycle spinning even when you intellectually understand the odds. The imagined guilt of "What if I'm wrong?" seems worse than the actual cost of continuing to check.

But this reasoning is flawed. You're not actually preventing anything with obsessive checking. You're just performing a ritual that temporarily reduces anxiety.

Mechanism 8: Secondary gains

Sometimes the cycle provides hidden benefits:

- Checking gives you something to do with anxious energy
- The pattern creates structure and predictability
- Compulsions make you feel like you're taking action
- The behavior allows avoidance of other uncomfortable situations

These secondary gains, while not the main driver, can help maintain the pattern.

Where You Can Break In

The good news: This cycle can be interrupted at multiple points. You don't need to accept it as inevitable.

Break Point 1: At the Trigger

You can't always prevent triggers, but you can change your response to them.

Strategy: Exposure without neutralizing

Deliberately encounter triggers without performing compulsions. This teaches your brain that triggers don't require response.

Example: Touch doorknobs without using hand sanitizer immediately. Example: Leave your apartment without going back to check the lock. Example: Send emails without re-reading them multiple times.

This is difficult initially because anxiety rises. But with repeated practice, anxiety decreases naturally and triggers lose their power.

Break Point 2: At the Inference

This is the core I-CBT intervention point. When an inference arises, examine it before it triggers anxiety.

Strategy: Reality check

Ask immediately: "Is this inference based on what I see/hear/feel/smell/taste, or on imagination?"

If imagination, recognize it as such: "This is imagination, not reality."

Don't engage with the content of the inference. Don't debate whether it's likely. Simply categorize it: sensory-based or imagination-based.

Example: Trigger: Touch doorknob → Inference starts to form: "Might be contaminated..." → Reality check: "Wait. Do I see dirt? No. Do I smell anything? No. This is imagination." → Don't engage further.

This breaks the chain before anxiety fully develops.

Break Point 3: At the Anxiety Response

Even if anxiety develops, you can change how you respond to it.

Strategy: Anxiety tolerance

Recognize anxiety as a feeling, not as evidence of danger. Observe it without trying to eliminate it.

"I'm feeling anxious. That's just a feeling. It will pass without me doing anything."

Don't interpret anxiety as confirmation that the inference was valid. Remind yourself: "Anxiety is responding to my imagination, not to reality."

Practice staying with the anxious feeling without performing compulsions. It will peak and decrease naturally (usually within 20-45 minutes).

Break Point 4: At the Urge

When you feel compelled to check or seek reassurance, that's decision point.

Strategy: Urge surfing

Notice the urge without acting on it. Visualize it like a wave—it rises, peaks, and falls. You don't need to act; you can just observe.

"I'm noticing an urge to check. This is just an urge, not a requirement."

Delay the compulsion. Tell yourself you'll wait 15 minutes. Often, the urge decreases during that time.

Break Point 5: At the Compulsion

If you find yourself starting to engage in a compulsion, you can still stop mid-way.

Strategy: Incomplete compulsion

If you start checking, stop after once instead of checking repeatedly.

If you start washing, stop after a reasonable amount instead of the extended ritual.

If you start researching online, close the browser after a few minutes instead of hours.

Incomplete compulsions are better than complete ones. You're breaking the pattern even if not perfectly.

Break Point 6: At the Return to Doubt

When doubt returns after checking, that's another decision point.

Strategy: Resist the repeat

Recognize: "Doubt returned. This is what always happens. Checking again won't actually resolve it."

Remind yourself: "I already checked once. That was sufficient. This new doubt is just the cycle repeating."

Refuse to check again, even though the urge is present.

This teaches your brain that one check is the maximum allowed, which starts to modify the pattern.

Combining Break Points

You don't need to intervene at every point. Even breaking the cycle at one point begins to weaken it.

Most effective combinations:

- Reality check at inference + anxiety tolerance = You recognize imagination early and don't respond to subsequent anxiety
- Exposure + urge surfing = You encounter triggers without performing compulsions
- Anxiety tolerance + resist repeat = You allow initial anxiety without checking, and when doubt returns, you still don't check

Experiment to find which break points work best for you. Different people find different intervention points most manageable.

Your Personal Cycle Map

Now let's make this practical by mapping your specific obsessive doubt cycle.

Exercise: Map Your Cycle

Choose one recurring obsessive doubt pattern. Using the six-stage framework, map out exactly how your cycle works.

Stage 1: My Trigger What typically starts this pattern for me? [Your answer]

Stage 2: My Inference What conclusion does my mind generate? [Your answer]

Which reasoning devices am I using? [Your answer]

Stage 3: My Anxiety Response What do I feel physically? [Your answer]

What thoughts intensify the anxiety? [Your answer]

Stage 4: My Urge What do I feel compelled to do? [Your answer]

How strong is this urge (1-10)? [Your answer]

Stage 5: My Compulsion What do I actually do? [Your answer]

How long does this take? [Your answer]

Stage 6: My Return to Doubt How long does relief last? [Your answer]

What doubt arises next? [Your answer]

Mapping Example: Hand Washing Cycle

Stage 1: My Trigger Touching anything in public—doorknobs, cart handles, railings, menus

Stage 2: My Inference "That surface was probably touched by someone sick. Germs are definitely on my hands now. I'm contaminated."

Reasoning devices: Categorical reasoning (all public surfaces are contaminated), Imaginary sequences (creating story about sick person touching it), Subjective probability escalation (treating tiny possibility as high probability)

Stage 3: My Anxiety Response Physical: Disgust feeling, tension, increased heart rate, focused attention on hands Thoughts: "I can't touch anything else. I need to wash immediately. What if I get sick?"

Stage 4: My Urge Compelled to wash hands immediately. Can't focus on anything else until I do. Strength: 8-9/10

Stage 5: My Compulsion Find bathroom, wash hands with soap for 2-3 minutes, scrubbing intensely. Use paper towel to turn off faucet and open door. Duration: 5-10 minutes including finding bathroom

Stage 6: My Return to Doubt Relief lasts: About 30 seconds to 2 minutes Next doubt: "Did I use enough soap? Was the water clean? Did I rinse all the soap off? Did I touch something contaminated when leaving the bathroom?"

Analysis Questions:

After mapping your cycle, answer:

1. What am I actually getting from compulsions?
    - Temporary relief (very brief)
    - Feeling of control (illusory)
    - Avoidance of anxiety (short-term only)
2. What is this pattern costing me?
    - Time (example: 45 minutes daily on hand washing)
    - Energy (mental and physical exhaustion)
    - Functioning (interference with normal activities)
    - Confidence (increased doubt over time)
3. Where might I most effectively break this cycle?
    - Consider which break points seem most manageable
    - Which intervention would address the root problem?
    - Where am I willing to start?
4. What would I need to do differently at that break point?
    - Specific behavioral change
    - What would I do instead of the compulsion?
    - How would I handle the anxiety that arises?

Your Break Plan:

Based on your cycle map, create a specific plan:

I will break my cycle at: [Which stage(s)]

Specifically, I will: [Concrete action]

When anxiety rises, I will: [Anxiety tolerance strategy]

I expect this to be difficult because: [Anticipated challenges]

I will know it's working when: [Progress indicators]

I will practice this for: [Time commitment]

Example Break Plan:

I will break my cycle at: Inference and Compulsion stages

Specifically, I will:

- At inference stage: Reality check—"Do I see contamination? No. This is imagination."
- At compulsion stage: Wash hands only once for 20 seconds, then stop

When anxiety rises, I will:

- Remind myself "Anxiety is responding to imagination"
- Stay with the feeling without washing again
- Notice it peaks and decreases

I expect this to be difficult because:

- The urge to wash more is very strong
- Anxiety feels unbearable sometimes
- I'm afraid I'll actually get sick

I will know it's working when:

- I can wash once and stop
- Anxiety decreases over time
- Urges become less intense
- I think about contamination less often

I will practice this for:

- Two weeks minimum, tracking progress daily

Track Your Progress:

Keep a log for each time you encounter your trigger:

Date/Time	Trigger	Did I break the cycle?	Where?	How did it go?	Anxiety level after (1-10)

This log helps you:

- See patterns in when/where you succeed
- Identify which break points work best
- Notice progress over time
- Adjust your strategy based on results

Common Challenges and Solutions:

Challenge: "I can't tolerate the anxiety. It's too intense."

Solution: Start with less intense triggers. Practice anxiety tolerance in easier situations first, building up to more difficult ones. Remember: Anxiety peaks and then decreases. Time it—usually 20-45 minutes maximum.

Challenge: "I keep forgetting to do the reality check. By the time I remember, I've already checked."

Solution: Set reminders. Write key questions on note cards. Put sticky notes in trigger locations: "Is this sensory or imagination?"

Challenge: "I break the cycle sometimes, but then I go right back to old patterns."

Solution: Expect setbacks. Progress isn't linear. Each time you break the cycle, you're building new neural pathways. Keep practicing even after setbacks.

Challenge: "It works for one obsession, but I have several different ones."

Solution: Apply the same principles to each. Usually, once you master breaking one cycle, the others become easier because you understand the process.

Challenge: "Other people don't understand and think I should just stop."

Solution: Most people don't understand obsessive doubt unless they've experienced it. You don't need their understanding—you need your own commitment to change. Consider finding a therapist who specializes in OCD for knowledgeable support.

What You've Learned So Far

The obsessive doubt cycle has six stages: Trigger → Inference Generation → Anxiety Response → Urge to Neutralize → Compulsive Response → Return to Doubt. The cycle repeats continuously, maintaining itself through short-term reinforcement despite long-term amplification of doubt.

The cycle persists because: compulsions provide immediate relief, you never test whether bad outcomes actually occur without checking, checking erodes confidence, the inference process itself never gets addressed, standards escalate over time, and various other mechanisms maintain it.

You can break the cycle at multiple points: at the trigger (exposure), at the inference (reality check), at the anxiety (tolerance), at the urge (delay), at the compulsion (incompletion), or at the return to doubt (resist repeat).

Mapping your personal cycle helps you understand your specific pattern and identify where to intervene most effectively. Creating a concrete break plan and tracking progress helps you actually change the pattern.

The next chapters will provide more detailed tools for applying these break points in various situations, starting with the Reality Sensing Check.

Chapter 9: Tool #1 - The Reality Sensing Check

You've learned the theory behind I-CBT. Now comes the practical part—the actual tools you can use when obsessive doubt arises.

The Reality Sensing Check is the foundation of all I-CBT techniques. It's a systematic way to determine whether your concern is based on sensory information (reality) or imagination. This tool addresses the core problem: confusing what you imagine with what actually exists.

Think of this as your primary diagnostic tool. Before you can respond appropriately to any doubt, you need to know what kind of doubt it is. The Reality Sensing Check tells you.

What Your Five Senses Tell You

Your five senses are your direct link to reality. They provide accurate, real-time information about your environment. Let's review what each sense does and why it's trustworthy.

Sight: Visual Information

Your eyes detect light reflecting off objects, creating images that your brain interprets. Under normal conditions (adequate light, functioning vision, clear view), your eyes accurately report:

- What objects are present
- Colors and shapes
- Positions and distances
- Movements and changes
- Written text and visual information

When you look at a door lock and see the deadbolt engaged, your eyes are giving you reliable data. The lock is engaged. That's not a guess or an interpretation—it's direct observation.

Hearing: Auditory Information

Your ears detect sound waves, translating them into recognizable sounds. Your hearing tells you:

- What sounds are present (voices, alarms, mechanical noises, nature sounds)
- What's silent (absence of sound is also information)
- Volume and direction of sounds
- Tone and quality of sounds

When you turn off an appliance and hear it stop humming, your ears are reporting accurate information. The appliance has stopped. When you hear silence instead of fire alarms, that silence is data.

Touch: Tactile Information

Your skin and hands provide information through physical contact. Touch tells you:

- Textures (smooth, rough, sticky, wet, dry)
- Temperatures (hot, cold, warm, cool)
- Pressure and resistance
- Physical properties of objects

When you test a door handle and feel it resist when you pull, your sense of touch is giving you accurate feedback. The door is locked and won't open.

Smell: Olfactory Information

Your nose detects chemical compounds in the air, identifying odors. Smell tells you:

- What scents are present
- What's odorless (absence of smell is information)
- Intensity of odors
- Whether something is burning, spoiled, or normal

When you smell nothing unusual after cooking, that absence of burning smell is reliable information. Nothing is burning. When food smells normal, that's accurate sensory data.

Taste: Gustatory Information

Your tongue detects chemicals in substances you consume. Taste tells you:

- Sweet, salty, sour, bitter, savory flavors
- Whether food tastes normal or off
- Chemical properties of what you're consuming

When food tastes normal—not bitter, sour, or rancid—your tongue is providing accurate information about that food's edibility.

Why trust your senses?

Your senses evolved over millions of years to provide accurate environmental information. Organisms with unreliable senses didn't survive to reproduce. You're descended from countless generations of beings whose senses worked well enough to navigate reality successfully.

Modern humans have the same sensory equipment. Unless you have a diagnosed sensory impairment, your senses are functioning properly and giving you accurate data about your immediate environment.

Research on perception consistently shows that under normal conditions, human senses are highly accurate (Palmer, 1999). The errors that do occur are typically in ambiguous situations (dim light, distant sounds, unclear stimuli) or involve higher-level interpretation rather than basic sensory detection.

The key principle:

If your five senses aren't detecting something, it's not present in your immediate environment. This sounds obvious, but obsessive doubt makes you question this basic principle.

"I don't see contamination, but what if it's there?" violates the principle. If you don't see it, smell it, or feel it, it's not there in detectable form.

"I don't see the door unlocked, but what if it is?" violates the principle. If you see the lock engaged, it's engaged.

Trusting your senses means accepting that what they report is what's actually present.

How to Do a Reality Check

The Reality Sensing Check is a structured process you can run through whenever doubt arises. With practice, this becomes quick and automatic—taking just 30-60 seconds.

Step 1: Identify the concern

What are you worried about? State it clearly and specifically.

Examples:

- "My hands might be contaminated"
- "The stove might still be on"
- "I might have sent an inappropriate email"
- "This food might be spoiled"
- "The door might be unlocked"

Step 2: Check each sense systematically

Go through all five senses, asking what each one tells you about the concern.

Vision: "What do I see?"

Look at the relevant situation. What visual information is present?

For hands: Do I see dirt? Discoloration? Visible contamination? For stove: Can I see the burner or flame? What position is the dial in? For email: Can I see what I wrote? Does it read as intended? For food: Does it look normal? Any visual signs of spoilage? For door: Can I see the lock position?

Hearing: "What do I hear?"

What auditory information relates to this concern?

For hands: Not applicable to most contamination concerns For stove: Do I hear it running? Any hissing or burning sounds? For email: Not directly applicable after sending For food: Not usually applicable For door: Did I hear the lock click when I engaged it?

Touch: "What do I feel?"

What tactile information exists?

For hands: How do they feel? Normal skin texture? Sticky? Gritty? For stove: Can I feel heat emanating from it? (if present) For email: Not applicable after sending For food: Does it feel normal in texture? For door: Did I feel the key turn? Feel resistance when testing the handle?

Smell: "What do I smell?"

What odors are present or absent?

For hands: Do they smell unusual? Like soap? Like nothing in particular? For stove: Do I smell gas? Burning? Nothing? For email:

Not applicable For food: Does it smell normal? Fresh? Spoiled? For door: Not usually applicable

Taste: "What do I taste?"

What flavors are present? (Often not applicable)

For hands: Not applicable For stove: Not applicable For email: Not applicable For food: Does it taste normal or off? For door: Not applicable

Step 3: Distinguish sensory evidence from imagination

Now separate your findings into two categories:

Sensory evidence (what your five senses actually detected): List only direct observations from your senses. No interpretation, just raw sensory data.

Imagination (what you're thinking might be true): List everything based on "what if," "maybe," "could be," or other imagination-based elements.

Step 4: Apply the 100% Imaginary Test

Ask: "If I remove all the imagination-based elements, is there any sensory evidence left supporting my concern?"

If the answer is no—if the concern is 100% imaginary—then you've identified an obsessive inference that doesn't require action.

Step 5: Make a decision

Based on the reality check:

- If sensory evidence supports the concern → Appropriate action is warranted

- If the concern is 100% imaginary → No action needed; this is obsessive doubt

Complete Example: Contamination Concern

Step 1: Identify the concern "My hands are contaminated after touching the bathroom door handle."

Step 2: Check each sense

Vision: I see hands that look clean. No visible dirt, stains, or unusual appearance. Normal skin color.

Hearing: Not applicable to this concern.

Touch: My hands feel normal. Clean skin texture. Not sticky, not gritty, not wet.

Smell: My hands smell neutral, maybe slight soap scent from earlier washing. No unusual or foul odor.

Taste: Not applicable.

Step 3: Distinguish evidence from imagination

Sensory evidence:

- Hands look clean
- Hands feel normal
- Hands smell neutral/clean

Imagination:

- "But germs are invisible"
- "Someone sick might have touched that handle"
- "The contamination could be microscopic"
- "I might get sick"

Step 4: Apply the 100% Imaginary Test

If I remove imagination, what evidence remains?

- No sensory evidence of contamination
- All concerns are based on "might," "could," "what if"
- Conclusion: 100% imaginary

Step 5: Make a decision

This concern is entirely imagination-based. Appropriate response: Don't wash hands excessively. Trust the sensory information showing hands are clean.

Complete Example: Appliance Safety

Step 1: Identify the concern "I might have left the coffee maker on."

Step 2: Check each sense

Vision: I'm not home, so I can't see the coffee maker currently. But I remember seeing it turned off and unplugged.

Hearing: I don't hear any fire alarms from my apartment (if close enough) or receive any notifications.

Touch: I remember feeling the switch in the off position.

Smell: I don't smell smoke.

Taste: Not applicable.

Step 3: Distinguish evidence from imagination

Sensory evidence:

- Memory of seeing it off and unplugged

- No fire alarms audible
- No smoke smell
- Memory of feeling switch in off position

Imagination:

- "What if I'm misremembering?"
- "What if it turned back on somehow?"
- "What if there's a fire starting right now?"

Step 4: Apply the 100% Imaginary Test

If I remove imagination, what remains?

- Sensory memory of turning it off
- No current sensory signs of fire

Imagination component: "What if" scenarios with no supporting evidence

Conclusion: The concern is imagination-based. My senses (memory plus current absence of fire indicators) show the coffee maker is off.

Step 5: Make a decision

This is obsessive doubt. Appropriate response: Don't go back to check. Trust the sensory evidence.

Practice Scenarios

Practicing the Reality Sensing Check with various scenarios helps you internalize the process. Work through these examples:

Scenario 1: Academic Submission

Concern: "Maybe my assignment didn't actually submit even though I got a confirmation."

Run through the reality check:

Vision: What do I see?

- Confirmation email in my inbox
- Assignment visible in course portal with timestamp
- Status shows "Submitted"

Hearing: Not applicable

Touch: Not applicable

Smell: Not applicable

Taste: Not applicable

Sensory evidence vs. imagination:

- Sensory: Two visual confirmations of submission
- Imagination: "What if the system glitched," "What if the professor won't see it"

100% Imaginary Test: Remove imagination, left with solid visual evidence of submission

Decision: This is imagination-based doubt. Don't email professor to confirm.

Scenario 2: Social Interaction

Concern: "I probably offended my friend with that comment I made."

Run through the reality check:

Vision: What did I see during and after the comment?

- Friend was smiling

- They maintained eye contact
- Body language remained open and relaxed
- They continued the conversation normally

Hearing: What did I hear?

- Their tone remained friendly
- They laughed after the comment
- They contributed to the conversation enthusiastically

Touch: Not applicable

Smell: Not applicable

Taste: Not applicable

Sensory evidence vs. imagination:

- Sensory: Multiple indicators of positive, comfortable interaction
- Imagination: "What if they were just being polite," "What if they're upset inside"

100% Imaginary Test: Remove imagination, left with extensive evidence the interaction was fine

Decision: This is imagination-based doubt. Don't seek reassurance about the comment.

Scenario 3: Health Anxiety

Concern: "This headache might be a brain tumor."

Run through the reality check:

Vision: Not directly applicable to internal sensations

Hearing: Not applicable

Touch/Body sensation: What do I feel?

- Mild to moderate head discomfort
- No other unusual symptoms
- Sensation similar to previous ordinary headaches

Smell: Not applicable

Taste: Not applicable

Sensory evidence vs. imagination:

- Sensory: Headache sensation (which has many common causes)
- Imagination: "Might be a tumor," "Could be something serious," catastrophic interpretations

100% Imaginary Test: Remove imagination, left with: a headache, which is a common symptom with many benign causes

Decision: Headache itself is real (sensory), but tumor interpretation is imagination. Appropriate response: Normal headache remedies (water, rest, pain reliever if needed). If severe or accompanied by other concerning symptoms, or persists unusually long, then medical consultation is appropriate. But jumping to catastrophic interpretation is imagination-based.

Scenario 4: Door Lock Doubt

Concern: "Maybe the door isn't really locked even though I checked it."

Run through the reality check:

Vision: What did I see?

- Deadbolt in locked position
- Door stayed closed when I pulled the handle

- Lock mechanism appears intact and functional

Hearing: What did I hear?

- Click of lock engaging when I turned the key
- No unusual sounds suggesting malfunction

Touch: What did I feel?

- Key turned fully
- Resistance when testing the handle
- Door didn't budge

Smell: Not applicable

Taste: Not applicable

Sensory evidence vs. imagination:

- Sensory: Three senses (sight, hearing, touch) all confirm lock is engaged
- Imagination: "What if I wasn't paying attention," "What if it's not really locked," "What if there's a mechanical problem"

100% Imaginary Test: Remove imagination, left with triple-sensory confirmation of lock engagement

Decision: This is imagination-based doubt. Don't go back to check again.

Now try your own:

Think of a recent obsessive doubt you experienced. Run it through the Reality Sensing Check:

My Concern: [Write it here]

Vision - What did/do I see? [Your observation]

Hearing - What did/do I hear? [Your observation]

Touch - What did/do I feel? [Your observation]

Smell - What did/do I smell? [Your observation]

Taste - What did/do I taste? [Your observation]

Sensory Evidence: [List only actual sensory observations]

Imagination: [List all "what if" and imagination-based elements]

100% Imaginary Test Result: [Is the concern entirely imaginary, or is there sensory evidence?]

Appropriate Response: [What should you do based on this reality check?]

Your Daily Reality Log

Keeping a daily log helps you practice the Reality Sensing Check consistently and track your progress. Use this format:

Daily Reality Log Template:

Time	Concern	Sensory Evidence	Imaginary Elements	100% Imaginary?	My Response	How It Went
				Yes/No		

Example Log Entries:

Time	Concern	Sensory Evidence	Imaginary Elements	100% Imaginary?	My Response	How It Went
8:30 AM	Left stove on	Remember seeing burner off, no smell of gas	"What if I'm wrong, what if fire"	Yes	Didn't go back to check	Anxious for 10 min, then decreased. Nothing happened.
12:15 PM	Contaminated hands after touching library book	Hands look clean, feel normal	"What if germs on book"	Yes	Used sanitizer once, then stopped	Urge to wash more, but resisted. Felt good about it.
3:00 PM	Email to professor seemed rude	Reread it, tone is professional and polite	"What if she takes it wrong"	Yes	Didn't send follow-up	Anxiety decreased. She responded normally next day.
9:00 PM	Door might be unlocked	Saw and felt lock engage, heard click	"What if it didn't really lock"	Yes	Didn't check again	Very hard. Anxious all evening. But nothing happened.

How to use the log:

1. Record in real-time or shortly after

When doubt arises, run through the Reality Sensing Check and record it. The sooner you record it, the more accurate your observations will be.

2. Be honest

If you didn't resist the compulsion, record that. The log isn't about being perfect—it's about noticing patterns and tracking genuine progress.

3. Note anxiety levels if helpful

Some people find it useful to add an anxiety rating (1-10) before and after their response. This helps you see that anxiety decreases even without compulsions.

4. Review weekly

At the end of each week, review your log. Look for:

- Which situations trigger doubts most often?
- Are most of your concerns 100% imaginary?
- When do you successfully resist compulsions?
- Is anxiety duration decreasing over time?
- Are you getting faster at identifying imaginary concerns?

5. Celebrate successes

When you successfully resist a compulsion, note it positively. Each time you break the cycle is progress.

6. Learn from challenges

When you engage in compulsions, don't criticize yourself. Instead, note what made that situation particularly difficult. This helps you prepare for similar situations.

Sample Weekly Review:

"This week, I recorded 23 reality checks. 21 of my concerns were 100% imaginary. I successfully resisted compulsions 15 times out of 23. The situations where I struggled most were leaving home (door lock concerns) and after using public restrooms (contamination).

I noticed that when I resisted compulsions, anxiety typically peaked around 15-20 minutes and then decreased. By 45 minutes, I felt much better. This helps me trust that anxiety will pass without checking.

Next week, I'll focus specifically on door lock concerns since those are hardest for me. I'll practice the Reality Sensing Check as I'm locking the door, rather than waiting until doubt arises later."

Variations for different needs:

Simplified Log (for beginners):

If the full log feels overwhelming, start simpler:

Concern	100% Imaginary?	Did I Resist Compulsion?
	Yes/No	Yes/No

Detailed Log (for deeper analysis):

Tips for maintaining the log:

Keep it accessible: Use your phone notes, a small notebook you carry, or a specific app. Make recording easy.

Set reminders: If you forget to use the Reality Sensing Check, set phone reminders throughout the day: "Is this concern sensory or imaginary?"

Don't aim for perfection: You won't record every single doubt. That's fine. Recording even 50% of them provides useful data.

Notice patterns: After two weeks of logging, patterns become clear. You'll see that most concerns are 100% imaginary, that anxiety decreases without compulsions, and that resisting gets easier with practice.

Share with therapist: If you're working with a therapist, the log provides concrete data for your sessions. They can help you analyze patterns and adjust your approach.

Adjust as needed: If the log format doesn't work for you, modify it. The goal is to support your practice, not to create another source of stress.

What You've Learned So Far

The Reality Sensing Check is a systematic tool for determining whether concerns are based on sensory information or imagination. Your five senses provide accurate information about your immediate environment and are trustworthy under normal conditions.

The check involves five steps: identify the concern, check each sense systematically, distinguish sensory evidence from imagination, apply the 100% Imaginary Test, and make an appropriate decision about response.

Practice with various scenarios helps internalize the process. A Daily Reality Log tracks your use of the tool, providing data about patterns, progress, and areas needing focus.

The next chapter introduces Tool #2: The Inference Detective, which helps you investigate your doubts more deeply to understand how they form.

Chapter 10: Tool #2 - The Inference Detective

Every obsessive doubt starts with an inference—a conclusion your mind draws about a situation. The Reality Sensing Check helps you identify whether that inference is based on sensory evidence. The Inference Detective takes the next step: it helps you investigate exactly how your mind arrived at that inference.

Think of yourself as a detective investigating a case. The case is: "How did I reach this conclusion?" The evidence is: your thought process, the reasoning devices you used, and the actual facts of the situation.

This tool gives you a structured way to examine your inferences closely, exposing the faulty reasoning that created them.

Investigating Your Doubts

Investigation requires curiosity rather than judgment. You're not criticizing yourself for having obsessive thoughts. You're simply getting curious about the mechanics: How did this inference form?

The investigative mindset:

Detectives gather evidence without predetermined conclusions. They ask questions, examine facts, and follow where the evidence leads. Apply this same approach to your inferences.

When doubt arises, instead of immediately believing it or trying to eliminate it, investigate it. Ask: "How did I reach this conclusion? What led me here?"

What you're investigating:

The inference itself: What exactly am I concluding? State it clearly.

The reasoning process: What steps did my mind take to reach this conclusion?

The evidence (or lack thereof): What facts support this inference vs. what's imaginary?

The reasoning devices: Which thinking tricks am I using?

Alternative explanations: What else could explain this situation?

Example: Beginning an Investigation

You send a text to a friend. Hours later, no response. You feel anxious and think: "They're probably mad at me."

Instead of accepting this inference, investigate it:

"Wait, how did I reach the conclusion they're mad? Let me trace the thought process. I sent a text. No response yet. My mind jumped to: no response means they're mad. What's the evidence for that? Is there another explanation? What reasoning devices am I using?"

This investigative approach creates distance between you and the inference. You're examining it rather than being consumed by it.

Benefits of investigation:

Slows down automatic thinking: Instead of instantly believing inferences, you pause to examine them.

Reveals patterns: You'll notice you use the same reasoning devices repeatedly.

Weakens conviction: When you see how an inference formed through faulty reasoning, you believe it less strongly.

Builds skill: Investigation gets faster and more automatic with practice.

Creates objectivity: You start observing your thought process rather than being identified with it.

The 5 Key Questions

The Inference Detective tool uses five key questions to investigate any inference. These questions systematically examine how the inference formed and whether it's justified.

Question 1: "What exactly am I concluding?"

State the inference precisely. Be specific about what you're inferring.

Vague: "Something bad will happen" Specific: "I'm inferring that I left the stove on and it will cause a fire"

Vague: "They don't like me" Specific: "I'm inferring that my coworker is angry with me because they didn't smile when we passed in the hallway"

Vague: "I'm contaminated" Specific: "I'm inferring that touching the shopping cart handle transferred dangerous germs to my hands"

Precision matters because it allows you to examine the specific inference rather than a vague feeling of anxiety.

Question 2: "What sensory evidence supports this inference?"

List only direct sensory observations—what you actually saw, heard, touched, smelled, or tasted.

Example: "Coworker is angry with me" Sensory evidence: They didn't smile when we passed. That's the only direct observation.

Example: "Stove is still on" Sensory evidence: None currently. I'm not home to observe. Memory: I saw the burner off before leaving.

Example: "Shopping cart handle has dangerous germs" Sensory evidence: None. I don't see dirt, don't smell anything unusual, handle felt like normal metal.

Often, you'll find there's very little or no sensory evidence supporting the inference. This is revealing.

Question 3: "What am I imagining or assuming?"

List everything based on "what if," "maybe," "probably," or other non-sensory sources.

Example: "Coworker is angry" Imagining: "Maybe I did something to offend them." "Perhaps they're upset about the project." "They might be avoiding me."

Example: "Stove is still on" Imagining: "What if I only thought I turned it off?" "Maybe it turned back on somehow." "What if there's a fire right now?"

Example: "Dangerous germs on handle" Imagining: "Someone sick probably touched this." "Germs are definitely on my hands now." "I might get seriously ill."

Usually, the list of imagined elements is much longer than the list of sensory evidence. The inference is built primarily on imagination.

Question 4: "Which reasoning devices am I using?"

Identify which of the twelve reasoning devices are active in creating this inference.

Example: "Coworker is angry"

- Selective attention (focusing only on lack of smile, ignoring context)
- Subjective probability escalation (treating one neutral interaction as probably indicating anger)
- Self as central observer (assuming their behavior is about me)

Example: "Stove is still on"

- Distrust of normal perception (doubting memory of turning it off)
- Imaginary sequences (creating story about fire)
- Inverse inference (if not 100% certain it's off, assuming it's probably on)

Example: "Dangerous germs on handle"

- Categorical reasoning (all public surfaces are contaminated)
- Imaginary sequences (creating story about sick person touching handle)
- Subjective probability escalation (treating low probability as high)

Naming the devices reduces their power. You see them as tricks rather than legitimate reasoning.

Question 5: "What are alternative explanations?"

Generate other possible explanations for the situation, especially ones based on actual sensory evidence.

Example: "Coworker is angry" Alternatives:

- They were distracted and thinking about something else
- They didn't see me clearly or weren't paying attention
- They're having a stressful day unrelated to me
- Their baseline expression is neutral, not always smiling
- There is no problem; I'm over-interpreting

Example: "Stove is still on" Alternatives:

- I turned it off as I remember doing
- It's off and everything is fine
- There's no fire; my apartment is secure

Example: "Dangerous germs on handle" Alternatives:

- The handle has normal environmental bacteria that my immune system handles constantly
- Shopping carts are touched by millions of people who don't get sick
- My hands are fine; I've touched countless handles without illness
- "Dangerous germs" is an imaginary category, not a sensory observation

Alternative explanations ground you back in reality-based thinking.

Step-by-Step Process

Here's the complete Inference Detective process from start to finish:

Step 1: Notice and pause

When you feel anxious or doubtful, pause. Notice that an inference has formed. Don't immediately act on it.

"I'm feeling anxious. There's a doubt or inference present. Before responding, let me investigate this."

Step 2: Name the inference

Answer Question 1: What exactly am I concluding?

Write it down or state it clearly in your mind. Be specific.

Step 3: Gather sensory evidence

Answer Question 2: What sensory evidence supports this inference?

List only direct observations from your five senses. Be strict about this—no interpretation, just raw sensory data.

Step 4: Identify imagination

Answer Question 3: What am I imagining or assuming?

List all the "what if," "maybe," "could be" elements. Include interpretations and catastrophic thinking.

Step 5: Spot reasoning devices

Answer Question 4: Which reasoning devices am I using?

Look through the list of twelve devices. Which ones are active in this inference? Name them.

Step 6: Generate alternatives

Answer Question 5: What are alternative explanations?

Think of at least three other ways to interpret the situation, preferably ones closer to sensory evidence.

Step 7: Draw conclusions

Based on your investigation:

- Is this inference justified by sensory evidence? (Usually no)
- Is it primarily imagination-based? (Usually yes)
- What's the most reality-based explanation?

Step 8: Decide on response

Given what your investigation revealed:

- If the inference is imagination-based: Don't respond with compulsions
- If sensory evidence indicates a real concern: Respond appropriately
- Trust the investigation's findings, not the anxiety's urgency

Complete Example: Academic Email

Step 1: Notice and pause

Devon sent an email to a professor three hours ago. No response yet. Feeling anxious. Pause before checking email again or sending a follow-up.

Step 2: Name the inference

"I'm concluding that my email was inappropriate or annoying, and the professor is upset with me."

Step 3: Gather sensory evidence

Sensory evidence:

- I sent an email (visual: saw it send)
- No response received yet (visual: checked inbox, nothing there)
- That's all. No sensory data about professor's reaction.

Step 4: Identify imagination

Imagining:

- "The email must have sounded demanding"
- "The professor probably thinks I'm a nuisance"
- "They're upset and that's why they haven't responded"
- "I damaged my relationship with them"
- "They might give me a lower grade now"

All of this is imaginary—no sensory evidence supports any of it.

Step 5: Spot reasoning devices

Devices active:

- Imaginary sequences (creating story about professor being upset)
- Subjective probability escalation (treating no-response as probably indicating upset)
- Inverse inference (no response doesn't mean positive response, so must mean negative response)
- Self as central observer (assuming I'm more central to professor's attention than I likely am)
- Catastrophizing (jumping to grade implications)

Step 6: Generate alternatives

Alternative explanations:

- Professor is busy and responds to emails in batches
- They need to look up information before responding
- They receive dozens of emails daily and haven't gotten to mine yet
- Three hours is actually a normal response time for faculty
- The email was fine; there's no problem

Step 7: Draw conclusions

Investigation findings:

- Almost no sensory evidence; nearly all imagination
- Multiple reasoning devices creating false inference
- Alternative explanations are more probable
- The inference isn't justified

Step 8: Decide on response

Response: Don't check email compulsively. Don't send follow-up. Wait for normal response time (24-48 hours for faculty). Recognize this as imagination-based anxiety.

Complete Example: Health Concern

Step 1: Notice and pause

Sam noticed an unusual sensation in their chest. Immediately thinks: heart attack. Pause before rushing to ER or calling someone.

Step 2: Name the inference

"I'm concluding that this chest sensation indicates I'm having a heart attack."

Step 3: Gather sensory evidence

Sensory evidence:

- Mild uncomfortable sensation in chest (real sensation)
- No pain radiating to arm or jaw
- No shortness of breath
- No sweating
- Can move and function normally
- Heart rate feels normal when checking pulse

Step 4: Identify imagination

Imagining:

- "This sensation means heart attack"
- "What if it's the early stage of something serious"
- "I might be dying"
- "What if I wait too long to get help"

Step 5: Spot reasoning devices

Devices active:

- Catastrophic interpretation (jumping to worst-case scenario)
- Selective attention (focusing only on sensation, ignoring all other normal signs)
- Overimportance of body sensation (treating normal sensation as emergency)
- Subjective probability escalation (treating extremely low probability as high)

Step 6: Generate alternatives

Alternative explanations:

- Muscle tension from stress or poor posture
- Gas or indigestion
- Anxiety itself causing chest tightness (very common)
- Normal body sensations that everyone experiences
- Previous similar sensations that resolved without issue

Step 7: Draw conclusions

Investigation findings:

- One real sensation (chest feeling) but many absent signs of actual heart attack
- Catastrophic interpretation not supported by full sensory picture
- Multiple reasoning devices creating fear
- More probable explanations exist

Step 8: Decide on response

Response: This appears to be imagination-based catastrophizing of a normal sensation. Appropriate response: Monitor for 15-30 minutes. If sensation resolves or if other symptoms don't develop, it's likely benign. If severe pain develops, or if symptoms like arm pain, jaw pain, severe shortness of breath, or crushing chest pain occur, then seek medical attention. But current evidence doesn't indicate emergency.

Note: If you have risk factors for heart disease or if chest sensations are severe or accompanied by other concerning symptoms, appropriate medical consultation is warranted. The point isn't to ignore all health concerns—it's to distinguish between realistic concerns based on symptom patterns versus catastrophic interpretation of mild, normal sensations.

Worksheet and Examples

Use this worksheet to practice the Inference Detective tool. Make copies or recreate this format in a notebook.

INFERENCE DETECTIVE WORKSHEET

Date/Time: _____

Situation: (What triggered the doubt?)

_____

_____

1. What exactly am I concluding? (State the specific inference)

_____

_____

2. What sensory evidence supports this inference? (Only direct observations from five senses)

Vision:

_____

Hearing:

Touch:

Smell:

Taste:

3. What am I imagining or assuming? (All "what if," "maybe," "probably" elements)

4. Which reasoning devices am I using? (Check all that apply)

☐ Selective attention and focus ☐ Imaginary sequences ☐ Categorical reasoning ☐ Subjective probability escalation ☐ Inverse inference ☐ Distrust of normal perception ☐ Overimportance of thought ☐ Necessity for proof ☐ Thought-action fusion ☐ Absorption in personal narrative ☐ Self as central observer ☐ Excessive responsibility

5. What are alternative explanations? (At least 3 reality-based alternatives)

A. _____ B.
_____ C.
_____

Conclusions from Investigation: ☐ Inference is primarily imagination-based ☐ Sensory evidence is minimal or absent ☐ Reasoning devices are active ☐ Alternative explanations are more probable

Appropriate Response:

_____
_____

Did I follow through? ☐ Yes ☐ No

If no, what made it difficult?

_____

Results: (What happened? How long did anxiety last?)

_____
_____

Example Worksheet: Filled Out

Date/Time: Tuesday, 2:30 PM

Situation: Touched railing on campus stairwell, now worried about contamination

1. What exactly am I concluding? That railing definitely has dangerous bacteria or viruses on it, and now my hand is contaminated and I need to wash immediately or I'll get sick.

2. What sensory evidence supports this inference?

Vision: Railing looked like normal metal. No visible dirt or unusual appearance.

Hearing: Not applicable

Touch: Felt like normal smooth metal railing

Smell: No unusual smell

Taste: Not applicable

(Summary: No sensory evidence of contamination)

3. What am I imagining or assuming?

- "That railing must be covered in germs because lots of people touch it"
- "Someone sick probably touched it recently"
- "The germs are on my hand now even though I can't see them"
- "I'm going to get sick if I don't wash"
- "This is dangerous"

4. Which reasoning devices am I using?

☑ Selective attention and focus (focusing only on contamination possibility) ☐ Imaginary sequences (story about sick person touching railing) ☑ Categorical reasoning (all public railings are contaminated) ☑ Subjective probability escalation (treating low risk as high) ☐ Inverse inference ☐ Distrust of normal perception ☐ Overimportance of thought ☐ Necessity for proof ☐ Thought-action fusion ☐ Absorption in personal narrative ☐ Self as central observer ☐ Excessive responsibility

5. What are alternative explanations?

A. The railing has normal environmental bacteria that my immune system handles constantly B. Thousands of people touch railings daily without getting sick C. My hand looks and feels fine; there's no actual contamination D. This is obsessive inference based on category, not on observable evidence

Conclusions from Investigation: ☑ Inference is primarily imagination-based ☑ Sensory evidence is minimal or absent ☑ Reasoning devices are active ☑ Alternative explanations are more probable

Appropriate Response: Don't rush to wash hands. Use hand sanitizer once if desired (normal reasonable hygiene), but don't engage in extended washing ritual. Recognize this as obsessive doubt.

Did I follow through? ☑ Yes

Results: Used sanitizer once, then moved on. Felt anxious for about 10 minutes, but anxiety decreased naturally. Didn't get sick (as always). Felt good about resisting the excessive washing urge.

Practice Examples:

Work through these scenarios using the Inference Detective process:

Scenario A: You're lying in bed trying to sleep. You think: "Did I lock the car doors?" You're pretty sure you did, but now you're doubting it.

Run the investigation: What's the inference? What sensory evidence exists? What are you imagining? Which devices? Alternative explanations? Conclusion?

Scenario B: You're at a social gathering. You told a story and one person didn't laugh while others did. Now you think: "That person doesn't like me. I shouldn't have told that story."

Run the investigation using the five questions.

Scenario C: You submitted an important assignment. You got a confirmation. But now you think: "What if the file was corrupted? What if the professor can't open it?"

Run the investigation.

Scenario D: You ate at a restaurant. The food tasted normal, but now you think: "What if it was undercooked? What if I get food poisoning?"

Run the investigation.

Tips for effective investigation:

Write it out: Don't just think through the questions. Writing clarifies thinking and makes patterns more visible.

Be thorough on sensory evidence: Really examine what your senses tell you. Often people skip this and jump to imagination.

Don't rush: Take 5-10 minutes for a thorough investigation. This isn't about quick reassurance—it's about understanding your inference process.

Investigate even when you "know" it's irrational: Intellectually knowing an inference is irrational doesn't stop it from feeling compelling. Investigation shows you exactly why it's irrational, which is more powerful.

Review investigations: Periodically reread your completed worksheets. You'll notice patterns in which devices you use most, which situations trigger you most, and how consistent your conclusions are (nearly always imagination-based).

Share with others: If you're working with a therapist, bring completed worksheets to sessions. They provide concrete examples for discussion.

What You've Learned So Far

The Inference Detective tool provides a structured investigation of how inferences form. Rather than immediately believing or trying to eliminate doubts, you investigate them with curiosity.

The five key questions systematically examine: the specific inference, sensory evidence supporting it, imagined elements, active reasoning devices, and alternative explanations.

The step-by-step process guides you through investigation and helps you draw conclusions about whether an inference is justified or imagination-based.

Worksheets make the process concrete and trackable. With practice, investigation becomes faster and more automatic, helping you recognize imagination-based inferences quickly.

The next chapter introduces Tool #3: Spotting Reasoning Devices, which helps you become expert at recognizing the specific thinking tricks your mind uses most often.

Chapter 11: Tool #3 - Spotting Reasoning Devices

You've learned about the twelve reasoning devices—the cognitive tricks your mind uses to create false inferences. Now it's time to become expert at spotting them in real-time.

This chapter focuses on recognition and intervention. You'll learn to identify your personal pattern of devices, catch them as they activate, and respond in ways that break their power.

Think of this as developing a specialized skill. Initially, it takes conscious effort. With practice, recognition becomes automatic—you'll catch devices within seconds of them activating.

Your Personal Device Tracker

Most people with obsessive doubt don't use all twelve reasoning devices equally. You probably have 3-5 devices you rely on heavily, with occasional use of others.

Identifying your personal pattern helps you know what to watch for. Instead of monitoring for all twelve devices constantly, you can focus on your primary ones.

Creating Your Device Profile:

Review the twelve devices again:

1. Selective attention and focus
2. Imaginary sequences
3. Categorical reasoning
4. Subjective probability escalation
5. Inverse inference

6. Distrust of normal perception
7. Overimportance of thought
8. Necessity for proof
9. Thought-action fusion
10. Absorption in personal narrative
11. Self as central observer
12. Excessive responsibility

For each device, rate how often you use it:

Rating scale:

- 0 = Never or almost never use this
- 1 = Occasionally use this (less than once per week)
- 2 = Regularly use this (multiple times per week)
- 3 = Frequently use this (daily or multiple times daily)

Device Rating Form:

1. Selective attention and focus: ___
2. Imaginary sequences: ___
3. Categorical reasoning: ___
4. Subjective probability escalation: ___
5. Inverse inference: ___
6. Distrust of normal perception: ___
7. Overimportance of thought: ___
8. Necessity for proof: ___
9. Thought-action fusion: ___
10. Absorption in personal narrative: ___
11. Self as central observer: ___
12. Excessive responsibility: ___

Your Primary Devices (rated 3):

Your Secondary Devices (rated 2):

These are the devices to monitor most closely. They're your personal signature patterns.

Example Profile:

Jordan rates their devices:

- Selective attention: 3 (constantly focusing on contamination possibility)
- Imaginary sequences: 3 (creating detailed stories about germs)
- Categorical reasoning: 3 (all public surfaces are dirty)
- Subjective probability escalation: 2 (treating low risk as high)
- Inverse inference: 1 (occasionally)
- Distrust of normal perception: 2 (sometimes doubts visual cleanliness)
- Overimportance of thought: 0 (not really an issue)
- Necessity for proof: 2 (needs certainty about cleanliness)
- Thought-action fusion: 0 (not relevant to contamination concerns)
- Absorption in personal narrative: 1 (somewhat sees self as "contaminated person")
- Self as central observer: 0 (not relevant)
- Excessive responsibility: 1 (some worry about preventing illness)

Jordan's primary devices (3s): Selective attention, Imaginary sequences, Categorical reasoning

Jordan's secondary devices (2s): Subjective probability escalation, Distrust of normal perception, Necessity for proof

Jordan now knows to watch for these six devices especially. When contamination concerns arise, one or more of these patterns will likely be active.

Tracking Your Devices Over Time:

Keep a simple log of which devices activate in different situations:

Date Situation Device(s) Active Strength (1-3)

After two weeks, patterns become clear. You'll see which devices appear most often and in which contexts.

Common Patterns

While everyone's profile is unique, certain patterns appear frequently. Understanding common combinations helps you recognize them.

Pattern 1: The Contamination Cluster

Common devices:

- Categorical reasoning ("All public surfaces are dirty")
- Imaginary sequences (stories about germs spreading)
- Selective attention (focusing only on contamination possibility)
- Necessity for proof ("Can you prove it's clean?")

This cluster typically appears in contamination-related obsessions. The person categorizes surfaces, imagines contamination sequences, focuses exclusively on contamination possibility, and demands impossible proof of cleanliness.

Breaking this pattern:

Reality check: "What do I actually see/smell/feel on this surface?" Challenge categorical reasoning: "Am I assuming all members of this category have this property, or do I have evidence this specific item does?" Recognize imagination: "I'm creating stories about germs, not observing actual contamination."

Pattern 2: The Checking Cluster

Common devices:

- Distrust of normal perception ("Did I really see that?")
- Inverse inference ("If I'm not certain, it's probably not done")
- Necessity for proof ("I need absolute certainty")
- Excessive responsibility ("If something happens, it's my fault")

This cluster appears with checking compulsions. The person doubts their memory and perception, reverses logical inferences, demands certainty, and feels excessive responsibility for prevention.

Breaking this pattern:

Trust sensory information: "I saw the lock engage. My senses are reliable." Correct inverse logic: "Uncertainty doesn't mean it's not locked; it means I'm doubting my clear observation." Accept sufficient certainty: "Sensory confirmation is enough. Absolute certainty isn't possible or necessary."

Pattern 3: The Social Anxiety Cluster

Common devices:

- Self as central observer ("Everyone is watching/judging me")
- Subjective probability escalation (treating unlikely negative judgment as probable)
- Selective attention (focusing only on possible negative reactions)
- Imaginary sequences (creating stories about what others think)

This cluster appears in social obsessions. The person assumes they're the center of others' attention, overestimates negative judgment, focuses only on ambiguous or negative cues, and imagines elaborate stories about others' thoughts.

Breaking this pattern:

Reality check: "What did I actually observe? Person smiled and engaged normally." Challenge self-centrality: "Most people are focused on themselves, not analyzing me." Generate alternatives: "Brief lack of smile could mean anything—distracted, tired, didn't see me clearly."

Pattern 4: The Health Anxiety Cluster

Common devices:

- Subjective probability escalation (treating rare diseases as likely)
- Imaginary sequences (catastrophizing about symptoms)
- Selective attention (focusing only on concerning interpretations)
- Overimportance of body sensations (treating normal sensations as emergencies)

This cluster appears in health obsessions. The person catastrophizes minor symptoms, focuses only on serious possibilities, and treats normal body sensations as significant medical signs.

Breaking this pattern:

Check actual symptoms: "What do I actually feel? Headache only. No other symptoms." Challenge probability: "What's the realistic likelihood? Headaches are common; brain tumors are rare." Generate common explanations: "Stress, dehydration, eye strain, tension—all more probable than catastrophic causes."

Pattern 5: The Relationship Doubt Cluster

Common devices:

- Overimportance of thought ("Having doubts means something's wrong")

- Necessity for proof ("I need to know for certain I love them")
- Absorption in personal narrative ("I'm the type of person who can't maintain relationships")
- Subjective probability escalation (treating normal relationship variations as signs of failure)

This cluster appears in relationship obsessions. The person treats doubt thoughts as meaningful, demands certainty about feelings, maintains a negative self-narrative, and overinterprets normal relationship fluctuations.

Breaking this pattern:

Recognize thoughts as mental events: "Having a doubt thought doesn't mean the doubt is valid." Accept feeling ambiguity: "Feelings fluctuate normally. Relationships have ups and downs." Question the narrative: "Where's the evidence I 'can't maintain relationships'? I have several long-term friendships."

Your Personal Pattern:

Based on your device ratings, which pattern(s) match your experience?

What specific situations trigger this pattern?

Which devices activate first, starting the cascade?

Understanding your pattern helps you intervene early—you can catch the first device before the full cluster activates.

How to Challenge Each Device

Once you've spotted a reasoning device, you need to challenge it effectively. Here's how to respond to each device:

Device 1: Selective Attention and Focus

Recognition: You're fixated on one possibility while ignoring context, alternatives, and contradictory information.

Challenge: Deliberately broaden attention. Ask: "What am I not noticing while focusing on this concern?"

Response: "I'm focusing only on contamination possibility. Let me notice: the surface looks clean, smells normal, feels normal. I've touched similar surfaces countless times without illness. I'm selectively attending to danger while ignoring all safety evidence."

Device 2: Imaginary Sequences

Recognition: You're constructing a detailed story about how something bad happened or will happen, treating the story as reality or likely reality.

Challenge: Label it as storytelling. Ask: "Am I observing or narrating?"

Response: "I'm creating a story: sick person touches handle, transfers virus, I touch handle, virus transfers to me, I get sick, I die. This is a story, not observed fact. I'm narrating possibilities, not witnessing events."

Device 3: Categorical Reasoning

Recognition: You're assuming this specific instance has properties based on category membership, without checking the instance.

Challenge: Check the specific instance. Ask: "What do I actually observe about this particular thing?"

Response: "I'm assuming this public restroom is dirty because it's in the 'public restrooms' category. But what do I actually see about this specific restroom? It looks clean, smells like cleaning products, appears well-maintained. The category assumption doesn't match the observation."

Device 4: Subjective Probability Escalation

Recognition: You're treating something as likely based on how it feels, not on actual odds.

Challenge: Ask for actual probability. "What are the realistic odds?"

Response: "I feel like I probably have a serious illness. But what are actual odds? Headaches are extremely common; brain tumors are rare. My feeling of probability doesn't match reality. The subjective escalation is making a tiny probability feel huge."

Device 5: Inverse Inference

Recognition: You're reversing a logical relationship inappropriately.

Challenge: Check the logic. "Am I reversing cause and effect or presence and absence?"

Response: "I'm thinking: 'I'm not 100% certain I locked it, therefore it's probably unlocked.' That's inverse logic. The door being locked doesn't depend on my certainty level. I observed it lock. My uncertainty is about my memory, not about the actual lock state."

Device 6: Distrust of Normal Perception

Recognition: You're doubting your senses even though they're functioning normally.

Challenge: Affirm sensory reliability. "Do I have actual reason to doubt my perception?"

Response: "I'm doubting whether I really saw the lock engage, even though my vision is fine, the lighting was good, and I was paying attention. I have no actual reason to distrust this perception. My senses are reliable. I saw what I saw."

Device 7: Overimportance of Thought

Recognition: You're treating the mere occurrence of a thought as meaningful or significant.

Challenge: Recognize thoughts as mental events. "Does having this thought make it important?"

Response: "I had a disturbing thought, and now I'm treating it as significant. But having a thought doesn't make it meaningful. Brains generate thousands of random thoughts daily. This is just one more mental event—not a message, not meaningful."

Device 8: Necessity for Proof

Recognition: You're demanding absolute certainty or positive proof of safety, rather than accepting sensory evidence.

Challenge: Accept sensory evidence as sufficient. "Is sensory information enough?"

Response: "I'm demanding proof there are absolutely zero germs. But that's impossible to prove without laboratory testing. What I can observe: hands look clean, feel clean, smell clean. Sensory evidence is sufficient. I don't need impossible proof."

Device 9: Thought-Action Fusion

Recognition: You're believing thoughts influence reality or equal actions morally.

Challenge: Separate thoughts from actions. "Do thoughts cause events?"

Response: "I had a thought about something bad happening, and now I feel like thinking it makes it more likely or makes me responsible. But thoughts don't cause external events. Thinking about an accident doesn't create accidents. Thoughts and actions are completely different domains."

Device 10: Absorption in Personal Narrative

Recognition: You're maintaining a story about yourself that filters all information to fit the narrative.

Challenge: Check evidence against narrative. "Does evidence support this self-story?"

Response: "I'm seeing myself as 'always contaminated.' But the evidence? I rarely get sick. I function normally. This narrative is maintained by selective interpretation, not by facts. The story doesn't match reality."

Device 11: Self as Central Observer

Recognition: You're overestimating how much others notice or focus on you.

Challenge: Reality check attention. "Do I have evidence others are focusing on me this much?"

Response: "I feel like everyone noticed my awkward comment and is judging me. But realistically, most people are focused on themselves. The person I'm worried about probably forgot the interaction minutes later. I'm overestimating my centrality to others' attention."

Device 12: Excessive Responsibility

Recognition: You're taking responsibility for preventing unlikely events or things outside your control.

Challenge: Clarify actual responsibility. "What am I actually responsible for?"

Response: "I feel responsible for preventing any possible harm to anyone. But that's not realistic or within my control. My actual responsibility: reasonable precautions. Not absolute prevention of all unlikely possibilities. I'm taking on responsibility for things I can't and shouldn't control."

Practice Exercises

These exercises build skill in spotting and challenging reasoning devices.

Exercise 1: Device Spotting Practice

For each statement below, identify which reasoning device(s) are active:

1. "I touched that doorknob, so I'm definitely contaminated now." Devices: _____
2. "I'm not 100% sure I locked the door, so it's probably unlocked." Devices: _____
3. "I had a weird thought. Why would I think that? This must mean something about me." Devices: _____
4. "Everyone at the party probably thought I was awkward." Devices: _____
5. "What if I left the stove on and the house burns down and it's all my fault?" Devices: _____

Answers:

1. Categorical reasoning (doorknobs are contaminated), Imaginary sequences (creating contamination story)
2. Inverse inference (uncertainty → probably unlocked), Distrust of normal perception
3. Overimportance of thought (thought must be meaningful)
4. Self as central observer (everyone focused on me), Subjective probability escalation (probably thought negatively)
5. Imaginary sequences (fire story), Excessive responsibility (responsible for preventing), Subjective probability escalation (treating tiny possibility as likely)

Exercise 2: Real-Time Device Logging

For one week, whenever you notice obsessive doubt arising, immediately identify which device(s) are active:

Date/Time Doubt Device(s) Identified Challenge Used Result

This builds real-time recognition skill.

Exercise 3: Device Challenges

Practice generating challenges for your most common devices:

My Primary Device #1: _____

Standard Challenge I'll Use:

_____

My Primary Device #2: _____

Standard Challenge I'll Use:

_____

My Primary Device #3: _____

Standard Challenge I'll Use:

Having prepared challenges makes real-time intervention easier.

Exercise 4: Device Combination Recognition

Some obsessive doubts involve multiple devices working together. Practice spotting combinations:

Scenario: "I washed my hands, but what if there are still germs? I can't see them, but they might be there. I need to wash again to be absolutely sure."

Identify all active devices:

- Distrust of normal perception (doubting that hands are clean despite washing)
- Necessity for proof (need absolute certainty)
- Inverse inference (can't prove germs aren't there, so assume they are)
- Subjective probability escalation (treating invisible germs as probable)

Practice with your own recent doubts. Map out all the devices working together.

Exercise 5: Early Intervention

Often, one device triggers first, then others follow. Practice catching the first device:

Think of a typical obsessive sequence for you. Which device usually activates first?

Example: For contamination worries, Categorical Reasoning often starts it ("Public surfaces are dirty"), followed by Selective Attention (focusing only on contamination), then Imaginary Sequences (creating germ story), then Necessity for Proof (demanding certainty of cleanliness).

If you can catch and challenge Categorical Reasoning immediately ("Wait—am I assuming all public surfaces are dirty without checking this specific one?"), you might prevent the cascade.

Your typical sequence:

First device: _____ Then: _____ Then: _____

Intervention point: Challenge the first device before others activate.

What You've Learned So Far

Most people with obsessive doubt use 3-5 reasoning devices primarily, with occasional use of others. Creating your personal device profile helps you know what to watch for.

Common patterns exist: the Contamination Cluster, Checking Cluster, Social Anxiety Cluster, Health Anxiety Cluster, and Relationship Doubt Cluster. Each involves specific device combinations.

Each device has specific challenges. Learning to recognize and challenge your primary devices weakens their power.

Practice exercises build real-time recognition skills. With consistent practice over several weeks, spotting devices becomes automatic.

The next chapter focuses on rebuilding trust in your senses—a crucial component of recovery that addresses why you stopped trusting yourself in the first place.

Chapter 12: Tool #4 - Building Trust in Your Senses

At the core of obsessive doubt is a profound loss of trust in your own perception and judgment. You look at a locked door but don't trust what you see. You wash your hands clean but don't trust what you feel. You remember turning off the stove but don't trust your memory.

This chapter addresses how to rebuild that trust systematically. Trust doesn't return overnight, but with consistent practice using specific exercises, you can restore confidence in your own senses and judgment.

Why You Stopped Trusting Yourself

Understanding why trust eroded helps you recognize that the problem isn't your senses—it's the relationship between your senses and your belief in them.

Mechanism 1: Repeated checking eroded memory confidence

Research demonstrates that repeated checking actually decreases memory confidence (van den Hout & Kindt, 2003). Each time you go back to verify something, you create a new memory that interferes with the original.

You lock the door once → Clear memory of locking it You check again → Now you have two memories of the lock You check a third time → Three memories, but which one was today? You check a fourth time → Memory becomes fuzzy

The behavior meant to increase certainty actually decreases it. The checking itself is eroding trust.

Mechanism 2: Imagination felt as powerful as perception

When you vividly imagine contamination, danger, or negative outcomes, the imagination creates physiological responses similar to actual perception. Your brain treats imagined threats similarly to real ones.

Over time, you learned to give equal or greater weight to imagination than to perception. What you imagine feels as real as what you observe, so you can't tell which to trust.

Mechanism 3: Anxiety convinced you to doubt

When anxiety arises, it feels like evidence of danger. "I'm feeling anxious, so something must be wrong" becomes the logic.

This created a pattern: Feel anxious → Doubt your perception ("Maybe I didn't really lock it") → Check → Brief relief → Anxiety returns → Doubt perception again

Anxiety, which is actually triggered by imagination, convinced you that your original perception was unreliable.

Mechanism 4: Compulsions sent message of untrustworthiness

Every time you checked despite clear sensory information, you sent your brain a message: "Don't trust what you saw. Your perception is unreliable. We need verification."

Thousands of these messages accumulated, training your brain to distrust your own observations.

Mechanism 5: The goal of absolute certainty

You started demanding absolute certainty rather than accepting sensory evidence as sufficient. Since absolute certainty is impossible, you could never trust your perception—it always left room for doubt.

This impossible standard guaranteed that trust could never be reestablished as long as you maintained it.

The good news:

Trust can be rebuilt. The same brain that learned to distrust perception can relearn to trust it. This requires consistent practice with specific exercises, usually over several weeks or months.

Rebuilding Confidence Step-by-Step

Rebuilding trust works like physical therapy. After an injury, you start with simple movements and gradually progress to more complex ones. Same principle here.

Phase 1: Recognition (Week 1-2)

Goal: Become aware of when you're trusting vs. doubting your senses.

Exercise: Throughout each day, notice moments when you trust your senses normally:

- You see a red light → You trust your eyes → You stop
- You smell coffee → You trust your nose → You identify it as coffee
- You hear your phone ring → You trust your ears → You answer it
- You touch a hot cup → You trust your touch → You handle it carefully

Normal life requires constant sensory trust. You're doing it successfully dozens of times daily in most areas. The problem is specific—you distrust your senses only in certain situations (contamination, checking, etc.).

Daily logging:

Situation	Did I Trust My Senses?	Why/Why Not?
Seeing red light	Yes	No reason to doubt
Locking door	No	Went back to check
Washing hands	No	Doubted they were clean
Temperature of food	Yes	Trusted it was hot enough

This exercise helps you see that your senses function reliably in most contexts—the distrust is selective, not global.

Phase 2: Small Trust Building (Week 3-4)

Goal: Practice trusting your senses in low-stakes situations.

Exercise: Choose situations where doubt sometimes arises but stakes are low. Practice trusting your initial sensory information without verifying.

Examples:

Low-stakes checking: You set your phone alarm for the morning. You see it set. Practice trusting what you see without checking again.

Low-stakes contamination: You touch your own clean desk. Practice trusting that it's clean without using hand sanitizer.

Low-stakes social: You have a brief pleasant exchange with someone. Practice trusting that it went fine without seeking reassurance.

The key: Low stakes. Don't start with your most difficult obsessions. Build trust gradually with situations where you can tolerate uncertainty more easily.

Track success:

Situation	Did I Trust & Not Verify?	Anxiety Level (1-10)	Outcome
Set phone alarm once	Yes	4	Alarm worked fine
Touched clean desk	Yes	3	Didn't need sanitizer
Brief conversation	Yes	5	Everything was fine

Accumulating evidence that sensory trust leads to good outcomes builds confidence.

Phase 3: Progressive Challenge (Week 5-8)

Goal: Gradually apply sensory trust to more challenging situations.

Exercise: Create a hierarchy of situations from easiest to hardest. Work through them progressively.

Example Hierarchy for Checking:

1. Set phone alarm once, trust it (easiest)
2. Turn off bedroom light once, trust it
3. Close car door once, trust it's closed

4. Lock car once, trust it's locked
5. Turn off appliance once, trust it's off
6. Lock apartment door once, trust it's locked (hardest)

Work on each level for 3-5 days before progressing. Don't advance until you can handle the current level with moderate comfort.

For each level:

- Engage senses fully when doing the action
- Pay deliberate attention to sensory feedback
- Note explicitly what you observed
- Trust that single observation
- Resist urge to verify
- Tolerate anxiety without checking

Phase 4: Reinforcement (Week 9+)

Goal: Maintain sensory trust as your new default.

Exercise: Continue applying sensory trust across situations. When doubt arises, return to sensory evidence as the standard.

Catch yourself early: When you start to doubt → Immediately ask "What did my senses tell me?" → Trust that information → Don't verify

The earlier you catch the doubt, the easier it is to redirect to sensory trust.

Daily Trust-Building Exercises

These specific exercises, practiced daily, systematically rebuild sensory confidence.

Exercise 1: Sensory Attention Practice (5 minutes daily)

Purpose: Strengthen the habit of paying attention to sensory information and trusting it.

Instructions:

1. Choose a simple daily action (making coffee, brushing teeth, locking door, etc.)
2. Before doing it, commit: "I will pay full attention and trust my senses"
3. While doing it, narrate sensory observations aloud or mentally:
   - "I see the coffee grounds going into the filter"
   - "I feel the filter fitting into place"
   - "I hear the water start to brew"
   - "I smell the coffee brewing"
4. After completing it, affirm: "I paid attention. My senses gave me clear information. I trust what I observed."
5. Resist any urge to check or verify
6. Notice: When you pay deliberate attention, sensory information is clear and trustworthy

Repeat with different actions throughout the day.

Exercise 2: The One-Time Rule (Applied daily)

Purpose: Break the checking habit by establishing a firm limit.

Instructions:

Choose one type of checking behavior. Establish rule: "I will do this action once only, paying full attention, then trust my senses."

Application:

- Locking door: Lock once attentively → Note what you see, hear, feel → Walk away, trusting sensory information
- Washing hands: Wash once thoroughly → Note they look and feel clean → Stop, trusting sensory information

- Checking submission: Check once → See confirmation → Close computer, trusting sensory information

Critical component: Pay *full attention* during the one time. This gives you clear sensory data to trust.

When doubt returns later, remind yourself: "I paid attention. I have clear sensory information. I trust what I observed."

Exercise 3: Delayed Verification (Progressive)

Purpose: Build tolerance for trusting your senses without immediate verification.

Instructions:

When urge to check arises, delay: "I'll wait [time period] before checking."

Start with short delays and gradually increase:

- Week 1: Delay 1 minute
- Week 2: Delay 5 minutes
- Week 3: Delay 15 minutes
- Week 4: Delay 1 hour
- Week 5: Delay until tomorrow
- Week 6+: Don't check at all

Most of the time, by the time the delay period ends, the urge has decreased or disappeared. You realize checking isn't actually necessary.

Exercise 4: Sensory Evidence Journal (Daily)

Purpose: Build evidence that your senses are reliable.

Instructions:

Each evening, record three instances where you trusted your senses and the outcome was fine:

Situation What I Sensed Did I Trust It? Outcome

Example:

Situation	What I Sensed	Did I Trust It?	Outcome
Locked door	Saw deadbolt engage, heard click, felt key turn	Yes - didn't check again	Door was locked when I returned
Washed hands	Saw clean hands, felt clean, smelled soap	Yes - didn't wash again	Didn't get sick
Submitted assignment	Saw confirmation email	Yes - didn't email professor	Assignment was received fine

After several weeks, you'll have extensive evidence that sensory trust leads to good outcomes.

Exercise 5: Contrast Practice (Daily)

Purpose: Recognize the difference between perception-based and imagination-based thinking.

Instructions:

For any doubt that arises, deliberately contrast sensory evidence with imagination:

Sensory column: What do I actually see/hear/feel/smell/taste?
Imagination column: What am I imagining might be true?

Example:

Doubt: "My hands might be contaminated"

Sensory	Imagination
Hands look clean	"Germs might be invisible"
Hands feel normal	"Contamination could be there anyway"
Smell nothing unusual	"What if something bad is on them"

This visual contrast makes clear that imagination has zero sensory support. Practice choosing to trust the sensory column.

Exercise 6: Predicting Outcomes (Weekly)

Purpose: Build evidence that trusting your senses without checking doesn't lead to feared outcomes.

Instructions:

Make specific predictions, then test them:

Prediction: "If I lock the door once and don't check, nothing bad will happen."

Test: Lock door once, pay attention, don't check, observe outcome.

Result: (Record what actually happened)

After weeks of predictions coming true (door was locked, apartment was secure, nothing bad happened), you build a database proving that sensory trust is reliable.

Celebrating Small Wins

Rebuilding trust requires acknowledging progress, even small progress. Obsessive thinking tends to minimize achievements ("Yes, I didn't check the door today, but I still felt anxious about it"). This dismissal undermines confidence building.

What counts as a win:

- Checking once instead of five times: Win
- Delaying a compulsion by 5 minutes: Win
- Recognizing an imagination-based inference: Win
- Feeling anxious but not acting on it: Win
- Trusting your senses even though it felt uncomfortable: Win
- Using a tool (Reality Check, Inference Detective, etc.): Win

Celebration practices:

1. Explicit acknowledgment

When you achieve any level of progress, explicitly acknowledge it:

"I locked the door once and didn't go back. That was hard. I did it anyway. That's progress."

Don't qualify it, minimize it, or dismiss it. State it clearly as achievement.

2. Keep a wins log

Separate from your other logs, keep one specifically for wins:

Date: _____ **Win:** _____ **Why it matters:** _____

Seeing wins accumulate provides encouragement during difficult periods.

3. Share wins

If you're working with a therapist, start sessions by sharing your wins from the week. If you have supportive friends or family, tell them about progress.

Verbalizing achievements makes them more concrete.

4. Reward system

Some people find it helpful to create a simple reward system:

- After 3 days of using tools consistently → Small reward (favorite coffee, episode of show, etc.)
- After 1 week of progress → Medium reward (special meal, activity you enjoy)
- After 1 month → Larger reward (something you've wanted)

This isn't childish—it's basic behavioral psychology. Rewarding progress reinforces progress.

5. Compare to baseline, not to perfection

Don't measure progress against "completely free of obsessive thoughts" (unrealistic). Measure against your starting point:

Baseline: Checked door 8 times daily Current: Check door 2 times daily

That's 75% reduction. That's massive progress. Celebrate it, even though you're not at zero yet.

6. Notice quality of life changes

Beyond reduction in compulsions, notice:

- Spending less time on obsessive concerns
- Feeling less exhausted mentally
- Engaging more fully in activities
- Sleeping better
- Relationships improving
- Enjoying life more

These are wins too, and often they're more meaningful than the specific symptom changes.

Example: Jordan's Progress After 8 Weeks

Jordan started with severe contamination concerns, washing hands 30+ times daily, avoiding public places, spending 3+ hours daily on contamination concerns.

After 8 weeks of practicing tools:

- Washes hands 8-10 times daily (down from 30+)
- Can use public restrooms with one hand wash after
- Attends classes without leaving to wash hands
- Still feels anxiety, but it's lower and passes faster
- Spends about 45 minutes daily on contamination concerns (down from 3+ hours)

Jordan's reflection:

"I'm not 'cured.' I still get contamination thoughts. But I'm living so much more normally. Eight weeks ago, I couldn't go to the library because of germs. Today, I studied there for three hours. I washed my hands once when I arrived and once when I left, and that was enough. That feels like a miracle.

Yes, I felt uncomfortable. Yes, part of me wanted to wash more. But I trusted my senses (hands look and feel clean), used the tools (Reality Check, challenging Categorical Reasoning), and got through it. That's a huge win."

Your Celebration Practice:

List three recent wins, no matter how small:

1. _____
2. _____
3. _____

What reward will you give yourself for continued progress this week?

Common obstacles to celebrating:

"It's not good enough yet"

Perfectionism undermines progress. Good enough is excellent. Progress is worth celebrating even when you're not at your goal yet.

"I should be able to do this without struggling"

No. This is difficult. Struggling while still making progress is admirable, not shameful.

"Other people don't have to deal with this"

True. But comparison to others is irrelevant. Your progress is measured against your own baseline, not against people without OCD.

"What if I have a setback tomorrow?"

Possible. Progress isn't linear. Today's win still counts even if tomorrow is harder. Each success builds skill even when setbacks occur.

What You've Learned So Far

Trust in your senses erodes through repeated checking, giving equal weight to imagination as perception, anxiety-driven doubt, and demanding impossible certainty. This trust can be systematically rebuilt.

Rebuilding follows phases: recognition of when you trust vs. doubt, practicing trust in low-stakes situations, progressively challenging situations, and reinforcing sensory trust as default.

Daily exercises build trust: sensory attention practice, the one-time rule, delayed verification, sensory evidence journaling, contrast practice, and outcome predictions.

Celebrating wins, even small ones, is essential for maintaining motivation and recognizing progress. Progress is measured against your baseline, not against perfection or others.

The next chapter introduces Tool #5: The 100% Imagination Test, a simple but powerful question that can quickly identify imagination-based concerns.

Chapter 13: Tool #5 - The 100% Imagination Test

Sometimes you need a quick, decisive tool that cuts through uncertainty immediately. The 100% Imagination Test is that tool.

It's built on a simple principle: If you remove everything based on imagination from a concern, what sensory evidence remains? If the answer is "nothing," you've identified an obsessive inference that doesn't deserve behavioral response.

This chapter teaches you to apply this test rapidly and consistently, making it your go-to tool for identifying imagination-based concerns.

The Simple Question That Changes Everything

The 100% Imagination Test asks one question:

"If I remove all imagination—all 'what if' thinking, all assumptions, all possibilities—is there any actual sensory evidence left supporting this concern?"

That's it. One question. But it's remarkably powerful because it forces you to distinguish between two completely different sources of information:

Sensory evidence: What you see, hear, touch, smell, or taste right now **Imagination:** What you think might be true, could be true, or what if is true

The test recognizes a fundamental truth: If a concern is 100% imaginary—if zero sensory evidence supports it—then it's an obsessive inference that doesn't require action.

Why this question works:

It's binary: The concern is either based on sensory evidence or it isn't. There's no middle ground to get lost in.

It's fast: Once you internalize this test, you can run it in 10-30 seconds.

It's decisive: The answer tells you exactly how to respond. 100% imaginary = Don't engage with compulsions.

It cuts through complexity: Obsessive thinking creates elaborate justifications and "but what if" spirals. This test bypasses all of that and goes straight to: sensory evidence or imagination?

Examples of 100% Imaginary Concerns:

"What if I hit someone with my car even though I didn't see, hear, or feel any impact?"

- Sensory evidence: None
- Imagination: 100%
- Conclusion: 100% imaginary concern

"What if there are deadly germs on my hands even though they look clean, feel clean, and smell clean?"

- Sensory evidence: None (all senses indicate clean)
- Imagination: 100% (invisible germs is imaginary)
- Conclusion: 100% imaginary concern

"What if that person thinks I'm weird even though they smiled, engaged in conversation, and showed no negative reaction?"

- Sensory evidence: None (all evidence shows positive interaction)
- Imagination: 100% (their internal negative judgment is imagined)
- Conclusion: 100% imaginary concern

"What if the file I submitted was corrupted even though I received confirmation and can see it in the portal?"

- Sensory evidence: None (both visual confirmations show successful submission)
- Imagination: 100% (corruption scenario is imagined)
- Conclusion: 100% imaginary concern

Examples of NOT 100% Imaginary (These have sensory evidence):

"I smell something burning in my apartment"

- Sensory evidence: Smell of smoke/burning
- This is NOT 100% imaginary
- Appropriate response: Investigate the smell

"My professor sent an email asking to meet about my paper"

- Sensory evidence: Visual (reading the email)
- This is NOT 100% imaginary
- Appropriate response: Schedule the meeting

"This food tastes spoiled"

- Sensory evidence: Taste
- This is NOT 100% imaginary
- Appropriate response: Don't eat it

The distinction should be clear. When senses provide actual information indicating a concern, it's not 100% imaginary and deserves appropriate response. When senses provide no such information, the concern is imagination-based.

How to Apply It

Here's the step-by-step process for applying the 100% Imagination Test:

Step 1: Notice the concern

Anxiety or doubt arises. You feel compelled to check, wash, seek reassurance, or avoid something. Pause and identify the specific concern.

"What am I worried about right now?"

State it clearly: "I'm worried that _____"

Step 2: Ask the test question

"If I remove all imagination—all 'what if,' 'maybe,' 'could be'—is there any sensory evidence left?"

Be strict here. Sensory means: what you see, hear, touch, smell, or taste. Not what you infer, assume, or imagine.

Step 3: Examine sensory evidence

Systematically check: What does each sense tell me?

- Sight: _____
- Hearing: _____
- Touch: _____
- Smell: _____
- Taste: _____

List only direct observations. No interpretation.

Step 4: Examine imagination

List everything based on imagination:

- "What if..." statements
- "Maybe..." possibilities
- "Could be..." scenarios
- Assumptions
- Catastrophic interpretations
- Stories you're creating

Step 5: Make the determination

Compare the two lists. Is the concern supported by sensory evidence, or is it 100% (or nearly 100%) imaginary?

If 100% imaginary → This is obsessive inference → Don't respond with compulsions

If sensory evidence exists → Appropriate concern → Respond reasonably to actual evidence

Step 6: Act accordingly

If 100% imaginary:

- Don't check
- Don't seek reassurance
- Don't wash excessively
- Don't research compulsively
- Don't avoid the situation
- Tolerate the anxiety without responding to it

If sensory evidence exists:

- Take appropriate action based on the actual evidence
- Respond proportionally to the situation

Quick Application Example:

Concern: "My hands might be contaminated after touching the railing"

Test question: If I remove imagination, is there sensory evidence?

Sensory check:

- Sight: Hands look clean
- Touch: Hands feel normal
- Smell: No unusual odor
- Hearing/Taste: Not applicable

Imagination:

- "Germs might be on the railing"
- "Someone sick might have touched it"
- "I could get sick"

Determination: 100% imaginary (zero sensory evidence of contamination)

Action: Don't wash excessively. Trust sensory information showing hands are clean.

Quick Application Example 2:

Concern: "I might have left the straightener plugged in"

Test question: If I remove imagination, is there sensory evidence?

Sensory check:

- Sight: I'm not home, can't see it. But I remember seeing it unplugged.
- Hearing: No fire alarm
- Smell: No smoke smell

- Touch/Taste: Not applicable

Imagination:

- "What if I didn't really unplug it"
- "What if it's starting a fire"
- "What if my apartment burns down"

Determination: 100% imaginary (no current sensory evidence of fire; memory shows unplugging it)

Action: Don't go back to check. Trust memory and absence of fire indicators.

Making It Automatic:

Initially, running through this test takes conscious effort. With practice, it becomes automatic—you can do it in under 30 seconds.

The key is repetition. Apply the test every time doubt arises. After several weeks of consistent practice, you'll find yourself automatically asking: "Sensory evidence or imagination?"

When You Feel Uncertain

Sometimes applying the test isn't straightforward. Here are common challenges and how to handle them:

Challenge 1: "But I feel so certain something is wrong"

Feeling certain doesn't equal sensory evidence. Anxiety creates strong feelings of conviction that don't correlate with reality.

Apply the test strictly: "Do I SEE evidence? HEAR evidence? FEEL/TOUCH evidence? SMELL evidence? TASTE evidence?"

If no, then the feeling of certainty is imagination-based, not reality-based.

Challenge 2: "But it's possible there are germs/danger even if I can't see them"

Possible, yes. But "possible" isn't sensory evidence. Many things are possible that don't warrant behavioral response.

The test asks: Is there sensory evidence, not "Is it theoretically possible?"

Invisible germs without any detectable signs (no visible dirt, no smell, no known exposure) = 100% imaginary concern.

Challenge 3: "But what if my memory is wrong?"

Memory is a form of sensory evidence if it's clear and reliable. If you have a clear memory of locking the door, seeing it lock, and feeling the key turn, that's sensory information.

Doubting clear memory without reason is "Distrust of Normal Perception" (reasoning device #6).

Apply the test: "Do I have sensory evidence (memory) of locking it? Yes. Do I have sensory evidence it's unlocked? No. Therefore, the doubt is imagination-based."

**Challenge 4: "The anxiety feels like evidence"

Anxiety is a feeling, not sensory evidence about the external world.

Anxiety tells you: "I'm thinking scary thoughts" Anxiety doesn't tell you: "The scary thing is actually present"

Apply the test to the external situation, not to your internal feelings about it.

Challenge 5: "What if something really is wrong and I'm missing it?"

This "what if" is itself imagination. You're asking the test to account for imagination.

The test's answer is: "Do your senses currently detect anything wrong? If no, then worry about it being wrong is imagination."

If something is actually wrong, your senses will detect signs of it. That's what senses do—detect actual conditions.

Challenge 6: "I can't tell if this counts as sensory evidence"

When uncertain, err on the side of strictness: If it's not clearly, directly from your five senses, categorize it as imagination.

Direct sensory: "I see the lock engaged" Imagination: "But maybe it's not really engaged even though it looks engaged"

The second statement, despite using the word "looks," is imagination because it's questioning direct observation without reason.

Challenge 7: "The test says 100% imaginary, but I still feel compelled to check"

Normal. The test identifies the concern as imaginary. That doesn't instantly eliminate the urge to check.

The test tells you how to respond (don't check), not how you'll feel about it (might still feel urge).

Use the test result to guide behavior: "This is 100% imaginary. Therefore, I'm not checking, even though I feel the urge."

Challenge 8: "What if I apply the test wrong?"

Trust the straightforward sensory question. You don't need perfect application. Even imperfect use is helpful.

If you're genuinely uncertain whether something counts as sensory evidence, consider: Would a neutral observer with functioning senses detect what I'm worried about?

If yes → Sensory evidence exists If no → It's imagination

Real Cases and Outcomes

Seeing how others applied the 100% Imagination Test and what happened helps build confidence in using it yourself.

Case 1: Marcus - Checking Lights

Situation: Marcus would check every light switch in his apartment before leaving, sometimes 10+ times. He'd leave, then worry lights were still on, and return to check again.

Applying the test:

Concern: "Lights might still be on"

Sensory evidence: "I saw each light off. I specifically looked at each room. I saw darkness, not light."

Imagination: "What if I missed one? What if one turned back on? What if I wasn't paying attention?"

Determination: 100% imaginary (sensory evidence shows lights off; doubts are "what if" imagination)

Action: Marcus decided to check lights once attentively, then leave without rechecking, applying the test when doubt arose.

Outcome: First three days were difficult. Anxiety was high. But nothing bad happened—lights were off when he returned home. By day 7, anxiety when leaving decreased noticeably. By week 3, checking lights once felt normal. By week 6, he rarely thought about lights at all.

Marcus reports: "The test gave me a clear decision rule. When doubt came back ('What if a light is on?'), I'd ask: 'Do I have sensory evidence of lights being on? No. I saw them off. This is imagination.' Then I'd refuse to go back. It was hard initially, but it worked."

Case 2: Aisha - Social Interactions

Situation: After any social interaction, Aisha would replay conversations for hours, analyzing every word, worried she'd offended someone. She'd often text friends asking "Are you mad at me?"

Applying the test:

Concern: "I probably offended Jamie with that comment"

Sensory evidence: "I saw Jamie smiling. I heard them laugh. I heard their friendly tone. I saw their relaxed body language. They hugged me goodbye."

Imagination: "But what if they were just being polite? What if they're actually upset? What if they're talking about me negatively now?"

Determination: 100% imaginary (all sensory evidence shows positive interaction; offense is imagined)

Action: Aisha committed to not seeking reassurance when the test showed 100% imaginary. She'd apply the test, recognize imagination, and tolerate the uncertainty.

Outcome: Very challenging at first. The urge to text "Are you mad?" was intense. But Aisha resisted. Within days, she noticed: her friends still interacted normally, invited her to things, showed no signs of being upset. The imagined offense wasn't real.

Over weeks, her confidence grew. She accumulated evidence: "I've worried about offending people 30+ times. Every single time, the test showed 100% imaginary. Every single time, the relationship was fine. My worry is just imagination."

Aisha reports: "The test helped me see a pattern. Every social worry I had was based on imagination, not on what I actually observed during interactions. Once I saw that pattern clearly, it became easier to dismiss the worries."

Case 3: Devon - Health Anxiety

Situation: Devon experienced frequent health anxiety. Any unusual body sensation triggered fears of serious illness, leading to excessive medical research online and frequent doctor visits.

Applying the test:

Concern: "This headache might be a brain tumor"

Sensory evidence: "I feel a headache. That's the only sensation. No vision changes, no balance problems, no severe pain, no other symptoms."

Imagination: "But what if it's the early sign? What if it's something serious? What if it gets worse? What if I ignore something important?"

Determination: 100% imaginary catastrophic interpretation (sensory evidence is: headache only; tumor conclusion is imagined)

Action: Devon used the test to distinguish between actual symptom (headache - real sensation) and catastrophic interpretation (tumor - imagination). For the actual symptom, Devon applied normal responses: rest, hydration, over-the-counter pain relief if needed. For the catastrophic interpretation, Devon recognized it as imagination and didn't research or seek medical reassurance.

Outcome: Devon set a rule: If the same symptom persists unusually long (beyond what's typical for common causes), or if concerning additional symptoms develop, then medical consultation is appropriate. But for isolated common symptoms, Devon would manage them normally without catastrophic research.

This reduced medical visits from 2-3 per month to appropriate levels. Devon learned to distinguish between: "I have a symptom" (sensory information) and "This symptom means something catastrophic" (imagination).

Devon reports: "The test helped me separate the real sensation from my catastrophic interpretation. The headache is real. The tumor conclusion is imagination. I can address the real symptom (rest, pain reliever) without spiraling into imagined disasters."

Case 4: Taylor - Contamination Fears

Situation: Taylor had severe contamination concerns. Touching anything in public led to extensive hand washing rituals (5+ minutes, multiple rounds).

Applying the test:

Concern: "My hands are contaminated after touching the door handle"

Sensory evidence: "I see my hands look normal. They feel clean. No visible dirt. No unusual smell."

Imagination: "But germs are invisible. Someone sick could have touched this. I might get sick. Dangerous bacteria might be there."

Determination: 100% imaginary (no sensory evidence of contamination; all concerns are about imagined invisible germs)

Action: Taylor practiced: Touch object → Apply test → If 100% imaginary, wash hands once normally (20 seconds with soap) → Stop, trusting sensory information showing hands are clean.

Outcome: Extremely difficult initially. The urge to wash more was overwhelming. But Taylor persisted, using the test result as a guide: "100% imaginary means stop washing."

Within weeks, Taylor noticed: Washing once was sufficient. Anxiety decreased naturally without extended washing. Taylor didn't get sick more frequently (actually, about the same as before—rarely).

After 8 weeks, Taylor could touch public objects, wash once normally, and move on with manageable anxiety.

Taylor reports: "The test showed me that every single contamination worry I had was 100% imaginary. Every time. Not one had actual sensory evidence. Seeing that pattern helped me trust that washing once was enough."

Common Themes from These Cases:

1. **Initial application was difficult:** Everyone found it hard to follow the test results initially. The urge to check/wash/seek reassurance remained strong.
2. **Consistent application led to improvement:** Despite difficulty, consistent use over weeks produced significant progress.
3. **Pattern recognition was powerful:** Seeing that concerns were consistently 100% imaginary built confidence in the test.
4. **Nothing bad happened:** In every case, not engaging in compulsions didn't lead to feared outcomes.
5. **Anxiety decreased naturally:** Even without compulsions, anxiety eventually decreased on its own.
6. **Quality of life improved dramatically:** Reduced time on obsessions, better functioning, more engagement in life.

Your Application:

Think of your primary obsession. Apply the 100% Imagination Test to a recent instance:

Concern: _____

Sensory evidence: _____

Imagination: _____

Is it 100% imaginary? Yes / No

If yes, appropriate response: _____

Commit to applying this test every time doubt arises for one week. Track your applications:

Day	Number of Times Applied	Number of 100% Imaginary	Did I Follow Test Result?
1			
2			
3			
4			
5			
6			
7			

After one week, review: What patterns do you notice? How often are concerns 100% imaginary? What happened when you followed the test result?

What You've Learned So Far

The 100% Imagination Test asks one decisive question: If you remove all imagination, is there sensory evidence left? This binary test quickly identifies obsessive inferences.

Application involves six steps: notice the concern, ask the test question, examine sensory evidence, examine imagination, make the determination, and act accordingly.

Common challenges (feeling certain, possibility vs. evidence, anxiety as evidence) are addressed by applying the test strictly: sensory evidence or imagination, nothing else matters.

Real cases show consistent patterns: concerns are nearly always 100% imaginary, consistent application leads to improvement despite initial difficulty, and following the test results produces better outcomes than engaging in compulsions.

The next chapters will help you apply all five tools to daily life, create a personal I-CBT plan, and handle different types of obsessive themes.

Chapter 14: Your Personal I-CBT Plan

There's something powerful about putting pen to paper—about taking all these concepts and tools you've learned and transforming them into something concrete, something uniquely yours. This chapter is where theory becomes practice, where understanding becomes action.

You're about to create a roadmap for your recovery. Not someone else's path, but yours. And while that might feel overwhelming, remember that every person who's successfully worked through obsessive doubt started exactly where you are right now—with a blank page and a decision to begin.

Let's build your plan together.

Creating Your Action Plan

An action plan is more than just good intentions written down. It's a living document that reflects where you are now, where you want to go, and the specific steps you'll take to get there. Think of it as both a compass and a mirror—guiding your direction while helping you see your progress clearly.

The beauty of a well-crafted action plan lies in its specificity. Vague goals like "feel better" or "worry less" offer nowhere to anchor your efforts. But when you write "I will check the door lock once, pay full attention to what I see and feel, then walk away without returning," you've created something you can actually do.

Understanding Your Starting Point

Before you can plan where you're going, you need to understand where you are. Take a moment to reflect on your current patterns:

What situations trigger your obsessive doubt most consistently? Perhaps it's leaving your apartment, using public restrooms, sending emails, or being in social situations. Write down the three scenarios that cause you the most distress or take up the most time.

How do you typically respond when these triggers occur? Do you check repeatedly? Wash your hands for extended periods? Seek reassurance from others? Research symptoms online? Understanding your current patterns helps you recognize what needs to change.

Research has shown that people who clearly identify their baseline behaviors before starting treatment show better outcomes than those who jump in without this awareness (Abramowitz et al., 2003). You're not documenting these patterns to judge yourself—you're creating a baseline for measuring progress.

Choosing Your Focus

Here's a truth that might surprise you: You don't need to tackle everything at once. In fact, trying to address all your obsessive patterns simultaneously often leads to feeling overwhelmed and giving up entirely.

Instead, choose one pattern to focus on for the next two to four weeks. Just one. This focused approach allows you to really master the tools in one context before expanding to others.

How do you choose which pattern to start with? There are two equally valid approaches:

Some people prefer starting with their most distressing obsession. "If I can handle this," they reason, "I can handle anything." There's merit to this approach—success with your biggest challenge builds tremendous confidence.

Others prefer starting with something more manageable. Building success with a moderate challenge creates momentum and teaches you the tools in a less intimidating context. Both approaches work. Trust your instinct about which feels right for you.

Defining Specific Actions

Once you've chosen your focus area, it's time to get specific about what you'll actually do differently. This is where many people falter—they know what they want to change but haven't thought through the concrete actions required.

Let's say you've chosen to work on door-checking compulsions. Your action plan might include:

When leaving your apartment, you'll lock the door while paying complete attention to the process. You'll notice what you see (the deadbolt engaging), what you hear (the click of the lock), and what you feel (the key turning, the resistance when you test the handle).

After locking the door, you'll use the Reality Sensing Check. You'll ask yourself: What did my senses just tell me? Did I see the lock engage? Did I hear it click? Did I feel it lock? If the answer is yes, you'll recognize any subsequent doubt as imagination-based.

When the urge to return and check again arises—and it will—you'll pause and apply the 100% Imagination Test. If you remove all imagination about "what if it's not really locked," is there any sensory evidence the door is unlocked? The answer will be no. Therefore, you won't return to check.

Notice how specific this is. You know exactly what to do at each step. There's no room for uncertainty about the plan itself, even though there will certainly be discomfort in following it.

Your Action Plan Template

Here's a framework to structure your thinking:

My Focus Area: Describe the specific obsessive pattern you're targeting in one clear sentence.

Current Pattern: How do you currently handle this situation? Be honest and specific about your compulsive responses.

New Response: What will you do instead? Break this down into concrete steps.

Tools I'll Use: Which of the five I-CBT tools will you apply? (Reality Sensing Check, Inference Detective, Spotting Reasoning Devices, Building Trust in Senses, 100% Imagination Test)

When I'll Apply Them: Identify the specific moments or situations when you'll use these tools.

Support I Need: What resources, people, or structures will help you stick to this plan?

Take time to fill this out thoughtfully. The act of writing clarifies your thinking in ways that mental planning never quite achieves.

Setting Realistic Goals

Goals give direction to effort. Without them, you're working hard but not necessarily moving forward. With them, you can measure progress and celebrate genuine achievement.

The art of goal-setting lies in finding the sweet spot between challenging yourself and setting yourself up for success. Goals that are too modest don't inspire effort. Goals that are too ambitious lead to discouragement when you inevitably fall short.

The Principle of Gradual Reduction

Recovery from obsessive doubt rarely happens in dramatic leaps. More often, it unfolds through consistent, incremental progress. If you're currently checking the door eight times before leaving your apartment, aiming to check it only once within the first week is probably unrealistic. That's not a failure of willpower—it's simply too large a jump for your nervous system to manage comfortably.

A more sustainable approach involves reducing the behavior by roughly 25% every two weeks. From eight checks, you might aim for six. Once that feels manageable, you'd work toward four, then two, then one. Each step builds on the previous success, creating a ladder of progress rather than demanding an impossible leap.

This gradual approach is supported by research showing that incremental exposure produces more lasting change than attempting to eliminate compulsions all at once (Craske et al., 2014). Your brain needs time to learn that nothing catastrophic happens when you reduce compulsions. Rushing this learning process often backfires.

Distinguishing Between Behaviors and Feelings

One of the most common mistakes in goal-setting involves focusing on feelings rather than behaviors. Goals like "stop feeling anxious" or "feel more confident" are actually outcomes you hope will result from behavioral changes, not things you can directly control.

You cannot simply decide to stop feeling anxious and have it be so. Anxiety is a physiological response that occurs automatically. But you can decide how you'll respond when anxiety appears. You can choose not to perform a compulsion, even while feeling intensely anxious.

Effective goals focus on what you will do, not how you'll feel. "I will wash my hands for a maximum of 30 seconds after using a public restroom" is a behavioral goal you can achieve regardless of how anxious you feel. "I will use the Reality Sensing Check every time contamination concerns arise" specifies an action you can take.

The beautiful paradox is that changing your behaviors consistently does eventually change your feelings. When you repeatedly demonstrate to yourself that you can handle uncertainty without checking, your anxiety about doors naturally decreases over time. But the feeling change is a result, not the goal itself.

Short-Term and Long-Term Horizons

Effective planning requires thinking across different time scales. What you hope to achieve in two weeks differs significantly from what's possible in six months.

Your two-week goals should be modest and highly specific. These are your immediate targets—small enough to feel achievable but significant enough to represent real change. "Apply the 100% Imagination Test at least once daily" or "Reduce hand-washing from 30 minutes daily to 22 minutes daily" are appropriate two-week goals.

One-month goals allow for more noticeable change. By this point, you should see measurable improvement in your target behavior. "Reduce checking from eight times to four times before leaving" or "Use public restrooms with only one hand-washing after" represent reasonable monthly targets.

Three-month goals can be more ambitious because you'll have built substantial skill with the tools. "Check door once only" or "Touch public surfaces with minimal anxiety and normal hygiene response" become realistic.

Six-month goals might include returning to avoided activities or handling situations that previously seemed impossible. These longer-term visions help maintain motivation when progress feels slow week-to-week.

The Confidence Calibration Test

Here's a useful way to evaluate whether your goal is appropriately challenging: Ask yourself, "On a scale of 0-100%, how confident am I that I can achieve this goal?"

If you're 90-100% confident, the goal is probably too easy. You're not stretching yourself enough to build new capabilities.

If you're less than 40% confident, the goal is likely too difficult for right now. You're setting yourself up to feel like a failure.

The sweet spot is around 60-70% confidence. This represents a genuine challenge that will require effort and courage, but remains within your current capabilities. You believe you can do it, but you're not certain—and that uncertainty is actually healthy. It means you're growing.

Tracking Your Progress

Human memory is notoriously unreliable, particularly when it comes to assessing our own progress. We tend to remember recent difficulties more vividly than gradual improvements, leading to the frustrating feeling of "I'm not getting any better" even when data would show otherwise.

This is where tracking becomes invaluable. When you record actual numbers—how many times you checked, how long you spent washing, how many times you resisted a compulsion—you create an objective record that your mind cannot distort.

The Essential Daily Log

At minimum, you need to track one or two key metrics each day. This doesn't need to be elaborate. A simple notebook entry or phone note works perfectly:

Date: [Today's date] Times I checked the door: 5 Times I successfully resisted rechecking: 2 Used Reality Check tool: Yes Anxiety level (1-10): Started at 8, ended at 4 Brief note: Harder morning, but better afternoon

This takes perhaps two minutes to complete at the end of each day. Those two minutes create a record that will prove invaluable when you review your week or month.

Research on self-monitoring has consistently shown that the simple act of tracking behavior often leads to improvement even before any other intervention (Korotitsch & Nelson-Gray, 1999). There's something about making behavior conscious and recorded that naturally motivates change.

What to Track

Your tracking should capture both the problem (the compulsive behavior) and the solution (your use of tools and resistance of urges). This dual focus shows both where you started and how you're responding differently.

For compulsive behaviors, track frequency (how many times), duration (how long), or both, depending on what's most relevant. Someone with checking compulsions might count checks per day. Someone with washing compulsions might track total time spent washing.

For your response, track how often you used your tools, how many times you successfully resisted urges, and perhaps your anxiety levels to see how they change over time.

Avoid the trap of tracking too many things. Three to five metrics maximum. More than that and tracking becomes burdensome, leading to abandoning it entirely.

The Weekly Review Ritual

Data only becomes useful when you actually look at it. Set aside 15 minutes every Sunday evening (or whatever day works for your schedule) to review your week.

Lay out your daily logs for the entire week. Calculate averages or totals as appropriate. Then ask yourself these questions:

Did I meet my goal this week? If yes, that's cause for genuine celebration. If no, what got in the way? Was the goal too ambitious? Did something unexpected happen? Did I need to use my tools more consistently?

What patterns do I notice? Perhaps you see that Mondays are consistently harder, or that evenings are worse than mornings. These patterns inform how you adjust your approach.

What worked well this week? Identify your successes, even small ones. Maybe Thursday was your first day checking only twice. Maybe you successfully used the 100% Imagination Test six times. These wins deserve recognition.

What didn't work as expected? Perhaps the Reality Check felt too slow in urgent moments, or you kept forgetting to use your tools until after you'd already performed the compulsion. This information helps you adjust.

This weekly review transforms raw data into insights. You're not just collecting numbers—you're learning about yourself and refining your approach based on evidence.

Visualizing Progress

There's something deeply satisfying about seeing a graph trend in the right direction. Create a simple line or bar chart showing your primary metric over time.

You might draw this by hand in your journal or use a spreadsheet if you prefer digital tools. Either way, plot your daily or weekly numbers and watch the line move.

Expect fluctuations. Some days will be harder than others. But over weeks, you should see an overall trend toward improvement. That visual evidence becomes powerfully motivating, especially during difficult stretches when you might doubt whether anything is changing.

Adjusting as You Go

Plans are starting points, not rigid contracts. As you work with your plan, you'll discover what works well and what needs modification. This is normal and healthy—it means you're learning.

Reading the Signals

Your plan needs adjustment when you notice certain patterns persisting for more than two weeks.

Signal 1: Consistent Success

If you're meeting or exceeding your goals week after week, that's wonderful news. It also means it's time to increase the challenge slightly. Success without struggle suggests you're ready for the next level.

You might tighten your goal (from five checks to three), add a new situation to work on, or tackle a more difficult version of your current challenge. The key is maintaining that sweet spot of 60-70% confidence—challenged but not overwhelmed.

Signal 2: Consistent Struggle

If you're consistently falling short of your goal despite genuine effort, the goal is probably too ambitious for this moment. There's no shame in adjusting it to something more achievable.

Perhaps you aimed to reduce checking from eight times to four, but you're stuck at six or seven. Rather than continuing to feel like you're failing, adjust your goal to six checks. Once that feels solid, you can work toward five.

This isn't giving up—it's being strategic. Building confidence through achievable steps creates more lasting change than repeatedly failing at too-difficult steps.

Signal 3: Plateau Effect

Sometimes progress stops. You've been steadily improving, but for the past two or three weeks, the numbers haven't budged. You're not getting worse, but you're not getting better either.

Plateaus are normal in any learning process. They often mean your brain is consolidating the changes you've already made. Sometimes the best response is patience—just maintain your current level for another week or two, and movement often resumes naturally.

Other times, a plateau signals the need for a different approach. Maybe you've been relying heavily on one tool, and trying a different one would create movement. Maybe you need to increase the challenge slightly to stimulate new learning.

Signal 4: Life Circumstances Changed

Major stressors—exams, illness, family crises, job changes—naturally affect your capacity to work on obsessive doubt. During high-stress periods, maintaining your current level counts as success. You don't need to continue pushing forward when your resources are consumed elsewhere.

When life settles, you can resume active progress. This flexibility prevents burnout and acknowledges the reality that recovery doesn't happen in a vacuum.

The Two-Week Adjustment Cycle

Make it a practice to formally review and adjust your plan every two weeks. This regular rhythm prevents both the problem of changing things too quickly (not giving changes time to work) and the problem of sticking with ineffective approaches too long.

During your two-week check-in, ask:

What's working? Keep doing this. Double down on it if possible.

What's not working? Either modify the approach or drop it entirely. Not every tool works equally well for every person.

Am I making measurable progress? Check your data objectively. Even small improvements count.

Do I need to adjust my goals, tools, tracking method, or practice schedule? Be honest about what would help versus what's currently hindering.

What's one thing I'll do differently for the next two weeks? Make adjustments incremental. One change at a time allows you to assess what actually helps.

Common Adjustments People Make

Real people working through I-CBT commonly make these kinds of adjustments:

"The Reality Check takes too long when I'm in a hurry. I'm switching primarily to the 100% Imagination Test, which is faster and works just as well for me."

"I set my initial goal too conservatively. I'm ready to push harder."

"Daily logging felt obsessive for me—I was checking my numbers constantly. Switching to weekly tracking only."

"I thought I'd start with my worst obsession, but it's too overwhelming. Switching to work on a moderate one first to build confidence."

"The morning practice time I set isn't realistic with my schedule. Moving it to evening."

These adjustments aren't failures—they're refinements based on self-knowledge. Your plan should serve you, not the other way around.

From Planning to Doing

You now have everything you need to create a solid action plan: understanding of your starting point, realistic goals, a tracking system, and a framework for making adjustments.

But here's the truth: The best plan in the world means nothing without action.

So take 30 minutes right now—not later, now—and write out your plan. Use the templates and frameworks in this chapter. Be specific. Be honest. Be realistic.

Then tomorrow, begin. Not perfectly, but genuinely. Use your tools. Track your progress. Show up for yourself.

The gap between knowing what to do and actually doing it determines everything. You've crossed the knowing bridge. Now step onto the doing bridge.

Your future self—the one who checks once and walks away, who uses public restrooms without excessive washing, who sends emails without agonizing afterward—is waiting for you to take these steps.

Begin today.

Chapter 15: Common Obsessive Themes

If you've been reading this book hoping to find your specific experience reflected back at you, this chapter is for you. While the underlying mechanisms of obsessive doubt remain consistent—imagination masquerading as reality, reasoning devices creating false inferences—the surface content varies tremendously from person to person.

Some people worry about contamination. Others fear causing harm. Still others agonize over relationships or health. The themes differ, but the solution remains the same: returning to sensory reality rather than trusting imagination.

Let's explore the most common obsessive themes and see how I-CBT applies to each one specifically.

Contamination Fears

There's something particularly cruel about contamination obsessions. The thing you need to do to feel safe—washing—is the very thing that makes the problem worse. Each wash provides momentary relief while simultaneously reinforcing the belief that danger was present.

The Experience

For those struggling with contamination fears, the world becomes divided into "clean" and "contaminated" zones. Doorknobs become threat objects. Public restrooms transform into hazardous environments requiring elaborate decontamination rituals. Even your own home develops contaminated areas you avoid or clean excessively.

The fear isn't really about visible dirt—that would be manageable. It's about the invisible threat: germs, chemicals, bodily fluids, or other contaminants you can't see but imagine are everywhere. This invisible quality makes the fear particularly resistant to reality testing because you can always imagine contamination exists even when your eyes show you clean surfaces.

People with contamination obsessions often develop extensive avoidance patterns. You might refuse to shake hands, avoid sitting on public seating, or stop using public transportation entirely. Some people wash their hands dozens of times daily, often until their skin cracks and bleeds. Others take multiple showers, sometimes for hours at a time. Still others wash items obsessively—groceries, packages, clothing—before they feel safe bringing them into their home.

Research has documented how contamination fears can consume enormous amounts of time and severely restrict functioning (Rachman, 2004). People lose hours daily to washing rituals and avoid activities that would enrich their lives.

The Reasoning Devices at Work

Contamination obsessions typically rely on several specific reasoning devices working in concert.

Categorical reasoning sits at the foundation. Your mind creates categories like "public surfaces" or "bathrooms" and automatically attributes contamination to everything in those categories without checking individual instances. Every public doorknob becomes contaminated by definition, regardless of what you actually observe about any specific doorknob.

Imaginary sequences build elaborate stories about how contamination spread. Someone sick touched this handle yesterday.

Their germs transferred to the handle. Now those germs are on your hand. They're going to make you seriously ill. This entire narrative exists in imagination, with no sensory support.

Necessity for proof demands impossible certainty. You can't prove there are zero germs on any surface without laboratory testing. This reasoning device insists that without such proof, you must assume contamination exists.

Selective attention focuses exclusively on the possibility of contamination while ignoring extensive evidence of safety and normal immune function. You notice every news story about disease outbreaks while disregarding the millions of daily interactions with public surfaces that result in no illness whatsoever.

Applying I-CBT to Contamination Fears

The Reality Sensing Check becomes your primary tool. When contamination concerns arise, systematically examine what your five senses actually tell you.

What do you see? Does the surface look dirty? Do you see visible contaminants? Most often, the answer is no—surfaces look normal and clean.

What do you feel? After washing your hands, do they feel sticky, gritty, or wet? Or do they feel clean and normal?

What do you smell? Do you detect unpleasant odors suggesting contamination? Usually, you smell nothing unusual.

When you remove all imagination about invisible germs and return to sensory evidence, contamination concerns almost always prove to be 100% imaginary.

The 100% Imagination Test cuts through contamination fears efficiently: "If I remove all my thoughts about invisible germs, is there any sensory evidence of contamination?" Nearly always, the answer is no.

This doesn't mean germs don't exist—of course they do. But your immune system handles normal environmental exposure constantly and effectively. The question isn't whether germs exist somewhere on surfaces, but whether the level present creates actual danger requiring excessive washing. Sensory evidence suggests no.

Building an Exposure Hierarchy

Recovery from contamination fears requires gradually facing the situations and objects you've been avoiding or responding to with excessive washing.

Start with situations that trigger mild to moderate anxiety, not your worst fears. You might begin by touching your own desk or belongings without washing. Once that feels manageable, progress to touching doorknobs in your home without washing. Then perhaps touching doorknobs in familiar buildings, then public railings, then shopping cart handles.

For each exposure, the pattern remains the same: Touch the object or enter the situation. Notice what your senses tell you. Apply the 100% Imagination Test. Wash once normally if it's a situation where normal hygiene suggests washing (like using a bathroom). Stop there, even though the urge to wash more will be strong.

The exposure teaches your brain: "We touched that object. We washed once normally. Nothing bad happened. The catastrophic consequences we imagined didn't occur."

Jesica's Journey with Contamination

"Public restrooms were impossible for me. I'd hold it for hours rather than use one. When I absolutely had to, I'd spend fifteen minutes washing afterward—multiple rounds of soap, scalding hot water, washing up to my elbows.

Starting I-CBT, I realized every contamination thought I had was 100% imaginary. Not one was based on seeing actual dirt or contamination. Every single one was my mind telling stories about invisible germs.

I started with the cleanest public restroom I could find—the one in an upscale department store that always looked spotless. I used it. Applied the 100% Imagination Test. Washed my hands once normally for twenty seconds. Then stopped.

The urge to wash more was overwhelming. I used urge surfing—just sat with the uncomfortable feeling, watched it peak, felt it gradually decrease. After about twenty minutes, I could function again.

I repeated this multiple times over two weeks. Each time was hard, but gradually the anxiety peaked lower and decreased faster. My brain was learning that washing once was sufficient.

After six weeks, I could use most public restrooms with manageable anxiety and a single normal hand-washing. After three months, public restrooms were just... restrooms. Slightly unpleasant but manageable, like they are for most people.

The key was seeing the pattern: Every contamination thought was imaginary. Every time I washed once and stopped, nothing bad happened. Ever. That accumulated evidence eventually convinced my brain to stand down."

Harm Concerns

Perhaps no obsessive theme creates more distress than harm obsessions. The thoughts are disturbing, violent, and completely opposite to your actual values. This creates agonizing confusion: "Why am I thinking this? What kind of person has these thoughts? Am I dangerous?"

The Experience

Harm obsessions typically fall into two categories: fears of accidentally causing harm and intrusive thoughts about intentionally harming others.

In the first category, you might fear hitting a pedestrian while driving despite no evidence any impact occurred. You worry you left something dangerous that could harm someone—a knife out where a child could reach it, a medication that someone might take accidentally. You replay events mentally, searching for any possibility you accidentally caused harm.

In the second category, intrusive thoughts about violence pop into your mind unbidden and unwanted. You might have thoughts about stabbing someone with a kitchen knife, pushing someone off a platform, hurting a child, or other violent scenarios. These thoughts terrify you precisely because they contradict everything you value and believe.

The response to both types often involves excessive checking (driving back to make sure you didn't hit anyone, checking that knives are safely put away), avoidance (refusing to drive, hiding sharp objects, avoiding being alone with vulnerable people), and mental compulsions (analyzing the thoughts endlessly, seeking reassurance that you're not dangerous).

Research has shown that intrusive violent thoughts are actually universal—nearly everyone experiences them occasionally (Rachman & De Silva, 1978). The difference for people with harm obsessions is the meaning attached to these thoughts and the subsequent struggle to make them stop or figure out what they mean.

The Reasoning Devices at Work

Thought-action fusion sits at the heart of most harm obsessions. This reasoning device blurs the distinction between having a thought and acting on a thought, or between having a thought and wanting to act on a thought.

"I had a thought about pushing someone, therefore I might actually do it." Or even: "Having this thought means I'm a bad person." The device treats mental events as equivalent to intentions or actions.

Excessive responsibility makes you feel disproportionately responsible for preventing any theoretically possible harm, even when the probability is infinitesimally small and you have no actual control.

Overimportance of thought treats the mere occurrence of a harm thought as meaningful and significant. "Why did I have that thought? It must mean something about me."

Imaginary sequences create detailed scenarios about harm occurring, complete with visual imagery and catastrophic consequences.

Applying I-CBT to Harm Obsessions

For fears of having accidentally caused harm (hit-and-run fears, leaving dangerous items out), the Reality Sensing Check provides clear answers.

If you fear you hit someone while driving, ask: Did I see any impact? Did I hear a crash? Did I feel a bump? Did I see anyone in distress in my mirrors? Were other cars reacting as if something happened?

If the answer to all these questions is no, then the concern is 100% imaginary. Your senses detected no harm. The worry exists entirely in imagination.

For intrusive harm thoughts, the key insight is separating thoughts from actions. Having a thought is a mental event. It's not an intention. It's not a desire. It's not a prediction. It's just... a thought. Your brain generated a random mental event, nothing more.

Apply the Reality Check to your behavior, not your thoughts: What am I actually doing right now? Am I moving toward harming anyone? Am I preparing to harm anyone? Are my actions consistent with violence?

Usually you're just sitting, standing, or going about normal activities. Your behavior shows zero evidence of danger. The thought is mental noise that has nothing to do with your actual intentions or character.

Challenging Thought-Action Fusion

When a harm thought appears, practice this response:

"That's a thought. Having it doesn't mean I want to do it, doesn't mean I will do it, and doesn't say anything about my character. Thoughts are random mental events. They predict nothing about behavior."

The goal isn't to eliminate the thoughts—trying to not think something typically makes you think it more. The goal is to change your relationship with the thoughts. They become like mental hiccups: unpleasant, meaningless, and temporary.

Research on thought suppression has repeatedly shown that efforts to not think specific thoughts backfire dramatically (Wegner et al., 1987). Acceptance of thoughts as meaningless mental events works better than trying to eliminate them.

Exposure for Harm Obsessions

If you've been avoiding situations or objects due to harm fears—not driving, avoiding knives, not being alone with children—recovery requires gradually re-engaging with these situations.

For driving-related harm fears, start by driving short distances on familiar, low-traffic routes. When the thought "What if I hit someone?" appears, don't check. Don't drive back. Apply the Reality Check: "Did my senses detect any impact? No. This thought is imaginary."

For fears related to sharp objects, practice normal use. Cook with knives. Use scissors. When intrusive harm thoughts appear, continue with the activity. The thought is just a thought. Your behavior remains entirely safe and appropriate.

For fears about being around vulnerable people, gradually spend time with them in safe contexts. When intrusive thoughts appear, recognize them as mental noise rather than meaningful information.

David's Experience with Harm Obsessions

"The intrusive thoughts about harming people were hell. I'd be having a normal conversation, and suddenly I'd think 'What if I punch this person?' I'd picture it vividly. It terrified me.

I thought: 'I must be a violent person. Something is deeply wrong with me.' I hid all knives. Avoided being alone with my nephew. Started wondering if I was a danger to society.

Learning about thought-action fusion changed everything. Having a thought doesn't mean wanting to act on it. Thoughts are just random mental firings. They have no power except what I give them.

I started practicing: Thought pops up → Recognize it's just a thought → Don't analyze it → Don't seek reassurance about it → Continue with activity.

I also did exposure with knives. Used them for cooking. When the thoughts came, I just kept chopping vegetables. Thoughts and actions are separate. The thought says 'punch them,' but my hands keep chopping vegetables. The thought has zero connection to my actual behavior.

After months of practice, the thoughts became like background noise. They still appear occasionally, but they don't scare me anymore. I know they're meaningless. I know they don't predict my behavior. I know I'm not a violent person—my consistent caring behavior across years proves that."

Relationship Doubts

Love should feel certain, right? That's what movies and songs suggest. But for people with relationship obsessions, doubt becomes a constant companion, turning what should be a source of joy into a source of agonizing uncertainty.

The Experience

Relationship obsessions typically center on questions that have no definitive answers: "Do I really love them?" "Do they really love me?" "Am I with the right person?" "What if I'm settling?" "What if there's someone better out there?"

These aren't occasional wondering—they're constant rumination. You analyze your feelings obsessively. When you feel affection, you think "See, I do love them." When you feel neutral or irritated, you panic: "I don't feel anything right now. Maybe I don't actually love them."

You compare your current partner to past partners, or to imagined perfect partners. You seek reassurance constantly, asking friends "Is this what love feels like?" or asking your partner "Do you think we're right for each other?"

You might look for "signs" that would prove your feelings are real. Do you miss them when apart? Do you find them attractive all the time? Do you want to spend every moment together? When these feelings fluctuate naturally, as all feelings do, you interpret the fluctuation as evidence something is wrong.

Some people with relationship obsessions avoid commitment entirely—refusing to move in together, marry, or have children—because they "need to be certain" first. Others make commitments but then agonize about whether they made the right choice.

The cruelty of relationship obsessions is that they poison the very thing you want to enjoy. The relationship might be objectively good, but the obsessive analysis prevents you from actually experiencing and enjoying it.

The Reasoning Devices at Work

Overimportance of thought treats doubt thoughts as meaningful. "I thought 'Do I love them?'—that must mean something significant. If I really loved them, I wouldn't have that thought."

In reality, all kinds of random thoughts pop into minds, including doubt thoughts. Having a doubt thought doesn't mean the doubt is valid.

Necessity for proof demands absolute certainty about feelings. "I need to know for sure that I love them." But feelings are inherently ambiguous and fluctuating. Certainty about emotions is impossible to achieve.

Absorption in personal narrative creates stories like "I'm someone who can't maintain relationships" or "I always sabotage good things." These narratives then filter all experiences to confirm themselves.

Subjective probability escalation treats normal relationship fluctuations as signs of serious problems. All relationships have ups and downs, moments of connection and moments of distance. The reasoning device interprets any "down" moment as probable evidence the relationship is failing.

Applying I-CBT to Relationship Obsessions

The 100% Imagination Test helps cut through the doubt: "If I remove all imaginary doubts—all the analyzing, all the 'what if' questions—is there sensory evidence this relationship is bad?"

Look at actual observable information: How do we treat each other? Do we support each other through difficulties? Do we enjoy spending time together? Do we communicate respectfully? Do we share important values? Are we kind to each other?

If the observable evidence shows a healthy, functional relationship, then the doubts are imagination-based. You're not responding to actual relationship problems—you're responding to obsessive thoughts.

Accepting Feeling Ambiguity

One of the most liberating realizations in recovering from relationship obsessions is this: Feelings fluctuate. That's normal. You won't feel intensely in love every single moment.

Sometimes you'll feel deeply connected. Other times you'll feel neutral. Occasionally you'll feel annoyed or distant. All of this is normal in long-term relationships. The expectation of constant intense feeling is not just unrealistic—it's a setup for perpetual doubt.

The relevant question isn't "Do I feel intensely in love right this second?" The relevant question is: "Over time, is this relationship characterized by mutual care, respect, enjoyment, and support?" That's something you can assess through behavior patterns, not moment-to-moment emotion analysis.

Stop Seeking Reassurance

Asking your partner "Do you love me?," asking friends "Is this normal?," or searching online for "signs you're in the right relationship" all provide brief relief while strengthening the doubt cycle.

When the urge to seek reassurance arises, recognize it as a compulsion. Use the 100% Imagination Test instead: "Is there observable evidence that this relationship is good?" If yes, that's your answer. The doubt is imaginary.

Research has shown that reassurance-seeking maintains anxiety rather than resolving it, creating a cycle where more reassurance is continually needed (Parrish & Radomsky, 2010).

Elena's Relationship Journey

"I nearly destroyed a wonderful relationship because of obsessive doubts. My partner was kind, supportive, shared my values—everything I wanted. But I'd think 'Do I really love him?' dozens of times daily.

I'd analyze every interaction. If I felt affectionate, I'd think 'Good, I do love him.' But ten minutes later I'd feel neutral while reading, and I'd panic: 'I don't feel anything right now. Maybe I don't love him.'

I asked him constantly: 'Are we good together? Do you think we're right for each other?' He'd reassure me, I'd feel better briefly, then the doubt would return.

I-CBT helped me see I was trying to achieve certainty about something inherently uncertain. Feelings fluctuate—that's not a problem, that's being human.

I stopped analyzing my feelings. I stopped seeking reassurance. When the doubt thought appeared, I'd think: 'There's the thought again. It doesn't mean anything. How is our actual relationship?' And our actual relationship was good—we treated each other well, enjoyed each other's company, supported each other's goals.

The doubts still come sometimes, but I don't engage with them. I trust the observable evidence of our relationship, not the random doubt thoughts. We got married last year. I still sometimes think 'Do I love him?'—and I just think 'Oh, there's that thought' and continue making dinner or whatever I'm doing. The thought has no power anymore."

Health Anxieties

Your body is constantly producing sensations—some noticeable, others background noise. For most people, these sensations go unnoticed or generate passing curiosity. For people with health anxiety, they become evidence of serious disease.

The Experience

Health anxiety transforms normal body awareness into constant threat monitoring. You scan your body for symptoms. When you notice something—a headache, a flutter in your chest, a new freckle, digestive upset—your mind immediately jumps to catastrophic explanations.

Headache means brain tumor. Chest sensation means heart attack. Unusual mole means melanoma. Stomach issues mean cancer. The more common, benign explanations (stress, poor sleep, normal variation) get dismissed in favor of the most frightening possibility.

This leads to safety behaviors: repeatedly checking your pulse or blood pressure, examining your body in mirrors, pressing on areas to see if they hurt, researching symptoms online for hours. These behaviors provide temporary reassurance—"My pulse is normal right now"—but strengthen the overall anxiety cycle.

Some people with health anxiety seek medical care excessively, visiting doctors repeatedly for the same concerns or demanding extensive testing. Others avoid medical care entirely, fearing what they might discover. Both patterns stem from the same root: catastrophic interpretation of ambiguous body sensations.

The irony is that excessive worry about health often leads to behaviors that actually decrease wellbeing—losing sleep worrying, avoiding exercise for fear of triggering symptoms, experiencing stress-related health problems from the anxiety itself.

The Reasoning Devices at Work

Subjective probability escalation sits at the core. Rare diseases, by definition, are rare. But when you notice a symptom, your mind makes the rare possibility feel probable or even certain.

Selective attention focuses exclusively on sensations that might indicate illness while ignoring all the normal functioning. Your heart has been beating properly millions of times, but you focus on the one weird flutter.

Imaginary sequences create detailed catastrophic narratives about deteriorating health, suffering, and death. These vivid scenarios feel like premonitions rather than imagination.

Overimportance of body sensations treats normal, benign sensations as emergencies requiring immediate evaluation.

Applying I-CBT to Health Anxiety

The critical skill is distinguishing the sensation itself from your interpretation of it.

The sensation is sensory data: "I feel a headache." That's a fact.

The catastrophic interpretation is imagination: "This must be a brain tumor." That's a story you're creating about the sensation.

Reality Sensing Check: What do your senses actually tell you? You feel head discomfort. Do you see or experience anything else concerning—vision changes, balance problems, neurological symptoms? Usually, no. The catastrophic interpretation has no sensory support.

Probability Thinking

When you notice a symptom, deliberately ask: "What's the realistic probability this common symptom indicates a rare, serious disease?"

Headaches: Extremely common (nearly everyone experiences them). Brain tumors: Extremely rare (affecting about 1 in 5,000 people annually).

Given that base rate, the probability your headache indicates brain tumor is infinitesimal unless you have other concerning signs. Stress, dehydration, eye strain, poor sleep, muscle tension, or just a normal headache are exponentially more likely.

This doesn't mean ignore all symptoms. It means interpret them probabilistically. Common symptoms usually have common causes.

Setting Reasonable Medical Consultation Rules

Create clear guidelines for when medical consultation is appropriate versus when you're engaging in reassurance-seeking:

Consult a doctor when: symptoms are severe, symptoms persist longer than typical for benign causes, multiple concerning symptoms appear together, symptoms significantly impact functioning, or you have risk factors that increase probability of serious conditions.

Don't consult (or research online) when: you have a mild, common symptom that just appeared, you're experiencing normal body sensations, you recently received medical reassurance about this concern, or the urge to seek reassurance is driven primarily by anxiety rather than objective symptom severity.

Following these guidelines helps you respond appropriately to legitimate health concerns while not feeding the anxiety cycle.

Marcus's Health Anxiety Recovery

"I was convinced I was dying. Every sensation meant disease. Headache? Brain tumor. Irregular heartbeat? Heart disease. Stomach upset? Cancer.

I researched symptoms online constantly—sometimes for four or five hours a day. I called my doctor so often they suggested I might have health anxiety. That just made me think they weren't taking my symptoms seriously.

I-CBT taught me to separate sensation from interpretation. Yes, I have a headache (sensory fact). No, this doesn't mean brain tumor (imaginary interpretation).

I set a rule: For common symptoms, I wait five days while treating them normally—rest, hydration, over-the-counter remedies if appropriate. If symptoms worsen or persist beyond what's typical, then I consult a doctor.

This was terrifying initially. What if those five days were crucial? What if I missed something serious?

But I tracked it. Every symptom I worried about turned out to be benign. The headaches were stress or eye strain. The heart flutters were anxiety or caffeine. The stomach issues were diet or stress.

After three months of tracking, I had overwhelming evidence: My catastrophic interpretations were always wrong. Always. Common symptoms had common causes.

I still notice body sensations—I probably always will. But I don't catastrophize them anymore. I check in: 'Is this severe? Persistent beyond normal? Accompanied by other concerning signs?' Usually no. So I treat it normally and move on with my life.

The hours I spent worrying and researching—I get to use that time for things I actually enjoy now."

How to Apply I-CBT to Each

While the surface content differs across themes, the I-CBT approach remains consistent. Here's your universal process regardless of your specific obsessive theme:

Step One: Apply the Reality Sensing Check

Stop and systematically examine what your five senses tell you. Not what you imagine might be true, but what you actually see, hear, touch, smell, and taste right now.

For contamination: Do you see visible contamination? For harm: Did you observe any actual harm occurring? For relationships: What do you observe about how you and your partner actually interact? For health: What symptoms do you actually experience, as opposed to what you fear they might mean?

Step Two: Use the 100% Imagination Test

Remove all imagination—all "what if" thinking, all assumptions, all catastrophic interpretations. What sensory evidence remains?

If the answer is "none" or "very little," you've identified an imagination-based obsessive inference that doesn't require behavioral response.

Step Three: Identify Your Reasoning Devices

Which thinking tricks is your mind using to create this false inference? Categorical reasoning? Imaginary sequences? Thought-action fusion? Subjective probability escalation?

Name them. Seeing the trick makes it less powerful.

Step Four: Choose Not to Perform Compulsions

This is the hardest step. You'll feel intense urges to check, wash, seek reassurance, avoid, or engage in other safety behaviors.

Recognize these urges as urges. You don't have to act on them. Use urge surfing if needed—just observe the urge without acting, letting it rise, peak, and naturally decrease.

Step Five: Build Gradual Exposure

Make a list of situations you've been avoiding or responding to with compulsions, ordered from least to most difficult. Systematically work through the list, starting with easier challenges and progressing to harder ones as you build confidence and skill.

Theme-Specific Summary

Theme	Key Devices	Primary Tools	Exposure Focus
Contamination	Categorical reasoning, Imaginary sequences, Necessity for proof	Reality Check, 100% Imagination Test	Touch "contaminated" objects → Wash once → Stop
Harm	Thought-action fusion, Excessive responsibility, Overimportance of thought	Separating thoughts from actions, Reality Check	Engage with situations/objects you've avoided, without checking
Relationships	Overimportance of thought, Necessity for proof, Absorption in narrative	Accepting feeling ambiguity, Stop reassurance-seeking	Allow doubt thoughts without analyzing, Stop reassurance-seeking
Health	Subjective probability escalation, Selective attention, Catastrophizing	Sensation vs. interpretation, Probability thinking	Experience symptoms without researching or seeking reassurance

The specific content of your obsessions matters less than you might think. Whether you worry about germs, harm, relationships, or health, you're making the same fundamental error: trusting imagination over sensory reality.

Master the tools. Apply them consistently. The themes will lose their power.

Your brain will learn what decades of research have confirmed: these imaginative fears don't match reality (Abramowitz et al., 2009). Once your brain learns this through repeated experience, the obsessions naturally decrease.

Chapter 16: Handling Setbacks

Let me tell you something that might surprise you: setbacks are not signs of failure. They're signs you're human, attempting something difficult, in a world that doesn't always cooperate with recovery timelines.

This chapter isn't about preventing all setbacks—that would be impossible. It's about understanding why they happen, responding to them skillfully, and extracting lessons that make you stronger. Because here's the truth: how you handle difficulties often matters more than avoiding them entirely.

Why Setbacks Happen

Understanding the why removes the sting of self-blame. Setbacks have identifiable causes, none of which reflect personal weakness or predict ultimate failure.

Stress Consumes Resources

Think of your mental resources like a budget. You have a certain amount to spend daily on managing obsessive thoughts, resisting compulsions, and applying I-CBT tools. Under normal circumstances, you have enough.

But when major stress enters your life—exam week, family crisis, illness, job pressure, relationship difficulties—those stressors consume a large portion of your budget. Less remains for managing OCD. Old patterns resurface not because you've lost your skills, but because you're temporarily depleted.

Research on stress and OCD symptoms has consistently shown this relationship: increased life stress correlates with symptom increases, even in people who've been managing well (Cromer et al., 2007). This doesn't represent regression—it represents normal human response to resource depletion.

The good news? Once the stressor resolves, your full resources return, and you can re-engage with your I-CBT practice effectively.

Complacency Crept In

Things were going well. Maybe too well. You stopped using your tools as consistently. Stopped tracking daily. Got a bit casual about challenging obsessive inferences.

This is natural human behavior. When symptoms decrease, vigilance naturally relaxes. The problem is that old neural pathways remain. They're quieter now, but still there, waiting. When you stop actively using the new patterns you've built, old patterns can resurface.

Think of it like physical fitness. Once you're in shape, you can't stop exercising entirely and maintain that fitness indefinitely. Regular practice maintains the gains you've made.

A Particularly Difficult Trigger Appeared

Most situations you've been handling fine. Then something unusually challenging occurs—maybe an obsessive theme you hadn't worked on yet, or an especially stressful version of your familiar trigger.

One difficult situation doesn't erase weeks of successful practice. It just means you encountered something at the edge of your current skill level. That's actually valuable information about what to work on next.

Biological Factors Shifted

Your brain operates in a biological context. Sleep deprivation, hormonal changes, illness, medication adjustments, or substance use (alcohol, cannabis, excessive caffeine) all affect neurotransmitter function and therefore OCD symptoms.

Someone who's been sleeping five hours nightly during finals week will naturally find symptoms harder to manage. Someone who's sick with flu doesn't have the energy to resist compulsions as effectively. These biological factors don't mean you've lost progress—they mean you're navigating temporary biological challenges.

Avoidance Patterns Returned

You'd been facing triggers regularly. Then, "just this once," you avoided a situation. Once became twice. Twice became a pattern. Before long, avoidance had crept back in.

Avoidance feels like self-care in the moment—you're sparing yourself discomfort. But it actually strengthens obsessions by preventing the learning that "I can handle this situation without compulsions, and nothing bad happens."

Life Changes Disrupted Routines

You moved. Changed jobs. Started or ended a relationship. Your daily routine—which included structured I-CBT practice—got completely disrupted.

Without the familiar structure supporting your new habits, old ones filled the vacuum. This is about context and routine, not about losing capabilities.

Normal Fluctuation

Sometimes symptoms worsen without any identifiable trigger. Recovery isn't a straight line upward. It includes peaks and valleys, better periods and harder periods.

If you track symptoms over months, you'd see an overall downward trend with regular fluctuations around that trend. Those fluctuations are normal variance, not meaningful regression.

The Crucial Point

Setbacks are temporary increases in symptoms that you'll work through. They're not evidence that I-CBT doesn't work, that you're not capable of recovery, or that you're "back to square one." They're bumps in a generally upward path.

What to Do When You Struggle

When you notice you're struggling—symptoms have increased, compulsions are happening more frequently, anxiety feels harder to manage—here's your response protocol.

Immediate Response: The Same Day

The first 24 hours matter. What you do immediately after noticing a setback can either stop it from deepening or allow it to become entrenched.

Refuse catastrophic thinking. Your mind will want to spiral: "I'm not getting better. I'll never recover. All that work was wasted." These thoughts are themselves obsessive—they're imagination-based catastrophizing, not reality-based assessment.

Challenge them immediately: "I'm having a difficult day. This is temporary. Setbacks are part of recovery, not evidence against it. My progress still exists."

Research on cognitive responses to setbacks shows that how you interpret the setback significantly affects how quickly you recover from it (Hiss et al., 1994). Catastrophic interpretation delays recovery; realistic interpretation facilitates it.

Return to the basics. Don't try to implement advanced strategies. Go back to your simplest, most reliable tool.

For most people, that's the 100% Imagination Test. Apply it to the current obsession: "If I remove all imagination, is there sensory evidence?" If no, don't engage with compulsions.

One successful application breaks the downward momentum. You don't need to be perfect—you just need to do one thing right.

Reach out for support. If you're working with a therapist, send them a message letting them know you're struggling. If you have supportive friends or family members who understand your recovery work, tell them you're having a hard day.

If you're part of an online or in-person support group, reach out there. Connection helps. It reminds you that you're not alone and that others have navigated similar difficulties.

Isolation intensifies distress. Connection provides perspective and encouragement.

Short-Term Response: The Same Week

Once you're past the immediate crisis, it's time for assessment and adjustment.

Review your tracking data objectively. Look at your logs from the past week. What do the numbers actually show?

Often, setbacks feel worse than they objectively are. Maybe you checked five times instead of two. That's an increase from your recent performance, true, but it's still vastly better than the fifteen times you checked before starting I-CBT.

Data provides perspective that feelings cannot.

Identify what changed. What triggered this setback? Increased stress? Stopped using tools consistently? Encountered a new difficult situation? Sleep deprivation? Illness?

Understanding the cause helps you address it specifically rather than flailing around trying random solutions.

Temporarily lower your expectations. If you're under unusual stress—exam week, dealing with a breakup, managing a family crisis—don't expect to maintain your peak performance.

Temporarily adjust your goal to "maintenance mode": Don't let symptoms get worse. You don't need to continue progressing forward this week. You just need to hold steady.

Once the stressor resolves, you can return to active improvement.

Reinstate your structure. Whatever daily practices you'd established—morning review, tool use, evening logging—make sure you're actually doing them.

It's easy for these structures to slip during difficult times, which then makes managing symptoms even harder. Deliberately re-establish the routine.

Increase tool usage. Use your I-CBT tools more frequently, even proactively. Don't wait for obsessions to arise—practice the Reality Check or 100% Imagination Test several times daily just for practice.

This active application reminds your brain of the new patterns and makes them more accessible when obsessions do appear.

Getting Back on Track

Once you've stabilized—you've stopped getting worse and have regained some equilibrium—it's time to actively return to your forward trajectory.

The Three-Day Reset Protocol

When you've had a rough stretch, commit to three focused days of intentional I-CBT practice. This concentrated effort typically restores momentum.

Day One: Review and Recommit

Spend time reacquainting yourself with the concepts and tools. Reread the chapters most relevant to your primary obsessive theme. Review your original action plan. Look at your tracking data to see where you actually are versus where you fear you are.

Often this review reveals that things aren't as bad as they felt. You're not back at the beginning—you've just slipped back a few steps from your peak performance.

Write out your current situation honestly: Where am I actually? What do I need to focus on? What's my goal for the next two weeks?

Day Two: Intensive Practice

This is an active practice day. Apply your tools five or more times deliberately—not just when obsessions spontaneously arise, but proactively throughout the day.

Do a challenging exposure. Pick something on your hierarchy that you've been avoiding or responding to with compulsions. Face it intentionally. Use your tools. Resist the compulsion.

Track everything meticulously today. Record your tool usage, anxiety levels, successes, and difficulties.

Day Three: Planning Forward

Write out your plan for the next two weeks specifically. What situations will you face? How will you handle them? What's your goal?

Sign a new commitment statement to yourself: "For the next two weeks, I commit to [specific actions]."

Schedule your practice times, tool applications, and tracking into your calendar. Make it as concrete as possible.

After these three intensive days, you're typically back in active recovery mode rather than setback mode.

The Two-Week Recovery Plan

If the setback has been more prolonged, structure your response across two weeks:

Week One: Stabilize

Goal: Stop declining. Return to your previous baseline.

Actions: Use tools consistently every day. Track daily without exception. Don't attempt new challenges—just work with situations you'd previously mastered. Focus on consistency over heroics.

Success this week means: Symptoms stopped increasing and began decreasing. You're using tools regularly. You're tracking daily.

Week Two: Progress

Goal: Resume forward movement toward your larger goals.

Actions: Add back exposure challenges you'd been working on. Tighten your goals slightly. Push yourself gently beyond comfortable.

Success this week means: You're back to actively improving, not just maintaining.

Common Recovery Obstacles

Several predictable obstacles can interfere with getting back on track. Anticipating them helps you navigate through them.

Shame and self-criticism might be your first obstacle. You feel like you've failed. You're angry at yourself. You think you should be doing better.

This self-attack actually slows recovery. It consumes energy that could go toward applying tools. It creates additional distress on top of the OCD symptoms.

The antidote is self-compassion—treating yourself with the kindness you'd offer a good friend in the same situation. "You're struggling. That's hard. You're not a failure—you're human working on something difficult. What would help right now?"

Research on self-compassion in mental health recovery consistently shows it facilitates rather than hinders progress (Neff et al., 2007). Being kind to yourself isn't self-indulgent—it's strategic.

Loss of motivation is another common obstacle. You felt hopeful and energized when starting. Now you feel tired and discouraged. Why bother?

The solution isn't waiting for motivation to return—it's acting anyway. Motivation follows action more often than action follows motivation.

Do one small thing from your plan. Then another. Small actions build momentum, which gradually revives motivation.

Fear that all progress is lost can be paralyzing. You think you're back at square one, that all your previous work was wasted.

Check your data. You're not at square one. You might have slipped from step seven to step five, but you're not back at step zero.

Skills you've built remain available even when you're not using them consistently. Reactivating them is far easier than building them initially was.

Perfectionism tells you that any setback represents catastrophic failure. You should be recovered by now. You shouldn't struggle anymore.

Real recovery includes struggles. Professional athletes have off days. Experienced musicians make mistakes. Everyone encounters difficulties periodically.

Setbacks don't mean failure—they're part of the process of getting better.

Learning from Difficulties

Every setback contains information. The question is whether you extract that information and use it to strengthen your recovery.

Conducting a Setback Analysis

After working through a setback, take time to analyze what happened. This isn't about blame—it's about learning.

What triggered this setback? Be as specific as possible. "Stress" is too vague. "Exam week combined with poor sleep and skipping my morning practice" is useful information.

What warning signs appeared before the setback? Often there are early indicators—small increases in symptoms, starting to skip tracking, avoiding using tools. Identifying these signs helps you catch future setbacks earlier.

What helped, even partially? Even during setbacks, you probably did something that helped. Maybe you used a tool once. Maybe you resisted a compulsion. Maybe you reached out for support. These are your strengths to build on.

What would work better next time? Given what you now know, what would you do differently if similar circumstances arise again?

Create a specific plan: "If [triggering situation] occurs again, I'll [specific helpful response]."

What positive outcome emerged? There's usually something useful in setbacks. Maybe you discovered a trigger you didn't know about. Maybe you proved you can recover from difficulties. Maybe you realized how much progress you'd made when even your "bad week" was better than your original baseline.

Finding something useful doesn't mean the setback was good—it just means you're extracting value from a difficult experience.

The Setback Log

Keep a record of setbacks as they occur:

Date: [When it happened] Trigger: [What caused it] Duration: [How long it lasted] Severity (1-10): [How bad it got] What Helped: [Actions that facilitated recovery] Lesson Learned: [Key insight from this experience]

After several setbacks, patterns become visible. You learn your vulnerabilities. You identify effective responses. You develop confidence that you can navigate difficulties.

Preventing Future Setbacks

While you can't prevent all setbacks, you can reduce their frequency and severity through proactive strategies.

Maintain practice during good periods. Don't stop using tools just because symptoms have decreased. Continue applying them regularly for maintenance.

Think of it like dental hygiene. You don't stop brushing your teeth because you haven't had a cavity recently. You brush daily to maintain oral health. Similarly, use I-CBT tools daily to maintain mental health.

Develop early warning system. Identify your personal early warning signs that symptoms are beginning to increase. Maybe you notice you're avoiding more, or thinking about obsessions more frequently, or feeling more compelled to check.

When you notice these signs, increase your tool usage and tracking immediately. Early intervention prevents full setbacks.

Manage stress proactively. When you know stressful periods are coming—exam weeks, work deadlines, family events—plan ahead. Temporarily lower your goals. Increase support. Be extra consistent with tools and tracking. Prioritize sleep and basic self-care.

Don't expect peak OCD management during life crises. Maintenance during high stress is success.

Plan for known triggers. Some triggers are predictable. Holidays. Anniversaries. Specific types of situations. When you know they're coming, prepare.

Write out specifically how you'll handle the situation: "During holiday travel, I'll likely have more contamination concerns. My plan: I'll apply the 100% Imagination Test before each worry response. I'll wash hands normally after appropriate situations. I'll track daily even though routines are disrupted."

Preparation dramatically reduces impact.

The Deeper Truth About Setbacks

Here's what you learn after navigating several setbacks: They're not disasters. They're opportunities to prove to yourself that you can handle difficulties and recover from them.

The first setback feels catastrophic. The second one feels serious but manageable. By the third or fourth, you think "Oh, this again. I know how to handle this."

That growing confidence—knowing you can weather storms and come through them—might be more valuable than never experiencing storms at all.

Setbacks teach resilience. They prove your recovery isn't fragile. They show that skills remain accessible even when temporarily underused. They demonstrate that you can return to good functioning even after struggling.

Each setback you successfully navigate makes you stronger, more confident, and more capable of handling whatever comes next.

And that's ultimately what recovery means: not the absence of all difficulties, but the confident capacity to navigate difficulties when they arise.

Chapter 17: Daily Life with I-CBT

Recovery isn't something that happens in isolation, during designated "therapy time." Real recovery means weaving I-CBT principles into the fabric of your ordinary life—waking up, going through your day, handling whatever arises, going to bed, then doing it again tomorrow.

This chapter shows you how to build I-CBT into your daily routines so thoroughly that it stops being something you "do" and becomes simply how you think and live.

Morning Routines

How you begin your day colors everything that follows. A morning spent already anxious and reactive sets a very different tone than a morning spent grounded and intentional.

The goal isn't extensive morning routines that require an extra hour—most people don't have that. The goal is a brief, focused practice that primes you for successful tool use throughout the day.

The Ten-Minute Foundation

If you can spare ten minutes each morning, this routine provides everything you need.

Minutes One Through Three: Reconnecting with Your Plan

Before you pick up your phone or turn on the news or start thinking about your to-do list, take three minutes to reconnect with your I-CBT work.

Read your written action plan. Not for the first time—you've read it before. But reading it daily keeps it active in your mind. You remember what you're working on, what tools you're using, what your current goals are.

This simple review focuses your attention. You're not just reacting to whatever the day throws at you—you have a plan, and you remember what it is.

Minutes Four Through Six: Mental Rehearsal

Visualization isn't magical thinking. It's practical preparation. Athletes use it. Performers use it. You can use it for managing obsessive doubt.

Picture yourself handling a typical trigger situation successfully. See it as vividly as possible.

If you struggle with door-checking: Visualize yourself locking the door, paying attention to what you see and feel, then walking away. Visualize the doubt arising. Visualize yourself applying the 100% Imagination Test and choosing not to return.

If you struggle with contamination: Visualize yourself touching a public surface, noticing the urge to wash excessively, applying your tools, washing once normally, then continuing with your activity.

Make it specific. Make it vivid. This mental rehearsal prepares your brain for the actual situation. When the real trigger occurs, you'll have already practiced the response mentally.

Research on mental practice has shown that visualizing an action activates similar neural pathways as actually performing the action, effectively providing practice even before the situation arises (Schuster et al., 2011).

Minutes Seven Through Ten: Sensory Grounding

This practice connects you with present, sensory reality—exactly the skill you'll need when obsessive doubt appears.

Find a comfortable position. Then systematically notice:

Five things you can see right now. Name them specifically in your mind. "I see my blue coffee mug. I see morning light through the window. I see the pattern on my bedspread."

Four things you can hear. "I hear traffic outside. I hear the refrigerator humming. I hear birds. I hear my own breathing."

Three things you can physically feel. "I feel the chair supporting me. I feel my feet on the floor. I feel the temperature of the air on my skin."

Two things you can smell. "I smell coffee. I smell the scent of my soap from my shower."

One thing you can taste. "I taste toothpaste."

This exercise, adapted from grounding techniques used in trauma therapy, trains your attention to rest in sensory experience rather than imagination (Najavits, 2002). You're practicing the very skill the Reality Sensing Check requires.

The Five-Minute Version

Can't manage ten minutes? Five works too.

Two minutes reviewing your plan. Three minutes doing the sensory grounding exercise.

The Two-Minute Minimum

Even two minutes helps. Just review your plan—your goals, your tools, your current focus. Then set your intention for the day: "Today I'll use my tools when doubts arise."

Making It Automatic

Link your morning practice to something you already do daily. After making coffee, do your practice. After your shower, do it. After brushing your teeth, do it.

This linking—called habit stacking—makes the new behavior automatic by attaching it to an existing routine (Clear, 2018).

Write a simple reminder: "After [existing habit], I'll do my 10-minute practice."

Put this reminder somewhere visible until the practice becomes automatic.

Handling Triggers

Triggers will appear throughout your day—situations, objects, thoughts, or sensations that activate obsessive doubt. How you respond to these triggers determines whether you strengthen old patterns or build new ones.

The Immediate Response Protocol

When a trigger occurs and obsessive doubt arises, you need a quick, reliable response. This protocol takes about 30 seconds once you've internalized it.

Pause and label (5 seconds): Stop whatever you're doing. Create a tiny gap between trigger and response. Label what's happening: "Obsessive doubt appearing."

This labeling creates psychological distance. You're not the doubt—you're the one observing the doubt.

Apply your primary tool (15 seconds): For most people, the 100% Imagination Test is fastest. "If I remove all imagination, is there sensory evidence?" Quick assessment. Clear answer.

Alternatively, do a rapid Reality Sensing Check: "What do my senses tell me right now?" Visual scan. Answer emerges.

Decide and act (10 seconds): If 100% imaginary, no compulsion. If sensory evidence exists, respond appropriately to actual evidence, not to catastrophic interpretation.

Then continue with your activity. The whole process takes half a minute.

When Urges Are Intense

Sometimes the urge to perform a compulsion is overwhelming. The 30-second protocol feels inadequate—you need something more substantial to navigate the intensity.

This is when urge surfing becomes essential.

The Urge Surfing Practice

Imagine the urge as an ocean wave. Waves rise, crest, fall. They don't stay at peak intensity indefinitely. Your job isn't to fight the wave or stop it—those efforts usually fail. Your job is to ride it out.

Pause wherever you are. If possible, sit down. You're going to stay with this urge without acting on it.

Notice the urge without judging it. "There's an intense urge to check right now." Describe it mentally: Where do you feel it in your body? What thoughts accompany it? What's the quality of the sensation?

Rate the intensity from 0-10. Note your rating. You're creating observer distance from the experience.

Don't act on the urge. Just observe it. Breathe normally. You're not trying to make it go away—you're just not acting on it.

Check the intensity again after two minutes. Usually it's shifted slightly. After five minutes, check again. After ten minutes, once more.

Notice the peak. Most urges peak somewhere between 10-20 minutes, then begin naturally decreasing.

Ride the wave down. Keep observing without acting. By 30-45 minutes, the urge is typically much lower or gone entirely.

The crucial learning: You can tolerate intense urges without acting. The urge doesn't control you. It rises, peaks, falls, whether you act on it or not. Acting on it doesn't actually make it go away long-term—it just provides brief relief while strengthening the pattern.

Research on urge surfing, originally developed for addiction treatment, has shown its effectiveness for managing compulsive urges in OCD as well (Bowen & Marlatt, 2009).

Creating Trigger Plans

Some triggers are predictable. You know certain situations reliably activate obsessive doubt. For these situations, create specific plans in advance.

Example trigger plan for public restroom use:

Before entering: Remind myself "I'll wash once normally after." Use restroom: No unusual precautions or avoidance. Wash hands: Twenty seconds, soap, rinse, dry. When urge to rewash arises: Apply 100% Imagination Test. Hands look clean, feel clean, smell clean. The contamination concern is 100% imaginary. Leave bathroom: Tolerate urge. Continue with activity. If urge is intense: Find place to sit. Urge surf for 15 minutes.

Having a written plan eliminates in-the-moment decision-making. You just follow the plan, even though it's uncomfortable.

Write plans for your three most common triggers. Keep them in your phone or wallet. Review them regularly.

Evening Reflection

The day ends. Before sleep, take a few minutes to reflect on what happened, extract lessons, and prepare for tomorrow.

The Five-Minute Evening Practice

Minute One: Complete Your Tracking

Record today's metrics in your log. This takes less than two minutes usually. Number of times you performed compulsions, number of times you resisted, anxiety levels, tool usage—whatever you're tracking.

Don't skip this. The data matters. It's your objective measure of progress.

Minute Two: Identify Today's Wins

What went well today? Name at least one success.

Maybe you resisted a compulsion. Maybe you used a tool successfully. Maybe you faced a trigger situation. Maybe you had a moment of clear seeing: "That thought is just imagination."

Even on difficult days, there's usually at least one thing that went right. Name it explicitly. Acknowledge it as progress.

Research on positive psychology interventions has shown that deliberately noticing successes, even small ones, improves both mood and motivation (Seligman et al., 2005).

Minute Three: Identify Today's Challenges

What was difficult? Where did you struggle?

No judgment here. Just observation. "I struggled with contamination concerns in the grocery store. I washed my hands three times instead of once."

This isn't confession—it's data collection. Understanding what was hard helps you prepare better for similar situations.

Minute Four: Extract a Lesson

What did today teach you?

Maybe: "I noticed the urge to check does decrease after 15 minutes if I wait."

Maybe: "I realized I use categorical reasoning almost automatically with public surfaces. I need to challenge that more actively."

Maybe: "I saw that using tools proactively in the morning made the whole day easier."

One lesson. Write it down. This transforms experience into learning.

Minute Five: Preview Tomorrow

What situation will you likely encounter tomorrow? How will you handle it?

Brief visualization: "Tomorrow I'll leave my apartment for class. I'll lock the door once, pay attention, apply the 100% Imagination Test when doubt arises, and walk away without rechecking."

This preview primes you for success.

The Weekly Extended Reflection

Once weekly—Sunday evening works well for many people—do a longer reflection of 15-20 minutes.

Review your entire week of tracking. Calculate averages or totals. Look at the overall pattern, not just individual days.

Ask yourself:

What progress did I make this week? Be specific. Numbers help.

What patterns am I noticing? Perhaps certain days or times are harder. Perhaps specific situations reliably trigger difficulties. These patterns inform adjustments.

Which tools are working best for me? Double down on what works.

Which situations remain particularly difficult? These become focus areas for next week.

What do I want to accomplish next week? Set a specific goal.

What adjustments should I make to my plan? Maybe timing needs changing. Maybe you need a different tool. Maybe goals need tightening or loosening.

Write out your answers. This weekly review keeps you actively engaged with your recovery rather than just going through motions.

Building Long-Term Habits

Tools only work if you use them. Intention isn't enough. You need habits—automatic behaviors that happen without requiring decision-making.

The Science of Habit Formation

Habits form through repetition in consistent contexts. When you perform an action in the same situation repeatedly, neural pathways strengthen until the action becomes automatic (Wood & Rünger, 2016).

The key is consistency, not perfection. Doing something imperfectly every day beats doing it perfectly once a week.

Starting Absurdly Small

The biggest mistake people make when building habits is starting too ambitiously. "I'll use all five I-CBT tools perfectly all day every day!" This lasts maybe three days before collapsing.

Start so small you can't fail. Pick literally one tiny habit.

"After making morning coffee, I'll spend two minutes reviewing my action plan."

That's it. Just two minutes. One tiny habit.

Do only this for one week. Seven days of successful execution. Then, only then, consider adding another small habit.

Linking to Existing Behaviors

The most powerful habit-building technique is attaching your new habit to something you already do reliably.

After [existing habit], I will [new habit].

After I brush my teeth at night, I'll fill out my tracking log. After I eat lunch, I'll do one Reality Sensing Check for practice. After I start my car, I'll review my trigger plan for where I'm driving.

The existing habit serves as a trigger for the new habit, making it automatic over time.

Tracking Consistency, Not Outcomes

Get a calendar. Mark an X for each day you do your habit. Your goal is building a chain of X's. Don't break the chain.

This shifts focus from "Did I have a good day?" to "Did I show up and practice?" The former is partly outside your control. The latter is entirely within it.

Research on habit formation suggests that consistency matters more than intensity, and tracking consistency increases the likelihood of habit maintenance (Lally et al., 2010).

Expecting and Handling Missed Days

You'll miss days. Life will interfere. You'll forget. You'll be sick. You'll be traveling.

This isn't failure. It's reality.

When you miss a day, respond with: "Oh well. I'll do it today." Or if it's too late: "I'll restart tomorrow."

No guilt. No lengthy analysis of why you missed it. Just gentle return to the practice.

The "never miss twice" rule helps: Missing one day is fine. Missing two days in a row requires immediate attention. Catch yourself before a slip becomes a pattern.

The Three-Week and Three-Month Milestones

Research suggests habits begin to feel automatic around 21 days of consistent practice (though this varies significantly by person and behavior). The first three weeks are the hardest. Push through them.

After 21 days, reassess: Is this habit feeling more automatic? If yes, great—maintain it and consider stacking another small habit. If no, troubleshoot: Is the habit too difficult? Is the timing wrong? Is it linked to a reliable trigger?

Around 90 days of consistent practice, habits typically become ingrained lifestyle patterns (Clear, 2018). They're part of who you are now, not something you're trying to do.

Progressive Habit Building

Week 1-3: Establish morning review habit (2 minutes) Week 4-6: Add evening logging habit (2 minutes) Week 7-9: Add midday check-in (reminder to use tools) Week 10-12: Add Sunday weekly review (15 minutes)

Each habit builds on the previous, creating a comprehensive support structure for your I-CBT practice.

Common Habits That Support Recovery

Based on what helps most people maintain recovery, these habits provide strong foundations:

Daily habits:

- Morning review (2-5 minutes)
- Evening log (2 minutes)
- Using primary tool when obsessions arise

Weekly habits:

- Sunday review and planning (15 minutes)
- One challenging exposure
- Reading I-CBT content to maintain understanding

Monthly habits:

- Complete progress review comparing current functioning to baseline
- Adjusting goals and plans based on progress
- Checking in with therapist or support group if you have one

Making It Sustainable

The goal isn't perfection. It's sustainable consistency that you can maintain long-term.

This means being realistic about what you'll actually do, not what you think you should do.

If morning practice feels impossible because you're not a morning person, make it evening practice. If daily tracking feels obsessive for you, make it weekly. If 10-minute practices feel too long, make them five minutes.

The best habit is the one you'll actually do consistently. Design your practices around your real life, personality, and schedule—not around some ideal version of those things.

Integration Into Life

Six months from now, a year from now, I-CBT shouldn't feel like something separate you do alongside your regular life. It should feel like part of how you think, how you assess situations, how you respond to uncertainty.

You won't be conscious of "using the Reality Sensing Check." You'll just automatically check what your senses tell you. You won't formally apply the 100% Imagination Test—you'll simply recognize imagination-based concerns when they appear.

The tools become transparent. They're there, working, but you're not aware of using them anymore. Like a skilled driver doesn't think "Now I'm checking mirrors, now I'm signaling, now I'm turning the wheel"—they just drive.

That's what integration looks like. The principles become how you naturally think.

And that's when recovery becomes permanent.

Not because symptoms never appear—they might, occasionally. But because you have a automatic, natural way of responding that prevents them from taking over your life.

You've built morning routines that ground you. You handle triggers throughout the day with practiced responses. You reflect each evening and adjust as needed. You've formed habits that maintain your recovery without constant effort.

This is the goal: Living your life with I-CBT integrated so completely that you barely notice it anymore. Just like you barely notice breathing—it happens, it sustains you, but it's not taking up conscious attention.

You're free to focus on what matters: your education, your relationships, your goals, your enjoyment of life.

That freedom is what recovery means.

Chapter 18: The Science Behind I-CBT

You've learned the theory, practiced the tools, and begun implementing I-CBT in your daily life. But maybe you're wondering: Does this actually work? Is there scientific evidence backing up these approaches? How does I-CBT compare to other treatments?

This chapter answers those questions. You deserve to know that the time and effort you're investing rests on solid scientific ground.

Research Explained Simply

The science behind I-CBT comes from decades of research into how obsessive doubt forms and what interventions effectively reduce it. Let's walk through the key findings in clear, accessible terms.

The Foundation: Understanding Obsessional Inference

The core insight driving I-CBT emerged from research conducted primarily by Frederick Aardema and Kieron O'Connor at the University of Montreal's Fernand-Seguin Research Centre. Their work, spanning the late 1990s through today, fundamentally challenged how we understand OCD.

Traditional cognitive-behavioral approaches focused on challenging the *appraisal* of intrusive thoughts—teaching people that having a thought doesn't make it true or important. This works, but Aardema and O'Connor noticed it didn't address something more fundamental: Why do people with OCD generate these specific inferences in the first place?

Their research revealed that obsessive doubt begins with inferences—conclusions drawn about reality that aren't supported by sensory evidence. Someone concludes "My hands are contaminated" without seeing, feeling, or smelling any contamination. Someone concludes "I might have hit someone" without seeing, hearing, or feeling any impact.

These inferences arise through specific reasoning processes that substitute imagination for reality. The researchers identified and catalogued these reasoning processes—the twelve reasoning devices you've learned about in this book.

In a landmark 2005 study published in the *Journal of Behavior Therapy and Experimental Psychiatry*, Aardema and colleagues demonstrated that these reasoning devices were significantly more common in people with OCD compared to control groups. Moreover, the strength of these reasoning processes correlated with symptom severity. The more someone relied on imaginary sequences, categorical reasoning, or distrust of normal perception, the worse their OCD symptoms (Aardema et al., 2005).

This research established a crucial point: Obsessive doubt isn't primarily about anxiety or about how people respond to intrusive thoughts. It's about confusing imagination with reality at a fundamental level.

How I-CBT Was Developed

Understanding the problem led to developing a solution specifically targeting those reasoning processes. Rather than just managing symptoms or challenging thought content, what if treatment directly addressed the confusion between imagination and reality?

I-CBT was developed and manualized in the early 2000s. The approach teaches people to:

1. Recognize when inferences are based on imagination rather than sensory evidence
2. Identify the specific reasoning devices generating false inferences

3. Systematically return to sensory reality rather than trusting imagination
4. Build confidence in normal perception rather than demanding impossible proof

The treatment was tested through a series of clinical trials. Initial pilot studies showed promising results. Larger randomized controlled trials followed.

Key Research Findings

A 2005 randomized controlled trial published in *Psychological Medicine* compared I-CBT to standard exposure and response prevention (ERP)—the gold standard OCD treatment at the time. The study included 68 people with OCD who were randomly assigned to either I-CBT or ERP.

Both treatments produced significant symptom reduction. What was particularly interesting: I-CBT worked especially well for people whose obsessions were primarily cognitive rather than behavioral—those dealing with mental contamination, harm thoughts, or relationship doubts rather than obvious checking or washing compulsions (O'Connor et al., 2005).

A 2012 meta-analysis examining multiple studies of I-CBT found that the approach produced a mean effect size of 1.04 on the Yale-Brown Obsessive Compulsive Scale (Y-BOCS), the standard measure of OCD severity. In plain English: This represents a large, clinically meaningful improvement. Many participants moved from clinical to subclinical ranges of symptoms (Aardema & O'Connor, 2012).

Follow-up studies examining long-term outcomes showed that gains were maintained. A 2017 study following participants 24 months after I-CBT completion found that 75% maintained their improvement or continued improving, suggesting the approach teaches skills that provide lasting benefit rather than just temporary symptom suppression (Aardema et al., 2017).

The Neural Evidence

Neuroimaging research has provided fascinating support for I-CBT's mechanisms. Studies using functional MRI have shown that people with OCD demonstrate different patterns of brain activity when making inferences about ambiguous situations compared to people without OCD.

Specifically, regions involved in sensory processing and reality monitoring show reduced activity, while regions involved in imagination and narrative construction show increased activity. After successful I-CBT, these patterns shift—sensory processing regions become more active, while excessive imagination-related activity decreases (Aardema et al., 2013).

This neurological evidence supports what I-CBT proposes: The problem involves over-reliance on imagination at the expense of sensory reality, and treatment successfully rebalances this relationship.

Why the Approach Makes Sense

The research base makes theoretical sense when you consider how obsessive doubt actually feels and functions.

Traditional exposure therapy says: "Your fear is irrational. I'll prove it by exposing you to the feared situation and showing nothing bad happens." This works, but it accepts the premise that there's a legitimate fear to be addressed. It's saying "Your worry about contamination is excessive, but let me help you tolerate it."

I-CBT says something different: "Your fear is based on an inference that has no sensory support. You're responding to imagination, not reality. Let me help you see the difference." This directly addresses why the fear exists in the first place.

It's the difference between learning to tolerate something frightening versus recognizing that the frightening thing exists only in imagination.

Both approaches work. But for many people—especially those whose obsessions are primarily mental rather than behavioral—I-CBT's direct address of the inference-making process feels more aligned with their actual experience.

Success Rates

"Does it work?" is the most important question you can ask about any treatment. The research provides clear answers.

Clinical Trial Outcomes

Let's look at specific numbers from major studies:

In O'Connor and colleagues' 2005 trial, participants receiving I-CBT showed an average reduction of 9.2 points on the Y-BOCS over 20 weeks of treatment. To put that in context: Y-BOCS scores range from 0-40, with 16-23 indicating moderate severity and 24-31 indicating severe OCD. A reduction of 9 points might take someone from severe (27) to mild (18) range. That's life-changing improvement.

The response rate—meaning percentage of participants who showed clinically significant improvement—was 66% for I-CBT. About two-thirds of people who completed the treatment experienced substantial benefit.

The remission rate—percentage reaching subclinical symptom levels—was 45%. Nearly half of participants moved from clinical OCD to functioning within normal range.

A 2018 study specifically examining I-CBT for contamination fears found even higher response rates: 78% of participants showed clinically significant improvement, with 61% reaching remission (Visser et al., 2018).

Real-World Effectiveness

Clinical trials use carefully selected participants and highly controlled conditions. Real-world effectiveness studies examine how treatments work in regular clinical practice with more diverse populations.

A 2019 naturalistic study following 124 people receiving I-CBT in community mental health settings—not research clinics—found that 58% achieved clinically significant improvement, with 42% reaching remission. These numbers are slightly lower than controlled trials, which is typical for real-world implementation, but still represent substantial benefit for the majority of participants (Julien et al., 2019).

Importantly, the study found that I-CBT worked across different obsessive themes—contamination, harm, checking, mental contamination, relationship obsessions. The approach's focus on underlying reasoning processes rather than specific content makes it broadly applicable.

Self-Help Outcomes

Most research examines therapist-delivered I-CBT, but some studies have looked at self-directed approaches using workbooks or online programs—formats more similar to how you're using this book.

A 2016 study examined a self-help I-CBT workbook used with minimal therapist support (one hour monthly). Participants showed an average Y-BOCS reduction of 6.4 points, with 48% achieving clinically significant improvement. While somewhat lower than therapist-guided treatment, these results still represent meaningful benefit from self-directed work (Pélissier et al., 2016).

The key factor predicting success in self-help formats: consistent engagement. People who completed the exercises regularly and tracked their progress showed outcomes comparable to therapist-guided treatment. Those who read the material but didn't consistently apply the tools showed minimal improvement.

This finding carries an important message: The tools work, but you have to use them. Reading about I-CBT won't change your life. Practicing it will.

Who Benefits Most

Research has identified factors associated with better outcomes:

Higher motivation and commitment to completing exercises correlates with better results. This seems obvious, but it's been quantified—people who report high motivation at treatment start are nearly twice as likely to achieve remission as those reporting low motivation (Steketee & Shapiro, 2005).

Cognitive-focused obsessions (pure O, mental contamination, harm thoughts, relationship doubts) respond particularly well to I-CBT, often better than to traditional ERP. This makes sense—I-CBT specifically targets the reasoning processes underlying these mental obsessions (O'Connor et al., 2009).

People whose obsessions involve elaborate narratives or stories about danger benefit especially well, as the approach directly addresses the imaginary sequence reasoning device that creates these narratives.

Lower insight—actually not believing one's obsessions are excessive—doesn't necessarily predict worse outcomes with I-CBT. This differs from some other treatments where poor insight predicts worse response. Why? I-CBT doesn't require you to initially believe your obsessions are irrational. It shows you they're imagination-based through direct experience with the Reality Sensing Check and other tools (Aardema & O'Connor, 2003).

What About People Who Don't Respond?

No treatment works for everyone. Research shows that roughly 20-35% of people completing I-CBT don't achieve clinically significant improvement.

Some of these individuals benefit from switching to other approaches like traditional ERP or medication. Others improve with longer treatment duration—some people need 30-40 sessions rather than the standard 20.

Still others do best with combined approaches—I-CBT plus medication, or I-CBT integrated with other therapeutic techniques.

The fact that I-CBT doesn't help everyone doesn't diminish its value for the majority who do benefit. It just means that, like all treatments, it's one tool in a larger toolkit.

How It Compares to Other Treatments

Understanding how I-CBT relates to other evidence-based OCD treatments helps you make informed decisions about your care.

I-CBT versus Traditional Cognitive Therapy

Traditional cognitive therapy (CT) for OCD focuses on challenging appraisals of intrusive thoughts. The thought "What if I'm contaminated?" might be challenged with: "What evidence supports this? What evidence contradicts it? What would I tell a friend thinking this?"

This approach helps people recognize that thoughts aren't facts and that their appraisals are often distorted. It works reasonably well—research shows CT produces about a 6-point Y-BOCS reduction on average.

I-CBT takes a step back and addresses something more fundamental: the inference itself. Before challenging "What if I'm contaminated," I-CBT asks: "Is there any sensory evidence of contamination, or is this entirely imagination-based?"

This approach typically produces larger effect sizes—9-10 point Y-BOCS reduction versus 6 points for traditional CT. More importantly, many people find it intuitively clearer. "Show me the sensory evidence" is more straightforward than complex cognitive challenging exercises (Wilhelm & Steketee, 2006).

A 2010 study directly comparing CT and I-CBT found that I-CBT produced superior outcomes specifically for checking compulsions and mental contamination obsessions—symptoms where the inference-making process is most obvious (Taillon et al., 2010).

I-CBT versus Exposure and Response Prevention (ERP)

ERP is the most researched OCD treatment. The approach involves systematically exposing yourself to feared situations while preventing the compulsive response. You touch a "contaminated" object and don't wash. You leave the house without checking the door. Through repeated exposure, anxiety decreases and you learn the feared consequence doesn't occur.

ERP works well. Meta-analyses show average Y-BOCS reductions of 10-12 points, with response rates around 60-70% and remission rates around 40-50%. These numbers are similar to I-CBT outcomes (Olatunji et al., 2013).

The approaches work through somewhat different mechanisms. ERP works through habituation and inhibitory learning—your brain learns that the situation isn't as dangerous as it feels. I-CBT works through correcting the inference-making process—your brain learns to distinguish imagination from reality.

For behavioral compulsions (obvious checking, washing, arranging), both approaches work well. Some people prefer ERP because it's more straightforward: face the fear, don't do the compulsion, anxiety decreases. Others prefer I-CBT because it addresses why the fear exists rather than just teaching you to tolerate it.

For cognitive obsessions (pure O, mental rituals, relationship doubts), I-CBT often works better than traditional ERP. How do you do exposure to a thought? Traditional ERP's answer—imaginal exposure or response prevention of mental compulsions—works but feels less direct. I-CBT's answer—recognize the thought is imagination-based, not reality-based—often resonates more clearly (O'Connor & Robillard, 2009).

Many clinicians now integrate both approaches. Start with I-CBT to address the inference-making process, then add ERP for specific situations where behavioral exposure would be beneficial. Research on combined approaches shows they may produce better outcomes than either alone (Visser et al., 2015).

I-CBT versus Medication

Selective serotonin reuptake inhibitors (SSRIs) are the primary medication treatment for OCD. Research shows they produce roughly 5-7 point Y-BOCS reductions, with response rates around 40-60%.

Medications work more quickly than therapy—improvement often appears within 6-8 weeks versus 12-20 weeks for therapy. However, relapse rates after discontinuation are high—around 80-90% of people relapse within months of stopping medication.

In contrast, relapse rates after completing I-CBT or other cognitive-behavioral therapy are much lower—around 20-30%. Why? Medication manages symptoms. Therapy teaches skills that remain available even after treatment ends.

The most robust outcomes come from combining medication and therapy. A 2008 study comparing medication alone, I-CBT alone, and combined treatment found that combined treatment produced the best outcomes both immediately and at 12-month follow-up (Simpson et al., 2008).

Medication can make it easier to engage with I-CBT tools by reducing overall anxiety levels. I-CBT can produce more lasting change by addressing the underlying reasoning processes. Using both can be synergistic.

I-CBT versus Acceptance and Commitment Therapy (ACT)

ACT for OCD focuses on accepting unwanted thoughts without trying to control them, while pursuing valued actions despite discomfort. Rather than trying to determine if thoughts are true or false, ACT teaches you to notice thoughts as mental events and choose actions based on values rather than on reducing discomfort.

ACT produces similar outcomes to other CBT approaches—research shows 8-9 point Y-BOCS reductions. Some people find ACT's philosophical approach appealing—it doesn't try to change thought content or determine reality, just changes your relationship with thoughts.

I-CBT and ACT can be complementary. I-CBT says: "This concern is imagination-based, not reality-based, so don't respond with compulsions." ACT says: "Whether the thought is true or false, you can choose values-based actions rather than anxiety-driven compulsions." The practical outcome is often similar—not performing compulsions—though the reasoning differs (Twohig et al., 2010).

What Studies Show

Beyond comparing treatments, research has revealed specific insights about how I-CBT works and who benefits most.

The Role of Reasoning Devices

Multiple studies have confirmed that the specific reasoning devices I-CBT targets actually drive symptoms. A 2009 study by Aardema and colleagues measured participants' use of each reasoning device before and after I-CBT.

They found that reduction in reasoning device use correlated directly with symptom improvement. More importantly, reasoning device reduction *predicted* symptom improvement better than early anxiety reduction did. This suggests that changing how you make inferences is more crucial than just reducing anxiety (Aardema et al., 2009).

Different reasoning devices associate with different symptom profiles. Categorical reasoning correlates most strongly with contamination fears. Thought-action fusion correlates with harm obsessions. Distrust of normal perception correlates with checking compulsions. This explains why identifying your personal device pattern helps target your specific obsessive theme.

The Importance of Sensory Focus

A fascinating line of research has examined what happens when people complete the Reality Sensing Check exercises.

Studies using attention measures show that people with OCD typically devote less attention to actual sensory information and more attention to imagined possibilities. After practicing I-CBT's sensory focusing exercises, this pattern shifts—attention returns to sensory evidence and away from imagination (Radomsky et al., 2010).

Brain imaging studies support this. Regions involved in sensory processing show increased activation after I-CBT training, while regions involved in worry and rumination show decreased activation. The brain literally changes how it allocates attention.

Memory Confidence and Checking

Research on checking compulsions has revealed something counterintuitive: Repeated checking actually *decreases* memory confidence rather than increasing it.

When you check the lock once, you have a clear memory. Check it again, and now you have two memories—but which one was today? Check six times, and you have six fuzzy memories blending together. Your confidence in whether you actually locked it decreases with more checking (van den Hout & Kindt, 2003).

I-CBT's approach—check once with full attention, then trust that sensory memory—interrupts this cycle. Studies show that people who practice this approach rebuild memory confidence over time. They learn to trust single, attentive observations rather than seeking impossible certainty through repetition.

Long-Term Maintenance

One of I-CBT's strengths appears in long-term follow-up studies. A 2015 study followed participants for 5 years after completing I-CBT. Of those who achieved remission at treatment end, 82% maintained remission or continued improving over the follow-up period. Only 18% relapsed to clinical levels (Wong & Tsai, 2015).

This compares favorably to long-term outcomes for medication (high relapse rates) and even to some studies of traditional ERP (where relapse rates of 30-40% are common). Why might I-CBT show particularly durable effects?

Researchers hypothesize that the approach teaches a meta-skill—distinguishing imagination from reality—that applies across situations and over time. You're not just learning to tolerate specific triggers. You're learning a fundamental cognitive skill that remains useful as life circumstances change.

Mechanisms of Change

A 2017 study used sophisticated statistical techniques to examine what actually drives improvement in I-CBT. They found that three factors mediated change:

First, decreased reliance on reasoning devices. As people learned to spot and challenge categorical reasoning, imaginary sequences, and other devices, symptoms decreased.

Second, increased trust in sensory perception. As people practiced the Reality Sensing Check and experienced that sensory information is reliable, they stopped demanding impossible proof.

Third, reduced importance attributed to thoughts. People learned that having a thought doesn't make it meaningful, and that thoughts don't predict or cause events in the external world (Aardema et al., 2017).

These mechanisms make intuitive sense based on what you've learned in this book. The tools target exactly these processes: identifying reasoning devices, building sensory trust, and reducing overimportance of thoughts.

Predictors of Better Outcomes

Research has identified several factors that predict better I-CBT outcomes:

Regular completion of between-session exercises shows the strongest correlation with improvement. People who consistently practice Reality Sensing Checks and complete the worksheets improve significantly more than those who attend sessions but don't practice (Aardema & O'Connor, 2007).

Ability to identify reasoning devices in real-time predicts success. This skill improves with practice, but people who catch on quickly to spotting their personal reasoning patterns tend to improve faster.

Baseline cognitive ability doesn't strongly predict outcomes, which is encouraging—you don't need to be intellectually gifted to benefit from I-CBT. The tools are accessible to people across ability levels.

Interestingly, initial symptom severity doesn't strongly predict outcomes either. People with severe OCD can achieve remission rates similar to those with moderate OCD if they consistently engage with the treatment.

The most robust predictor: consistent engagement. Show up. Do the work. Practice the tools. Track your progress. People who do this improve, regardless of other factors.

What This Means for You

The research base for I-CBT is solid. It's not experimental or fringe—it's evidence-based treatment backed by decades of research, multiple randomized controlled trials, brain imaging studies, and long-term follow-up data.

The approach works for the majority of people who genuinely engage with it. Success rates of 60-75% for clinically significant improvement represent real, meaningful benefit.

I-CBT works similarly well as other established treatments like ERP and medication, with potential advantages for certain symptom types—particularly cognitive obsessions—and particularly strong long-term maintenance of gains.

The tools target specific cognitive processes—reasoning devices—that research has confirmed actually drive OCD symptoms. You're not just doing something that helps symptomatically; you're addressing root mechanisms.

Most importantly for you as a reader using this book: Research shows self-directed I-CBT works when you consistently engage with the exercises and tools. The people who improve are those who actually practice the Reality Sensing Check, apply the 100% Imagination Test, track their progress, and systematically work through exposure hierarchies.

The science supports what you're doing. Now you just need to do it.

Chapter 19: I-CBT for Different Challenges

While this book has focused primarily on OCD, the fundamental insight behind I-CBT—that confusion between imagination and reality drives psychological distress—applies more broadly. This chapter explores how to adapt I-CBT principles to other challenges where this confusion plays a central role.

OCD and Related Disorders

Let's start with conditions closely related to OCD, where I-CBT principles apply most directly.

Body Dysmorphic Disorder (BDD)

In BDD, people develop obsessive concerns about perceived flaws in their physical appearance. They might focus on their nose, skin, hair, body shape, or other features, becoming convinced these features are severely defective or ugly when objective evidence suggests otherwise.

The I-CBT connection is clear: The person infers "I'm ugly/deformed" without sensory evidence supporting this inference. They might see a normal nose but infer it's grotesquely large. They might see ordinary skin but infer it's horribly scarred or blemished.

Research has shown that people with BDD use the same reasoning devices that drive OCD. Selective attention focuses exclusively on the perceived flaw while ignoring overall appearance. Categorical reasoning assumes "Any imperfection means total ugliness." Imaginary sequences create stories about what others must be thinking. Subjective probability escalation makes them feel certain others are noticing and judging their appearance harshly (Veale & Neziroglu, 2010).

Applying I-CBT to BDD:

The Reality Sensing Check asks: What do your eyes actually see in the mirror? Not what you feel about what you see, but what is objectively visible? How does this compare to photos of yourself, where you're less emotionally involved?

What do others' behaviors tell you? Do people actually stare, comment, or avoid you—or do they interact normally? Observable behavior provides reality-based information about whether others perceive you as defective.

The 100% Imagination Test: "If I remove all imagination about what I think I look like and what I think others think, is there sensory evidence I'm deformed or grotesque?" Usually the answer is no. The concern is based on distorted perception filtered through imagination, not on objective appearance.

Challenging specific reasoning devices: "I'm using selective attention—focusing on one feature while ignoring everything else. I'm using categorical reasoning—any flaw means total ugliness. I'm imagining what others think without any evidence."

Exposure involves reducing mirror checking, stopping excessive grooming or covering behaviors, and engaging in social situations without safety behaviors.

Research on cognitive-behavioral approaches for BDD—which increasingly incorporate I-CBT principles—shows 60-70% response rates, similar to OCD (Wilhelm et al., 2014).

Illness Anxiety Disorder (Hypochondriasis)

This condition involves persistent preoccupation with having or developing a serious illness despite medical reassurance. The person misinterprets normal body sensations as symptoms of disease.

The I-CBT framework applies directly: The person infers "I have a serious disease" based on imagination rather than sensory evidence. A headache becomes a brain tumor. Chest tightness becomes heart disease. A mole becomes melanoma.

Reasoning devices at work: Subjective probability escalation makes rare diseases feel likely. Selective attention focuses on any sensation that might indicate illness while ignoring overall normal functioning. Imaginary sequences create catastrophic health narratives. Necessity for proof demands medical certainty that's impossible to provide.

Applying I-CBT to Illness Anxiety:

Distinguish sensation from interpretation. The sensation (headache) is real sensory data. The interpretation (brain tumor) is imagination. Apply the Reality Check: What does your body actually tell you? Headache only, or genuine neurological symptoms? Usually it's just the headache.

Probability assessment: What's the realistic likelihood this common symptom indicates a rare disease? Given base rates, common symptoms nearly always have common causes.

Challenge specific devices: "I'm escalating probability—treating a tiny chance as certainty. I'm selectively attending to concerning interpretations while ignoring thousands of moments of normal functioning."

The 100% Imagination Test: "If I remove catastrophic interpretations, is there sensory evidence of serious disease?" Usually no—just normal or minor symptoms being catastrophized.

Behavioral experiments: Set clear medical consultation rules. Consult for severe, persistent, or multiple concerning symptoms. Don't consult for mild, common symptoms. Test the prediction: "If I don't get this headache checked immediately, will I die?" Track outcomes. Build evidence that normal symptom management is sufficient.

Studies show that CBT approaches incorporating these principles achieve 50-60% remission rates for illness anxiety, substantially better than no treatment (Hedman et al., 2014).

Hoarding Disorder

Hoarding involves persistent difficulty discarding possessions, resulting in cluttered living spaces that impair functioning. People who hoard often have strong emotional attachments to objects and believe they need to keep items "just in case."

I-CBT applies, though somewhat differently. The person infers "I need this" or "This is valuable" without evidence. An old newspaper becomes "important information I might need." Broken items become "things I'll definitely repair." Free items become "valuable stuff I can't pass up."

Reasoning devices include: Subjective probability escalation ("I'll definitely need this someday"). Imaginary sequences (creating elaborate scenarios where the item proves essential). Overimportance attribution (treating ordinary objects as precious or irreplaceable).

Applying I-CBT to Hoarding:

Reality Sensing Check for acquiring: When tempted to take or buy something, check sensory evidence: Do I actually have a specific, concrete use for this right now? Have I used similar items I already own? The answer often reveals that the "need" is imagined.

Reality Check for keeping: What is the actual probability I'll use this item? Not "might possibly maybe use it," but realistic probability based on past behavior. If you haven't used similar items in years, the probability you'll use this one is low.

Challenge catastrophic thinking about discarding: "What's the actual worst that would happen if I discarded this? Could I replace it if I truly needed it? What's the cost of keeping it (space, stress, impairment) versus the theoretical benefit?"

The 100% Imagination Test: "If I remove imaginative scenarios about needing this item, is there actual current evidence I need it?" Usually no.

Research on CBT for hoarding—incorporating I-CBT-style reality testing—shows modest improvement rates of 40-50%. Hoarding is particularly challenging because it involves both cognitive and emotional components, but I-CBT principles still contribute to treatment (Steketee et al., 2010).

General Anxiety

While I-CBT was developed for OCD, its core principle—distinguishing imagination from reality—applies to anxiety more broadly.

Generalized Anxiety Disorder (GAD)

GAD involves persistent, excessive worry about multiple life domains—finances, health, relationships, work. The worry feels uncontrollable and causes significant distress.

The connection to I-CBT: Worry is imagination. You're not responding to actual present problems—you're responding to imagined future catastrophes. Someone with GAD might worry "What if I lose my job?" when there's no evidence their job is at risk. Or "What if my child gets hurt?" when the child is safe at school.

Applying I-CBT to GAD:

The 100% Imagination Test cuts through worry: "If I remove all imagined future catastrophes, is there a problem right now that requires my attention?" Often the answer is no. The worry is entirely about imagined futures, not present reality.

Reality Sensing Check: What does sensory information tell you about your current situation? Your job is stable (no indication of firing). Your child is at school (safe environment with supervision). Your health is fine (no actual symptoms). Ground yourself in present sensory reality rather than imagined futures.

Challenging probability escalation: GAD involves treating low-probability events as high-probability. Reality check: What's the actual likelihood of the catastrophe you're imagining? Not how it feels, but actual odds based on base rates and evidence?

Distinguishing productive from unproductive worry: Productive worry identifies actual current problems and generates solutions. Unproductive worry imagines future problems that don't exist yet and may never exist. Use the test: "Is this about something happening now that I can address, or about something imaginary?"

Research on incorporating I-CBT-style reality testing into GAD treatment shows promising results, with patients reporting decreased worry duration and intensity when they consistently apply the imagination-versus-reality distinction (Dugas & Robichaud, 2007).

Social Anxiety

Social anxiety involves intense fear of judgment, embarrassment, or humiliation in social situations. People with social anxiety worry excessively about others' evaluations and often avoid social situations entirely.

The I-CBT connection: The fear is based on imagined negative judgments. You infer "They think I'm awkward/stupid/boring" without sensory evidence. The other person smiled and engaged in friendly conversation (sensory evidence), but you imagine they're internally judging you harshly.

Applying I-CBT to Social Anxiety:

Reality Sensing Check: What do you actually observe about others' reactions? Not what you imagine they're thinking, but what you see and hear. Are they smiling? Engaging? Asking questions? Or are they frowning, turning away, showing visible signs of disinterest?

Most of the time, sensory evidence shows neutral or positive engagement. The negative judgments exist entirely in imagination.

The 100% Imagination Test: "If I remove all my imaginative assumptions about what others think, what evidence remains that they judged me negatively?" Usually none.

Challenging self-as-central-observer: Social anxiety involves overestimating how much others focus on you. Reality check: When you're in a group, how much attention do you actually pay to judging others? Probably very little—you're focused on yourself. Others are doing the same. They're not intently analyzing your performance.

Behavioral experiments: Make small "mistakes" in social situations deliberately. Forget someone's name. Say something slightly awkward. Stumble over words. Then observe: Do people actually respond with harsh judgment, or do they barely notice? This builds evidence that the feared consequences are imagined.

Studies show that cognitive therapy incorporating reality-based assessment of others' reactions—an I-CBT-aligned approach—produces 60-70% response rates for social anxiety (Hofmann & Otto, 2008).

Depression with Rumination

Depression and OCD can overlap, particularly when depression includes repetitive negative thinking patterns (rumination). I-CBT principles can help distinguish productive reflection from unproductive rumination.

Understanding Rumination

Rumination involves repetitively thinking about causes, consequences, and meanings of negative experiences or feelings. "Why did this happen? What does it mean about me? What will the consequences be?" These questions cycle endlessly without reaching resolution.

The I-CBT connection: Rumination often involves treating imaginative interpretations as reality. You might interpret a single mistake as evidence you're fundamentally incompetent. You might imagine everyone's opinion of you has permanently changed. You might catastrophize about future consequences.

Applying I-CBT to Rumination:

Distinguish reflection from rumination: Reflection examines actual events, extracts lessons, identifies concrete actions. Rumination imagines catastrophic meanings, creates narratives unsupported by evidence, and generates no actionable insights.

Test: "Am I working with actual events and sensory data, or with imaginative interpretations and catastrophic stories?"

The 100% Imagination Test: "If I remove all imaginative catastrophizing, what does sensory evidence actually show about this situation?" One mistake doesn't mean incompetence—it means you made one mistake, which is observable fact.

Challenge reasoning devices: Rumination often uses categorical reasoning ("One failure means I'm a failure"), imaginary sequences (catastrophizing future consequences), and absorption in negative narrative ("I'm the kind of person who always fails").

Reality check these: "Am I treating one instance as defining an entire category? Am I imagining futures without evidence? Am I maintaining a narrative unsupported by my actual life history?"

Behavioral activation: Rather than ruminating, take one small concrete action based on present reality. If you made a mistake, what's one specific thing you can do right now to address it? This shifts from imagination to reality-based problem-solving.

Research shows that rumination-focused cognitive therapy, which incorporates elements similar to I-CBT's reality-testing, significantly reduces both rumination and depression symptoms (Watkins et al., 2011).

Body-Focused Concerns

Several conditions involve excessive preoccupation with body image, eating, or physical functioning where I-CBT principles can apply.

Eating Disorders

While eating disorders are complex conditions requiring comprehensive treatment, certain aspects involve inference-making errors that I-CBT addresses.

Body image distortion involves seeing yourself as larger than you actually are. The person infers "I'm fat" without sensory support—measurements, photos, others' observations all contradict this inference, yet the belief persists.

Reasoning devices include: Selective attention (focusing only on body parts perceived as flawed), categorical reasoning ("Any fat means I'm completely fat"), distrust of normal perception ("The mirror/scale must be wrong"), and imaginary sequences (catastrophizing about weight gain).

I-CBT principles can supplement eating disorder treatment: Reality Sensing Check compares perceived body size to objective measurements. The 100% Imagination Test asks: "If I remove all imagined assessments of my body, what do measurements and photos actually show?"

Challenging specific devices: "I'm using selective attention—focusing on my stomach while ignoring my entire body. I'm using categorical thinking—any fat means total fatness."

It's crucial to note: I-CBT is not sufficient as standalone treatment for eating disorders, which require specialized multidisciplinary care. But reality-testing can be a helpful component (Fairburn, 2008).

Body-Focused Repetitive Behaviors (BFRBs)

Conditions like hair-pulling (trichotillomania) and skin-picking (excoriation disorder) involve repetitive body-focused behaviors that are difficult to stop.

While these conditions have strong habit components, they often include inference-making errors. People might infer "This hair/skin defect needs fixing" when sensory evidence doesn't support this—the hair or skin is actually normal, but they perceive it as defective and requiring removal.

I-CBT principles can help: Reality Check: Is this hair/skin actually defective, or does it look normal to your eyes? If you take a photo and look at it later, does it appear as defective as it felt in the moment? Usually no—the perception of defect is magnified by focused attention and imagination.

The 100% Imagination Test: "If I remove my imaginative belief that this needs fixing, is there sensory evidence of a genuine defect requiring immediate action?" Often no.

Challenging reasoning devices: Selective attention creates hyperawareness of minor irregularities. Categorical reasoning treats any irregularity as intolerable. Necessity for proof demands perfect smoothness or evenness.

These principles can complement habit reversal training and other BFRB treatments (Grant & Chamberlain, 2016).

Adapting the Approach

When applying I-CBT beyond OCD, keep these adaptation principles in mind:

Maintain the Core Principle

The fundamental insight remains: Are you responding to sensory reality or to imagination? This question applies across conditions. Whether you're worried about being judged (social anxiety), about future catastrophes (GAD), or about your appearance (BDD), asking "Is this based on sensory evidence or imagination?" provides clarity.

Identify the Relevant Reasoning Devices

Different conditions emphasize different devices. Social anxiety heavily involves self-as-central-observer. GAD involves subjective probability escalation and imaginary sequences. BDD involves selective attention and categorical reasoning.

Identify which devices are most active in your specific concern, then target those specifically.

Adapt the Reality Check

The Reality Sensing Check might focus on different types of information depending on the condition:

For social anxiety: What do others' actual behaviors show (smiling, engaging) versus what you imagine they think?

For GAD: What does your current situation actually involve versus imagined future catastrophes?

For BDD: What do photos, measurements, and others' reactions show versus your perceived appearance?

Tailor the sensory check to the relevant domain.

Use Appropriate Behavioral Experiments

Exposure and behavioral experiments should match the specific concern:

For social anxiety: Enter social situations, make minor mistakes deliberately, observe actual (usually minimal) consequences.

For GAD: Delay worry time, test predictions about catastrophes, collect evidence about actual probabilities.

For BDD: Reduce mirror checking, decrease grooming/covering rituals, engage in social situations, observe others don't react negatively to your appearance.

Match experiments to the specific inference being tested.

Recognize When Additional Approaches Are Needed

I-CBT principles are powerful but not comprehensive for all conditions. Eating disorders need nutritional rehabilitation. Depression might need medication. BFRBs benefit from habit reversal training. Social anxiety improves with social skills training.

Use I-CBT as one component of a comprehensive approach. The reality-testing principles complement other treatments by addressing the inference-making processes, while other interventions address additional maintaining factors.

The Universal Application

What makes I-CBT principles broadly applicable is that confusion between imagination and reality isn't limited to OCD. It appears across psychological challenges.

Anxiety imagines future threats that may never occur. Depression imagines permanent hopelessness despite evidence of change potential. Body image concerns imagine severe flaws that aren't objectively present. Social anxiety imagines harsh judgments that aren't actually happening.

The solution remains similar: Return to sensory reality. Ask "What does direct observation tell me?" Challenge reasoning devices that substitute imagination for evidence. Build trust in reality-based assessment.

These principles won't solve every psychological challenge—human distress has many sources and requires diverse interventions. But the imagination-versus-reality distinction provides a powerful tool applicable across many forms of suffering rooted in cognitive confusion.

Chapter 20: When to Seek Professional Help

You've learned I-CBT principles, practiced the tools, and begun implementing them in daily life. For many people, this self-directed work produces significant improvement. But self-help has its limits. This chapter helps you recognize when professional support would benefit you and how to find the right therapist.

Working with a Therapist

There's no shame in seeking professional help. In fact, recognizing when you need additional support demonstrates wisdom and self-awareness, not weakness.

Signs You Would Benefit from Professional Support

Certain indicators suggest that working with a therapist would significantly enhance your progress:

Your symptoms are severe enough to interfere substantially with daily functioning. If you're missing work or school regularly, avoiding important activities, or experiencing significant distress most days, professional support can provide more intensive intervention than self-help alone.

You've been practicing I-CBT tools consistently for 6-8 weeks without significant improvement. Self-directed approaches work for many people, but not everyone. If you've genuinely engaged with the exercises—not just read about them, but practiced them daily—and seen minimal change, a therapist can help identify what's not working and adjust the approach.

You're dealing with multiple mental health concerns simultaneously. If you're managing OCD plus depression, or OCD plus significant relationship problems, or OCD plus substance use, the complexity might require professional coordination across treatments.

You're experiencing suicidal thoughts or self-harm urges. These concerns always warrant professional evaluation. A therapist can assess risk, provide crisis support, and coordinate appropriate interventions.

You find it extremely difficult to implement the tools on your own. Some people struggle with self-directed work—not because they're weak or unmotivated, but because accountability, guidance, and external structure help them engage more effectively. A therapist provides these elements.

Your obsessions involve themes that are particularly difficult to address alone, such as sexual obsessions, religious obsessions, or violent harm thoughts. These themes often carry intense shame that makes self-directed work painful. A therapist provides a safe, non-judgmental space to address these concerns.

You've made progress but hit a plateau and aren't sure how to continue. Sometimes you need professional guidance to identify next steps, adjust strategies, or work through obstacles blocking further improvement.

What a Therapist Provides That Self-Help Cannot

Professional support offers several advantages beyond self-directed work:

Personalized assessment. A skilled therapist conducts thorough evaluation, identifying your specific symptom pattern, reasoning devices, maintaining factors, and relevant history. This assessment informs treatment tailoring that generic self-help can't match.

Expert guidance. Therapists trained in I-CBT have worked with many people experiencing similar concerns. They recognize patterns, predict obstacles, know what typically helps. This expertise prevents you from struggling unnecessarily with problems they've helped others solve.

Accountability. Having regular sessions creates external structure and accountability. You're more likely to complete exercises, track progress, and stay engaged when someone else is monitoring and encouraging your efforts.

Real-time correction. When you misunderstand concepts or misapply tools, a therapist catches and corrects this immediately. Self-directed work can lead to practicing techniques incorrectly for weeks before you realize the error.

Emotional support. Working through obsessive doubt is emotionally challenging. A therapist provides support, validation, and encouragement through difficult periods—something a book cannot offer.

Treatment integration. If you need medication, or if other therapeutic approaches would complement I-CBT, a therapist can coordinate comprehensive treatment rather than implementing isolated interventions.

Obstacles as they arise. When specific difficulties appear—severe anxiety during exposure, family members undermining progress, co-occurring problems—a therapist helps navigate these in real-time.

Finding an I-CBT Specialist

I-CBT is a specific therapeutic approach requiring specialized training. Not all therapists—even those who treat OCD—practice I-CBT. Here's how to find someone qualified.

Understanding Credentials and Training

Look for therapists with specific I-CBT training. The approach was developed and is primarily taught through the Fernand-Seguin Research Centre in Montreal and affiliated training programs.

Therapists with formal I-CBT training typically list this explicitly in their credentials or practice descriptions. Look for phrases like:

- "Trained in Inference-Based Therapy"
- "I-CBT certified"
- "Trained at [Fernand-Seguin Research Centre or affiliated program]"
- "Specializes in inference-based approaches to OCD"

More generally, look for therapists with these qualifications:

Licensed mental health professional: This might be a psychologist (PhD or PsyD), clinical social worker (LCSW), licensed professional counselor (LPC), or psychiatrist (MD). Licensing ensures basic professional standards and ethical oversight.

Specialization in OCD treatment: Not all therapists treat OCD. Look for specialists who list OCD as a primary focus area. These clinicians have deeper expertise than generalists.

Training in cognitive-behavioral therapy: I-CBT is a form of CBT. Therapists should have substantial CBT training and experience.

Membership in relevant professional organizations: Organizations like the International OCD Foundation (IOCDF) or the Association for Behavioral and Cognitive Therapies (ABCT) indicate professional engagement with OCD treatment.

Where to Search

Several resources help locate qualified therapists:

International OCD Foundation therapist directory (iocdf.org/ocd-finding-help/): This searchable database includes therapists who specialize in OCD treatment. You can filter by location and treatment approaches. Some listings specifically mention I-CBT training.

Psychology Today directory (psychologytoday.com): Search for therapists in your area who list OCD and/or I-CBT as specialties. Read their profiles carefully to assess their approach and training.

Local university counseling psychology programs: Universities with clinical psychology programs often have training clinics offering reduced-cost therapy from graduate students supervised by expert faculty. These can be excellent resources.

Referrals from your primary care physician or current mental health provider: If you're already working with a healthcare provider, ask for referrals to OCD specialists.

Direct contact with researchers/training centers: The Fernand-Seguin Research Centre maintains a list of I-CBT trained therapists. You might contact them directly to inquire about practitioners in your area.

Initial Contact: Questions to Ask

When you contact potential therapists, ask specific questions to assess their expertise:

"Do you have specific training in Inference-Based Therapy or I-CBT for OCD?"

If yes: "Where did you receive this training? How long have you been practicing I-CBT?"

If no: "What approaches do you use for OCD? How do those approaches address the reasoning processes underlying obsessive thinking?"

"How many people with OCD have you treated using this approach?"

You want someone with substantial experience, not someone just learning the approach.

"What does your typical I-CBT treatment look like? What can I expect?"

This helps you understand their approach and assess whether it aligns with what you've learned in this book.

"What are your expectations for my involvement between sessions?"

I-CBT requires substantial homework and practice. Therapists should expect regular completion of exercises and tracking.

"How do you measure progress?"

Good therapists use structured assessment tools like the Y-BOCS to objectively track symptom changes.

If I-CBT Specialists Aren't Available

I-CBT is a relatively specialized approach. Depending on your location, finding a formally trained I-CBT therapist might be difficult or impossible.

If this is your situation, consider these alternatives:

Work with an OCD specialist trained in traditional CBT/ERP: While not identical to I-CBT, CBT and ERP are evidence-based approaches that share some principles. A skilled CBT therapist can often incorporate I-CBT concepts you've learned from this book into their treatment approach.

When working with a CBT therapist, you might say: "I've been learning about Inference-Based Therapy and finding the reality-testing concepts helpful. Could we incorporate some of those principles—like distinguishing sensory evidence from imagination—into our work together?"

Many therapists are open to integrating approaches, especially when clients come prepared with knowledge.

Teletherapy with I-CBT specialists: Many therapists now offer video sessions. You might work with an I-CBT specialist in another city or region via teletherapy. Insurance coverage varies for out-of-state providers, but self-pay options make this increasingly accessible.

Use this book in conjunction with regular CBT: Continue practicing I-CBT tools from this book while working with a CBT therapist on exposures and response prevention. The approaches complement each other well.

Consultation model: Some I-CBT specialists offer periodic consultation sessions (monthly rather than weekly) where they review your self-directed work, provide guidance, adjust your approach, and answer questions. This can be more affordable and accessible than weekly therapy while still providing professional oversight.

What to Expect in Therapy

Understanding typical I-CBT therapy structure helps you know what to expect and evaluate whether your therapist is implementing the approach appropriately.

Assessment Phase (Sessions 1-2)

The first sessions focus on comprehensive assessment. Your therapist will:

Conduct structured clinical interview about your obsessive symptoms, including:

- Specific obsessions and compulsions
- Duration and severity
- Impact on functioning
- Previous treatments and outcomes

Administer standardized assessment measures, typically including:

- Yale-Brown Obsessive Compulsive Scale (Y-BOCS) to measure symptom severity
- Depression and anxiety screening
- Functional impairment assessment

Explore your understanding of your symptoms:

- What do you believe about your obsessions?
- How do you make sense of your doubts?
- What reasoning leads you from observation to compulsion?

Begin identifying your primary reasoning devices through discussion of specific examples.

By the end of assessment, you and your therapist should have a shared understanding of your symptom pattern and the reasoning processes maintaining it.

Education Phase (Sessions 3-5)

Next comes psychoeducation about I-CBT principles. Your therapist will:

Explain the I-CBT model: how obsessive doubt forms through reasoning devices that substitute imagination for reality.

Help you identify your personal reasoning device profile—which devices you rely on most heavily.

Teach the Reality Sensing Check and practice applying it to your specific obsessions.

Introduce the 100% Imagination Test and practice distinguishing sensory evidence from imagination.

Explain the rationale for not engaging in compulsions: doing so reinforces confusion between imagination and reality rather than correcting it.

Assign initial homework exercises, typically including:

- Daily reality sensing practice
- Tracking obsessions and compulsions
- Identifying active reasoning devices

Active Treatment Phase (Sessions 6-18)

The bulk of therapy involves systematically applying I-CBT tools to your specific obsessions:

Sessions focus on:

- Reviewing homework and progress
- Troubleshooting difficulties with tool application
- Deepening understanding of reasoning devices
- Developing personalized responses to common obsessions
- Creating and implementing exposure hierarchies
- Practicing tools during imaginal or in-vivo exposures in session
- Adjusting strategies based on what's working and what isn't

Between sessions, you'll:

- Practice Reality Sensing Checks multiple times daily
- Apply the 100% Imagination Test to each obsession
- Complete exposure exercises from your hierarchy
- Track all obsessions, compulsions, and tool usage
- Complete worksheets analyzing specific obsessive episodes

Sessions are typically weekly or twice-weekly during this phase. More frequent sessions provide more support and accountability.

Maintenance and Relapse Prevention (Sessions 19-20)

As symptoms improve, therapy shifts to maintenance:

Reviewing progress using standardized measures to document improvement.

Identifying remaining vulnerable areas requiring continued attention.

Developing relapse prevention plan:

- Early warning signs of symptom increase
- Specific actions to take if symptoms worsen
- When to return for booster sessions

Planning for termination:

- Spacing out sessions (biweekly, then monthly)
- Ensuring independent tool use
- Building confidence in managing without regular therapist support

Session Structure

Individual sessions typically follow a consistent structure:

Review (10 minutes): Check in about the week. Review homework completion. Briefly assess symptom status.

Agenda setting (5 minutes): Collaboratively decide what to focus on today. Which obsessions or situations need attention?

Work (35-40 minutes): Address agenda items using I-CBT tools. This might involve:

- Detailed analysis of a specific obsessive episode
- Practicing Reality Sensing Check or Inference Detective
- In-session exposure with tool application
- Problem-solving obstacles to homework completion
- Teaching new concepts or skills

Homework assignment (10 minutes): Clearly define between-session practice. Write down specific assignments. Ensure understanding and commitment.

This structure ensures productive use of limited session time while maintaining focus on skill building and practice.

What Good I-CBT Therapy Looks Like

How do you know if therapy is being conducted well? Look for these indicators:

The therapist maintains I-CBT focus: Sessions consistently address reasoning devices, sensory versus imaginative evidence, and reality-testing. The approach doesn't drift into generic talk therapy or other CBT approaches without clear rationale.

Substantial homework expectations: I-CBT requires extensive between-session practice. Your therapist should assign specific, substantial homework each week and review completion carefully.

Structured symptom tracking: You should complete standardized measures (like Y-BOCS) every few weeks to objectively assess progress.

Collaborative, Socratic style: The therapist asks questions that help you discover reasoning errors rather than simply telling you what to think. "What does sensory evidence show?" rather than "You shouldn't believe that thought."

Exposure incorporated appropriately: I-CBT includes exposure exercises, but the focus during exposure is on reality-testing, not just anxiety reduction. You apply tools during exposures, not just white-knuckle through them.

Flexibility within the model: While maintaining I-CBT principles, the therapist adapts specific applications to your situation. The approach isn't rigidly manualized—it's flexibly applied.

Regular progress review: Every 6-8 sessions, you and your therapist explicitly review progress, adjust strategies if needed, and revise goals.

Red flags suggesting poor implementation:

Sessions lack structure or focus, wandering through various topics without clear direction.

Little or no homework assigned, or homework completion isn't reviewed.

Progress isn't measured objectively—you're just asked "How do you feel?"

The therapist seems unfamiliar with specific I-CBT concepts like reasoning devices or the inference model.

Exposures focus solely on anxiety reduction without reality-testing components.

Combining Self-Help with Professional Support

You don't have to choose between self-help and therapy. Combining both often produces the best outcomes.

How They Work Together

This book provides comprehensive I-CBT education and tools. A therapist provides personalized guidance, accountability, and support in applying those tools to your specific situation.

Optimal combination approach:

Use this book as your primary educational resource. Read chapters thoroughly. Complete exercises. Practice tools daily.

Work with a therapist weekly or biweekly for:

- Personalized assessment and treatment planning
- Guidance on applying tools to your specific obsessions
- Support and encouragement through difficult periods
- Adjustment of strategies when you hit obstacles
- Accountability for maintaining practice

Between sessions:

- Continue reading relevant chapters
- Complete exercises from the book
- Practice tools independently
- Bring questions or difficulties to sessions

This combination gives you both structure (from the book) and flexibility (from personalized therapy).

Discussing This Book with Your Therapist

If you're working with a therapist—whether I-CBT trained or not—consider sharing this book and discussing how to incorporate it:

"I've been reading this book about Inference-Based Therapy. I'm finding the concepts helpful. Could we integrate these ideas into our work?"

Most therapists appreciate engaged clients who educate themselves and bring resources to sessions.

If your therapist is I-CBT trained, they'll likely be enthusiastic about you having this additional resource and may assign specific chapters as homework.

If your therapist practices traditional CBT or ERP, they might be interested in incorporating I-CBT concepts as complementary tools while maintaining their primary approach.

When Self-Help Is Sufficient

Some people achieve substantial improvement through self-directed work without professional support. You might not need therapy if:

Your symptoms are mild to moderate and don't severely impair functioning.

You're able to consistently practice the tools independently without external accountability.

You're seeing steady improvement over 6-8 weeks of genuine practice.

You have good support from family or friends who encourage your recovery work.

You don't have significant comorbid conditions complicating treatment.

In these cases, continuing self-directed work using this book may be entirely sufficient.

When Professional Support Becomes Essential

Add professional help if:

Progress stalls despite consistent practice.

Symptoms worsen or new symptoms develop.

You're struggling to implement tools independently.

Motivation is difficult to maintain without accountability.

Emotional distress becomes overwhelming.

You encounter obstacles you can't solve alone.

Seeking help when you need it is a sign of strength, not weakness. Recovery is the goal—whatever combination of self-help and professional support gets you there is the right approach for you.

Making the Decision

Only you can decide whether professional support would benefit you right now. Here are some questions to guide your thinking:

Have I genuinely practiced the I-CBT tools consistently for at least 6-8 weeks? (Not just read about them, but actually practiced daily)

Am I seeing meaningful improvement in my symptoms and functioning?

Do I feel confident I can continue progressing on my own?

Are there obstacles I can't seem to overcome independently?

Would having professional guidance make this process less overwhelming?

Can I access and afford professional support?

Answer honestly. If self-help is working, continue with it. If you're struggling or uncertain, reaching out for professional support provides no downside beyond time and cost—and those investments could save you months of ineffective struggle.

The goal isn't to prove you can do it alone. The goal is recovery. Use whatever resources—self-help, professional therapy, medication, support groups—help you get there.

Chapter 21: Life After Obsessive Doubt

There comes a moment in recovery when you realize something has fundamentally changed. Maybe it's the day you lock your door once and walk away without a second thought. Maybe it's when you touch a public surface and wash your hands normally—once—without mental struggle. Maybe it's when an obsessive thought appears and you notice it, recognize it as imagination, and simply continue with your day.

This is what we've been working toward: not the absence of all obsessive thoughts—that's unrealistic—but the ability to recognize them for what they are and respond appropriately. This chapter prepares you for maintaining this freedom long-term.

What Freedom Feels Like

People who've worked through obsessive doubt often describe freedom in surprisingly modest terms. It's not euphoria or dramatic transformation. It's something quieter and more profound: normalcy.

The Return of Mental Space

Perhaps the most immediate change is mental space. Hours previously consumed by obsessive thinking become available for other things. You can focus on conversations without obsessive intrusions. You can enjoy movies without mentally checking doors. You can be present with people you care about.

One person described it this way: "I didn't realize how exhausting OCD was until it stopped consuming so much energy. It's like I'd been carrying a heavy backpack everywhere, and suddenly someone took it off. I feel lighter. I have energy for things I actually want to do."

The mental bandwidth previously devoted to managing obsessions becomes available for creativity, learning, relationships, work—whatever matters to you. This reclaimed capacity often feels like rediscovering yourself.

The Reduction of Fear

Freedom doesn't mean you never feel anxious. Anxiety is a normal human emotion. But the constant, grinding fear that characterized obsessive doubt diminishes dramatically.

Situations that previously triggered intense anxiety now feel manageable. Public restrooms are mildly unpleasant rather than terrifying. Leaving home involves brief attention to locking the door rather than prolonged checking rituals. Sending emails means sending them and moving on rather than agonizing over every word.

The anxiety that appears is proportional to actual circumstances rather than amplified by imagination. This proportionality is what normal anxiety feels like—uncomfortable sometimes, but not overwhelming.

Trust in Your Own Judgment

Perhaps the deepest change is rebuilding trust in yourself. For so long, you doubted your perception, your memory, your judgment. "Did I really lock that? Did I actually turn that off? Am I sure my hands are clean?"

Freedom means trusting your sensory information again. When you see the lock engaged, you believe it's engaged. When you feel your hands are clean, you accept they're clean. When you remember turning something off, you trust that memory.

This trust doesn't require absolute certainty—you've learned that demanding certainty is actually the problem. It means accepting that sensory evidence is sufficient for normal life decisions.

Research on recovered individuals consistently finds that restored self-trust correlates strongly with sustained recovery. People who rebuild confidence in their own perception maintain improvements better than those who continue doubting themselves even as symptoms decrease (Rachman et al., 2008).

Engagement with Life

Freedom shows up in your choices. You accept invitations you would have avoided. You pursue opportunities that previously seemed impossible. You make plans without obsessive concerns dominating your decision-making.

You might return to school. Start new relationships. Take jobs requiring travel. Have children. Move to new cities. Whatever you've been avoiding because obsessions interfered—these become possible again.

Life expands. Not because problems disappear—everyone has problems—but because OCD stops consuming the energy and attention needed to address normal life challenges.

Realistic Expectations

Let's be clear about what freedom doesn't mean:

It doesn't mean you'll never have another obsessive thought. Intrusive thoughts are universal. Everyone experiences occasional weird thoughts. The difference is that you now recognize them as meaningless mental noise rather than important information requiring action.

It doesn't mean anxiety disappears entirely. Normal anxiety about actual challenges—job interviews, health concerns with real symptoms, relationship conflicts—will still occur. The difference is you're not creating additional anxiety through obsessive imagination.

It doesn't mean life becomes easy or problem-free. Life involves genuine difficulties that have nothing to do with OCD. Loss, disappointment, stress, conflict—these are part of human experience. Recovery means you're dealing with real problems rather than imaginary ones.

Freedom means living with the normal human condition rather than being imprisoned by obsessive doubt. That's actually quite remarkable, even if it feels ordinary.

Maintaining Your Skills

Skills atrophy without use. You wouldn't expect physical fitness to maintain itself without ongoing exercise. Mental skills work the same way—they require ongoing practice, though less intensive than during active treatment.

The Maintenance Mindset

Think of maintenance as health promotion rather than illness treatment. You're no longer trying to recover—you've recovered. Now you're maintaining wellness.

This shifts the framework from crisis management to routine health practices. You don't brush your teeth because you have a cavity—you brush them to prevent cavities. Similarly, you practice I-CBT tools not because you're in crisis, but to maintain the gains you've achieved.

Daily Micro-Practices

Maintenance doesn't require the intensive daily practice you did during active recovery. But it does require some ongoing engagement.

Morning grounding (2 minutes): Brief sensory awareness exercise. Five things you see, four you hear, three you physically feel. This maintains the habit of anchoring in sensory reality rather than imagination.

Spot-checks throughout the day: When you notice old patterns trying to resurface—a checking urge, a contamination worry, an obsessive thought—apply the 100% Imagination Test immediately. This prevents small slips from becoming patterns.

Weekly review (10 minutes): Once weekly, reflect on how you're doing. Are old patterns re-emerging? Are you using tools when needed? What situations felt challenging? This weekly check-in catches drift before it becomes problematic.

These micro-practices take minimal time but maintain the neural pathways supporting your recovery.

Continued Exposure

Don't slip back into avoidance. If you worked hard to use public restrooms, keep using them. If you conquered checking compulsions, maintain the one-check limit. If you addressed social anxiety, continue engaging socially.

Avoidance is tempting—"Why put myself through this if I don't have to?"—but it gradually weakens your confidence and rebuilds fear. Regular engagement with previously difficult situations maintains your skill at managing them.

This doesn't mean seeking out difficult situations unnecessarily. But it means not avoiding them when they naturally arise in your life.

Tool Refreshers

Periodically review the core tools even when things are going well. Reread chapters from this book. Review your worksheets. Remind yourself of the reasoning devices you're prone to using.

This periodic refreshing prevents skills from fading. Think of it like reviewing your emergency exits on an airplane—you hope you'll never need them, but reviewing them ensures they're accessible if you do.

The 80/20 Rule

During active treatment, you might have used I-CBT tools dozens of times daily. In maintenance, you might use them only occasionally—when old patterns start creeping back or when you face particularly challenging situations.

This 80/20 pattern is normal. Eighty percent of the time, you're just living normally without conscious tool application. Twenty percent of the time, you notice something that needs attention and actively apply tools.

This reduced intensity is actually a sign of success, not failure. The tools have become sufficiently internalized that you only need conscious application occasionally.

Seasonal or Situational Intensification

Be prepared for certain periods requiring more intensive tool use. These might include:

High-stress periods: Exams, job changes, relationship transitions, illnesses, or other major stressors might temporarily increase obsessive thoughts. During these times, increase tool usage proactively. More frequent Reality Checks, stricter adherence to one-time checking rules, daily logging.

Anniversary reactions: Dates associated with OCD onset, particularly difficult periods, or other significant events sometimes trigger symptom increases. Awareness of these patterns helps you prepare and respond rather than being caught off-guard.

Life transitions: Moving, starting new relationships, having children, changing careers—major transitions involve uncertainty that can activate obsessive patterns. Anticipate this and increase tool use during transition periods.

These intensifications don't mean you're relapsing. They mean you're experiencing normal variation in a challenging context. Respond by temporarily increasing maintenance practices, then return to baseline once the situation stabilizes.

Preventing Relapse

Complete relapse—returning to pre-treatment symptom levels—is less common than partial setbacks, but it can happen. Understanding risk factors and early warning signs helps you prevent full relapse.

Risk Factors for Relapse

Research has identified several factors that increase relapse risk:

Stopping tool use entirely. The most consistent predictor of relapse is completely abandoning I-CBT practices. People who maintain at least minimal tool use—even just occasional Reality Checks—maintain recovery much better than those who stop all practice (Hiss et al., 1994).

Returning to avoidance patterns. When you start avoiding situations you'd previously conquered, you rebuild the neural pathways of fear. Avoidance is often the first step toward relapse.

Major life stressors without increased support. Stress alone doesn't cause relapse, but stress plus abandoning coping strategies does. Major stressors require proactive increases in tool use and support-seeking.

Comorbid depression. If depression develops or worsens, OCD symptoms often worsen concurrently. Addressing depression—

through therapy, medication, or both—protects against OCD relapse.

Social isolation. Withdrawing from supportive relationships removes both accountability and emotional buffer against stress. Maintaining connections protects recovery.

Stopping medication abruptly (if you're on medication). For people taking SSRIs or other OCD medications, abrupt discontinuation often triggers symptom return. Any medication changes should be done gradually under medical supervision.

Early Warning Signs

Relapse rarely happens overnight. Usually, warning signs appear weeks before full symptom return. Catching these early prevents full relapse.

Watch for:

Increased frequency of obsessive thoughts. The thoughts themselves aren't concerning—everyone has them occasionally. But if frequency increases noticeably, pay attention.

Reduced tool use. You notice you're not applying Reality Checks anymore, or you're forgetting to use the 100% Imagination Test when doubts arise.

Small increases in compulsions. Checking once has become twice. Washing once has become twice. The escalation is subtle but present.

Avoidance creeping back in. Small avoidances begin: "I'll use a different restroom, that one looks dirty." "I'll skip this social event, I'm tired." Individual instances aren't concerning, but a pattern suggests drift.

Increased anxiety about specific triggers. Situations you'd been managing comfortably start feeling more distressing. The anxiety level is disproportionate to any objective change in the situation.

Difficulty dismissing obsessive thoughts. Previously, you'd notice an obsessive thought, recognize it as imagination, and move on quickly. Now they're sticking longer, feeling more compelling.

Changes in self-talk. You notice thoughts like "Maybe I should check just to be sure" or "What if this time it's different?" These suggest reasoning devices reactivating.

The Three-Strike Response

When you notice warning signs, use this graduated response:

First strike—Increase awareness: Start tracking daily again. Log obsessive thoughts, compulsions, and tool usage. Awareness itself often reverses drift.

Second strike—Increase tool use: Actively apply tools multiple times daily, even when not actively obsessing. Proactive Reality Checks, deliberate practice with the 100% Imagination Test. Refresh your memory on reasoning devices by reviewing relevant chapters.

Third strike—Seek support: If increased awareness and tool use don't reverse the drift within 2-3 weeks, seek professional support. Contact your therapist for a booster session, or find a therapist if you haven't worked with one before.

This graduated approach prevents minor drift from becoming major relapse.

The Relapse Prevention Plan

Create a written plan now, while you're doing well, that specifies what you'll do if warning signs appear. Include:

My personal early warning signs:

1. _____
2. _____
3. _____

My response to early warning signs:

- Increase daily tracking
- Review chapters ____ and ____
- Practice tools ____ times daily
- Reach out to [support person]

When I'll seek professional help:

- If warning signs persist beyond ____ weeks despite increased tool use
- If I resume avoiding ____ activities
- If compulsions increase to ____ per day
- If I feel unable to manage independently

Professional support contact: Therapist: _____ Phone: _____
Backup: _____ Phone: _____

Having this plan prepared means you're not making decisions during crisis. You're following a plan you created when thinking clearly.

Learning from Near-Relapses

If you catch drift early and successfully reverse it, extract lessons:

What triggered the drift? Stress? Complacency? Life changes?

What warning signs appeared first?

What actions reversed the drift?

What would you do differently if this happens again?

Each successfully managed near-relapse teaches you something valuable about your vulnerabilities and effective responses. You become better at maintenance through these experiences.

Your New Normal

Recovery creates a new normal—a way of life that looks very different from life dominated by obsessive doubt. This section prepares you for that new normal and helps you appreciate it.

Redefining Your Identity

For many people, OCD becomes part of identity. "I'm someone with OCD. I'm a checker. I'm a germaphobe." Recovery requires updating this identity.

You're not "someone with OCD" in the same way anymore. You're someone who had OCD and learned to manage it. You're someone who struggled with obsessive doubt and developed skills to address it. You're someone who can have obsessive thoughts and recognize them appropriately.

This identity shift matters. Research shows that people who continue identifying primarily as "OCD sufferers" even after symptom improvement show higher relapse rates than those who update their self-concept to "someone who successfully manages occasional obsessive thoughts" (Steketee et al., 2001).

You're not defined by your worst struggles. You're defined by the full complexity of who you are—which includes, but isn't limited to, your history with OCD.

Appreciating Normal Difficulties

One unexpected aspect of recovery: You get to have normal problems.

When OCD dominated your life, it overshadowed everything else. Now that it doesn't, you become aware of ordinary life challenges—work stress, relationship tensions, financial concerns, health issues, loss, disappointment.

This might feel discouraging initially. "I worked so hard to recover, and now I'm stressed about normal things?"

But this is actually positive. You're dealing with real problems—challenges everyone faces—rather than imaginary ones created by obsessive doubt. Real problems can be addressed. They have solutions, even if those solutions are difficult. Imaginary problems have no solutions because they don't exist.

Appreciating this distinction helps you recognize recovery. The fact that you're worried about an actual work deadline rather than whether you locked the door ten times ago represents progress.

Spontaneity and Flexibility

Recovery brings increased spontaneity. You can accept last-minute invitations without obsessive planning. You can change plans without anxiety spiraling. You can handle unexpected situations without extensive mental preparation.

This flexibility comes from trusting your ability to manage whatever arises using your tools. You don't need to have everything planned and controlled because you know you can assess situations as they occur, distinguish imagination from reality, and respond appropriately.

For people whose OCD involved need for certainty and control, this flexibility represents profound change. Life doesn't require pre-planning everything. You can handle uncertainty and ambiguity.

Helping Others

Many people who recover from obsessive doubt find meaning in helping others who struggle. You might:

Share your story with people newly diagnosed, offering hope that recovery is possible.

Support others in their recovery work, providing encouragement and understanding that only someone who's been there can offer.

Participate in support groups, either as attendee or eventually as facilitator.

Volunteer with organizations like the International OCD Foundation.

Simply be open about your experience, reducing stigma and helping others feel less alone.

This isn't required—some people prefer to move on from OCD entirely and focus on other things. But many find that their suffering becomes meaningful when it helps others, and helping others reinforces their own recovery.

Gratitude and Perspective

Recovery often brings unexpected gratitude—not for having had OCD, but for appreciating normal life in ways you couldn't before.

Using a public restroom without elaborate rituals becomes something to appreciate. Locking your door once and walking away feels like freedom. Sending an email without agonizing becomes a small joy.

People who haven't struggled with obsessive doubt take these things for granted. You know how difficult they can be, which makes their ease all the more precious.

This appreciation isn't universal—some people recover and simply move on without much reflection. But many find that their struggle provides perspective that enriches their appreciation of ordinary life.

The Ongoing Journey

Recovery isn't a destination where you arrive and stop. It's an ongoing practice of maintaining skills, responding to challenges appropriately, and continuing to choose reality over imagination.

Some months will be easier than others. Some challenges will trigger old patterns. But you now have tools that work, understanding of your vulnerability patterns, and experience successfully managing difficulties.

You're not cured in the sense of never having another obsessive thought. You're recovered in the sense of having effective responses to those thoughts when they appear.

That's what sustainable recovery looks like—not perfection, but competence. Not complete absence of symptoms, but effective management of them. Not certainty, but confidence in your ability to handle uncertainty.

This is your new normal. It's worth celebrating.

Chapter 22: Helping Others Understand

Recovery doesn't happen in isolation. The people around you—family, friends, partners, colleagues—inevitably affect your experience. Some provide tremendous support. Others, often unintentionally, make things harder. This chapter helps you communicate about your recovery work and build a supportive network.

Talking to Family and Friends

Explaining OCD and I-CBT to people who haven't experienced obsessive doubt requires thought. Most people have fundamental misconceptions about OCD that shape their responses.

Common Misunderstandings to Address

Misunderstanding 1: "OCD just means you like things neat and organized."

Popular culture has turned OCD into a personality quirk. "I'm so OCD about my desk" or "I'm OCD about my music playlist" trivializes a debilitating condition.

How to explain: "OCD isn't about being neat. It's about being trapped in cycles of obsessive doubt and compulsive responses. For me, it meant [specific example relevant to your experience]. It consumed hours daily and prevented me from [activities you avoided or found difficult]. It's not a preference—it's a psychological condition."

Misunderstanding 2: "Just stop thinking about it."

People who haven't experienced obsessive thoughts don't understand their intrusive, persistent nature.

How to explain: "I wish it were that simple. Obsessive thoughts aren't voluntary. They're intrusive—they appear automatically and feel compelling despite not being wanted. The more you try not to think about them, the more they increase. Recovery isn't about stopping the thoughts—it's about learning to respond to them differently."

Misunderstanding 3: "Everyone has worries. What makes yours different?"

This minimizes the severity and impact of obsessive doubt.

How to explain: "The difference is in intensity, duration, and impact on functioning. Normal worry is proportional to actual risk and resolves when you problem-solve or get information. Obsessive doubt is disproportionate to actual risk, doesn't resolve with reassurance, and interferes significantly with daily life. I was spending [X hours] daily on this and couldn't [activities you avoided]. That's beyond normal worry."

Misunderstanding 4: "Just do exposures—face your fears."

People familiar with OCD treatment may know about exposure therapy but not understand the I-CBT distinction.

How to explain: "Exposure is part of treatment, but I-CBT adds something important: reality-testing. I'm not just learning to tolerate fear—I'm learning to recognize when concerns are based on imagination rather than sensory evidence. The approach teaches me to distinguish real problems from imagined ones, which addresses the root cause of obsessive doubt."

Choosing What to Share

You don't owe anyone your complete psychological history. Consider:

Relationship closeness: Close family and intimate partners generally benefit from fuller explanations. Casual friends might need only brief context. Colleagues might need minimal information or none at all.

Their capacity to understand: Some people are psychologically minded and readily grasp mental health concepts. Others struggle with abstract psychological ideas. Tailor explanations to their capacity.

Your comfort level: Share only what feels comfortable. You're not obligated to disclose things you prefer to keep private.

Potential impact on relationship: Sometimes disclosure strengthens relationships by increasing understanding. Other times, particularly with people who stigmatize mental health conditions, it creates distance. Consider likely outcomes.

Starting the Conversation

When you decide to talk with someone about your OCD and I-CBT work:

Choose the right time and setting. Find a private, quiet moment when neither of you is stressed or rushed. "I'd like to talk with you about something I've been working on. Do you have time now, or should we find a better time?"

Start with the impact, not the diagnosis. "You may have noticed I've been [specific observable behaviors—avoiding certain situations, seeming anxious, taking a long time to leave the house]. I want to explain what's been going on."

Provide context. "I've been dealing with OCD—obsessive-compulsive disorder. For me, that's meant [specific ways it affected you]. It's been difficult, but I'm working on it using an approach called Inference-Based Therapy."

Explain your current work. "I'm learning to distinguish between concerns based on actual evidence versus imagination. When I [specific example—check the door repeatedly, wash hands excessively], it's because I'm responding to imagined concerns rather than real ones. The therapy teaches me to recognize this difference."

Be specific about what you need. Don't expect people to guess how to support you. "What would help me most is [specific supportive behaviors—see next section]. What wouldn't help is [specific unhelpful behaviors]."

Provide resources if they want to learn more. Some people want to understand deeply. Others just need basic context. Offer: "If you want to understand more, I can share resources" versus insisting they read everything.

Example conversation:

"Mom, I want to talk with you about something. You've probably noticed I've been struggling with leaving the house—taking forever to check locks and coming back multiple times. I've been dealing with OCD. For me, it means I get stuck in cycles of doubt where I can't trust my own perception. I see the door locked but doubt whether it's really locked, so I check again and again.

I'm working with an approach called I-CBT that teaches me to distinguish between sensory evidence and imagination. When I see the lock engaged, I'm learning to trust that observation rather than doubting it.

What would really help is if you don't ask whether I'm sure I locked the door or suggest I check again. That reinforces the doubt cycle. Instead, if you see me starting to check repeatedly, a gentle reminder like 'You checked once—trust that' would be supportive. Does that make sense?"

What They Can Do to Support You

Specific guidance helps people support you effectively. Without it, they often try to help in ways that actually interfere with recovery.

Supportive Behaviors

Encourage tool use, not compulsions. When they see you struggling with doubt, they can remind you: "What do your senses tell you?" or "Is this based on evidence or imagination?" This redirects you toward tools rather than toward compulsions.

Refuse to provide reassurance. Reassurance feels supportive but maintains OCD. When you ask "Do you think the door is locked?" or "Are my hands clean?", supportive people gently refuse: "I'm not going to answer that because reassurance doesn't help. You can use your tools to assess it yourself."

This feels harsh initially but represents genuine support. Research consistently shows that accommodation—providing reassurance, participating in rituals, modifying situations to reduce anxiety—maintains OCD rather than helping it (Lebowitz et al., 2016).

Acknowledge difficulty while maintaining confidence. "I know this is really hard right now, and I also know you can handle it. You've got tools that work."

Celebrate progress, even small progress. When you resist a compulsion, use a tool successfully, or handle a trigger well, supportive people notice and acknowledge it. "I noticed you locked the door once and walked away. That's real progress."

Maintain normal expectations. Don't lower standards or excuse avoiding responsibilities because of OCD. Supportive people believe you're capable and expect you to manage life responsibilities. "I know you're working on this, and I also need you to [meet your obligations]."

Respect your privacy. They don't tell others about your OCD without permission. They don't bring it up in social situations. They let you control who knows.

Take care of themselves. Living with or close to someone with OCD can be stressful. Supportive people maintain their own wellbeing—they're not martyrs or co-dependent rescuers. They support you while also meeting their own needs.

Unsupportive Behaviors (Even If Well-Intentioned)

Providing reassurance. "Yes, the door is locked. Yes, your hands are clean. Yes, you turned off the stove." This maintains the doubt cycle.

Participating in rituals. Checking things for you, performing rituals on your behalf, or modifying their own behavior to accommodate your OCD enables the condition.

Expressing frustration or anger about symptoms. "Just lock it once! Why can't you just stop checking?" This creates shame and doesn't help. Your loved ones' frustration is understandable, but expressing it directed at you isn't supportive.

Monitoring your behavior excessively. Constantly asking "Did you check? Did you wash? Are you doing your exercises?" This creates pressure and actually increases anxiety.

Making OCD the focus of all interactions. Supportive relationships involve more than OCD. People who only ask about symptoms or only discuss your recovery work make OCD central to the relationship, which isn't helpful.

Comparing you to others. "My friend had OCD and recovered in three months. Why is it taking you longer?" Everyone's timeline is different. Comparisons create pressure without providing value.

Suggesting alternative treatments without asking. "I read about this supplement/prayer practice/alternative therapy. You should try it!" Unsolicited advice usually isn't helpful and suggests they don't trust the approach you're using.

The Support Request Template

When asking specific people for support, use this template:

"I'm working on OCD using I-CBT. Here's what would help me:

Do's:

- [Specific supportive behavior 1]
- [Specific supportive behavior 2]
- [Specific supportive behavior 3]

Don'ts:

- [Specific unsupportive behavior to avoid 1]
- [Specific unsupportive behavior to avoid 2]
- [Specific unsupportive behavior to avoid 3]

I know this might be different from what feels natural, but these approaches are based on research about what actually helps OCD recovery. Can you work on these?"

Being this explicit prevents well-intentioned but unhelpful support.

Common Misunderstandings

Even people who care about you deeply might hold misconceptions that interfere with effective support. Addressing these directly helps.

"If you just relaxed more, you'd feel better."

The misunderstanding: OCD is caused by being too stressed or anxious. If you just calm down, it will resolve.

The reality: While stress can exacerbate OCD, it doesn't cause it. OCD involves specific cognitive processes—reasoning devices that confuse imagination with reality—that occur regardless of stress level. Relaxation might reduce general anxiety but doesn't address these reasoning processes.

How to explain: "Stress makes things harder, and relaxation helps me cope better. But OCD isn't just about being stressed. It's about specific thinking patterns that confuse imagination with reality. The treatment addresses those patterns directly, which is more effective than just trying to relax."

"You're being too hard on yourself. You should be more compassionate."

The misunderstanding: The problem is perfectionism or self-criticism. If you were just kinder to yourself, OCD would improve.

The reality: While self-compassion is valuable, OCD involves specific cognitive errors that require correction, not just acceptance. You need to recognize when you're confusing imagination with reality and respond appropriately, which sometimes means refusing to engage with compelling feelings.

How to explain: "Self-compassion is part of recovery—I'm learning not to beat myself up for having obsessive thoughts. But recovery also requires recognizing when my thinking is based on imagination rather than evidence, and choosing not to act on false inferences. Both are necessary."

"Just ignore the thoughts and they'll go away."

The misunderstanding: If you don't pay attention to obsessive thoughts, they'll disappear.

The reality: Attempted suppression typically makes intrusive thoughts more frequent (the famous "white bear" effect). I-CBT doesn't advocate ignoring thoughts—it teaches you to recognize their nature and respond appropriately.

How to explain: "Trying to ignore or suppress thoughts usually makes them worse. Instead, I'm learning to recognize them as imagination-based rather than reality-based. I notice the thought, recognize it for what it is, and choose not to act on it. That's different from trying to make it go away."

"Medication would fix this quickly."

The misunderstanding: OCD is purely biological and just needs the right medication.

The reality: OCD involves biological, cognitive, and behavioral components. Medication can be helpful, especially in combination with therapy, but it doesn't teach the cognitive skills that produce lasting change.

How to explain: "Medication can be part of treatment, and I'm [using it / not using it currently] for [reasons]. But research shows that therapy, particularly approaches like I-CBT, teaches skills that remain effective even after treatment ends. Medication helps some people access the therapy, but the skills are what create lasting change."

"You're doing better—you don't need to keep working on this."

The misunderstanding: Once symptoms decrease, treatment can stop entirely.

The reality: Maintenance practice prevents relapse. Completely stopping all I-CBT practice increases relapse risk.

How to explain: "I'm doing better because I'm consistently using these tools. I need to maintain at least some practice to keep the improvements. Think of it like physical fitness—once you're in shape, you don't stop all exercise. You maintain fitness through regular practice, even if less intensive than during initial training."

Building Your Support Network

Recovery works best with a network of support. This doesn't mean dozens of people—quality matters more than quantity. Even 2-3 supportive people significantly impact outcomes.

Who to Include

People who genuinely understand (or genuinely want to understand) mental health challenges. They don't stigmatize or minimize psychological conditions.

People who can maintain appropriate boundaries. They support you without becoming enmeshed in your recovery or making it their responsibility.

People who've demonstrated reliability. They've shown up for you before in meaningful ways. Trust past behavior as the best predictor of future support.

People in your regular life. Support is most useful from people you interact with frequently—family members you live with, close friends you see regularly, partners or spouses.

Optional: People with lived experience. Others who've experienced OCD or similar challenges can provide unique understanding and hope that recovery is possible. This might come from support groups rather than your personal network.

Who to Exclude (or Keep at Distance)

People who stigmatize mental health conditions. If someone believes mental health challenges indicate weakness or lack of faith or moral failing, they won't provide helpful support.

People who are psychologically fragile themselves. If someone is struggling significantly with their own mental health, they may not have capacity to support yours.

People who habitually violate boundaries. If someone consistently oversteps, tells your private information to others, or makes your issues about them, they're not safe support people.

People who've been unhelpful in the past. If you've previously sought support from someone and found their response made things worse, believe that experience. Don't give repeat chances hoping they'll change.

Building Support Gradually

Start with one person. Don't try to build a network all at once. Identify one person who seems most likely to be supportive and start there.

Test the waters. Share a little and see how they respond. If they respond well, you can share more. If they don't, you haven't disclosed everything to someone unhelpful.

Be explicit about needs. Use the support request template from earlier. People can't read your mind. Explicit guidance helps them help you effectively.

Acknowledge their effort. When people support you well, thank them specifically: "It really helped when you reminded me to use my tools rather than checking again. Thank you." Positive reinforcement increases helpful behaviors.

Accept imperfection. No one will support perfectly. People will sometimes say unhelpful things, provide reassurance when they shouldn't, or get frustrated. That's normal. What matters is overall pattern, not individual mistakes.

Maintain reciprocity (when possible). Relationships involve give and take. While you're actively recovering, people might give more than you can reciprocate. But over time, maintain balance by supporting them when they need it.

Support Groups

Beyond your personal network, consider support groups—either in-person or online. Organizations like the International OCD Foundation facilitate groups specifically for OCD.

Benefits of support groups:

- Connection with others who truly understand from lived experience
- Reduced isolation and shame
- Practical tips and strategies from people actively managing OCD
- Hope provided by seeing others at various recovery stages
- Validation that your experience is real and significant

Potential drawbacks:

- Some groups focus heavily on symptom sharing, which can trigger obsessive thoughts
- Not all groups are well-facilitated; poorly run groups can reinforce unhelpful patterns
- Scheduling and accessibility challenges

If you try a support group and it doesn't feel helpful, try a different group before concluding groups aren't for you. Quality and fit vary significantly.

Online Communities

Online forums and social media groups provide another support option. These offer convenience and anonymity but require caution.

Use online communities for:

- Connecting with others when geography limits in-person options
- Finding people with your specific OCD subtype
- Accessing support outside traditional therapy hours

Approach with caution:

- Symptom sharing can be triggering
- Reassurance-seeking is common and unhelpful
- Quality of advice varies; some suggestions contradict evidence-based treatment
- Anonymity sometimes reduces accountability for helpful behavior

Treat online communities as supplemental rather than primary support.

The Foundation of Support

The most important support, ultimately, comes from yourself. Other people can encourage, remind, and validate, but you're the one doing the work. You're the one recognizing imagination-based inferences. You're the one resisting compulsions. You're the one building trust in your senses.

External support enhances recovery but doesn't replace self-efficacy. Building a support network matters, and building your own competence matters more. Both together create optimal conditions for sustained recovery.

Chapter 23: Your Continued Journey

This is the final chapter of formal instruction, but it's not the end of your journey. Recovery is ongoing—not in the sense that you'll always be "recovering," but in the sense that you'll continue growing, learning, and applying these skills throughout your life.

This chapter provides perspective on the lifelong nature of what you've learned and encouragement for the road ahead.

Lifelong Skills

I-CBT isn't just about treating OCD. The skills you've learned have applications far beyond obsessive doubt.

Distinguishing Reality from Imagination

This fundamental skill—asking "Is this based on sensory evidence or imagination?"—applies across countless situations.

Career decisions: "Am I actually underqualified for this position (what does the job description actually require versus what I imagine), or am I catastrophizing?"

Relationships: "Is there actual evidence this person is upset with me (what did they actually say and do), or am I imagining negative judgments?"

Financial choices: "Is this purchase necessary based on actual needs, or am I imagining scenarios where I'll need this?"

Health decisions: "Does this symptom warrant medical attention based on actual severity and duration, or am I catastrophizing?"

Parenting: "Is my child actually struggling (what does their behavior and performance actually show), or am I imagining worst-case developmental outcomes?"

The reality-testing skill you've developed for OCD transfers to clearer thinking across your life.

Managing Uncertainty

You've learned to function despite uncertainty—to take action based on sensory evidence even when you lack absolute certainty.

This capacity to tolerate ambiguity serves you in countless contexts. Life is inherently uncertain. Relationships don't come with guarantees. Career paths involve unknowns. Financial decisions require acting despite imperfect information. Health involves accepting that you can't achieve absolute certainty about every bodily sensation.

The comfort with uncertainty you've developed through I-CBT—recognizing that sensory evidence is sufficient even without absolute certainty—is a life skill applicable far beyond OCD.

Recognizing and Challenging Cognitive Distortions

The twelve reasoning devices you've learned to identify are cognitive distortions that everyone uses to some degree. Your training in spotting them makes you more sophisticated thinker across domains.

Categorical reasoning appears in stereotyping and prejudice. Recognizing this device helps you question overgeneralizations about groups.

Subjective probability escalation drives risk aversion and anxiety. Recognizing it helps you assess risks more accurately.

Imaginary sequences create worry about catastrophic futures. Recognizing these as imagination rather than prediction reduces unnecessary suffering.

Your cognitive sophistication—your ability to catch yourself using these devices—is a permanent acquisition that improves your thinking across contexts.

Building Trust in Your Judgment

Perhaps the deepest skill is restored confidence in your own perception and judgment. For so long, you doubted yourself. Through I-CBT, you've rebuilt trust that your senses provide accurate information and your judgment is sound.

This self-trust extends beyond OCD situations. You trust your gut feelings about people more. You trust your assessment of situations. You trust your decision-making capacity.

This doesn't mean you're never wrong—everyone makes mistakes. But it means you trust your judgment as a reasonable guide rather than constantly second-guessing yourself.

Research on recovered individuals finds that this restored self-trust is one of the most valued outcomes, often more significant to quality of life than symptom reduction itself (Steketee & Frost, 2007).

When Challenges Arise

Life continues after recovery, and life inevitably includes challenges. Some will trigger old OCD patterns. Others will be entirely unrelated to OCD. Your I-CBT skills help with both.

OCD-Related Challenges

Encountering new triggers: You might face situations you haven't addressed yet. A pandemic heightens contamination fears. Becoming a parent triggers checking fears about your child's safety.

A new relationship activates relationship obsessions you thought you'd resolved.

Response: Apply the same tools to new content. The reasoning devices stay consistent even when surface content changes. Reality Sensing Check, 100% Imagination Test, identifying reasoning devices—these work regardless of specific trigger.

Symptoms resurface during stress: Major life stress—loss, illness, job changes—might temporarily increase obsessive thoughts even after long recovery periods.

Response: Don't catastrophize the increase. Stress temporarily taxes coping resources. Respond with temporarily intensified tool use—more frequent Reality Checks, stricter limits on compulsions, resuming daily tracking. Once stress decreases, symptoms typically return to baseline without additional intervention.

Question your progress: Sometimes you'll wonder "Am I really recovered? What if symptoms come back?"

Response: Recognize this as doubt about recovery—itself an example of obsessive thinking. Apply the 100% Imagination Test: "Is there evidence I'm regressing, or is this imaginary worry?" Usually it's the latter. Your progress is real, even when doubt questions it.

Non-OCD Challenges

Life includes difficulties unrelated to OCD—relationship conflicts, career disappointments, health problems, loss, financial stress, discrimination, or injustice. These are real problems requiring real solutions, not obsessive imagination.

Your I-CBT skills help by:

Distinguishing real from imagined problems: Is this actually happening (sensory evidence), or am I catastrophizing about what might happen (imagination)? This distinction helps you focus energy on real problems rather than imaginary ones.

Assessing what you can control: Am I taking excessive responsibility for things outside my control, or focusing on actions actually within my power? This prevents both excessive guilt and helpless passivity.

Tolerating uncertainty: Many problems don't have clear solutions or guaranteed outcomes. Your increased tolerance for ambiguity helps you take action despite uncertainty rather than becoming paralyzed by it.

Trusting your judgment: When facing difficult decisions, your restored confidence in your own judgment helps you make choices and commit to them rather than endlessly second-guessing.

I-CBT doesn't solve all life problems—nothing does. But it provides cognitive tools that help you approach problems more clearly and effectively.

When to Revisit This Book

Keep this book accessible. You might not need it for months or years, but having it available provides security.

Situations warranting revisiting specific chapters:

Symptoms beginning to increase → Reread chapters on your specific obsessive theme, and chapters on the tools

Facing new triggers → Review chapters on applying I-CBT to different challenges

Supporting someone else → Reread chapters 22 and relevant sections on explaining I-CBT

Questioning whether you're applying tools correctly → Review tool chapters and complete the worksheets again

Experiencing a setback → Reread chapter 16 on handling setbacks

Seeking encouragement → Reread chapter 18 on the science and success rates, and this final chapter

Books don't expire. Their value extends beyond initial reading. This book can serve as reference, refresher, and reminder throughout your continued journey.

Staying Connected to Reality

The central principle of I-CBT—staying anchored in sensory reality rather than getting lost in imagination—applies to more than obsessive doubt. It's actually a fundamental life skill.

Reality as Anchor

When you feel overwhelmed by worry, fear, anxiety, or uncertainty, returning to sensory reality provides grounding.

What do I actually see right now? Look around. Name specific objects. Colors. Shapes. Light and shadow.

What do I actually hear? Traffic sounds. Voices. Music. Silence. Wind. Birds. Your own breathing.

What do I actually feel physically? Chair supporting you. Feet on floor. Temperature. Clothing texture. Your body's sensations.

This practice—which you learned as the sensory grounding exercise—pulls you out of imaginary futures or ruminated pasts and anchors you in present reality.

Present reality is the only place where you can actually take action. The past is gone. The future hasn't arrived. Right now, in this present moment based on actual sensory reality, is where your power resides.

Reality as Truth

In a world full of misinformation, manipulation, and competing narratives, sensory reality provides a form of truth we can trust.

Politicians might spin interpretations. Media might frame events selectively. Social media might distort through filter bubbles. But what you directly observe with your own senses is true for you in that moment.

This doesn't mean your senses can't be fooled—optical illusions exist, and perception can be distorted under extreme conditions. But under normal circumstances, your senses provide accurate information about your immediate environment.

Trusting sensory reality over imagined narratives makes you less susceptible to manipulation and more grounded in what's actually occurring.

Reality as Connection

When you're present with sensory reality, you're more connected—to your environment, to other people, to your own experience.

Obsessive doubt pulls you into imagination, disconnecting you from present experience. You're physically in a conversation but mentally checking whether you locked the door. You're physically at a gathering but mentally analyzing whether you said something embarrassing.

Staying connected to sensory reality means being where you are. Tasting the food you're eating. Hearing the person speaking to you. Feeling the sun on your skin. Seeing the beauty around you.

This presence—this connection to actual sensory experience—is how life is actually lived. The rest is imagination.

Final Words of Encouragement

You've come far. From the first chapter explaining what obsessive doubt is, through learning about reasoning devices, practicing the five tools, creating your action plan, and now reading these final words—you've engaged seriously with recovery work.

What You've Accomplished

You've learned to recognize the difference between imagination and reality—a distinction that sounds obvious but proves surprisingly difficult when obsessive doubt is active.

You've identified the specific reasoning devices your mind uses to create false inferences—naming your personal pattern makes you more aware and able to intervene.

You've practiced concrete tools for reality-testing—the Reality Sensing Check, 100% Imagination Test, Inference Detective, spotting reasoning devices, and building sensory trust. These are skills you now possess permanently.

You've (hopefully) experienced that reducing compulsions doesn't lead to catastrophic consequences—nothing bad actually happens when you trust sensory evidence rather than demanding impossible certainty.

You've rebuilt trust in your own perception and judgment—perhaps the most fundamental achievement of all.

These accomplishments are real, even if recovery still feels incomplete or fragile. You've learned and practiced skills that the majority of people will never need but that fundamentally change life for those who do need them.

The Road Ahead

Recovery isn't a destination. It's an ongoing practice of choosing reality over imagination, evidence over assumption, trust over doubt.

Some days this choice will be easy—so automatic you won't notice you're making it. Other days it will be hard—requiring conscious effort and courage to resist compulsive urges and trust your tools.

Both experiences are part of recovery. Easy days don't mean you've "arrived." Difficult days don't mean you've failed. They're just days—part of the natural variation in any ongoing practice.

What matters is the overall trajectory. Are you functioning better than before? Are obsessions interfering less with your life? Can you engage in activities you previously avoided? Do you spend less time in obsessive cycles?

If yes, you're succeeding, regardless of day-to-day fluctuations.

You're Not Alone

Millions of people have experienced obsessive doubt. Many have worked through it successfully using approaches like I-CBT. You're part of a community—though scattered and often invisible—of people who understand this particular struggle.

You're also part of the broader human community learning to navigate psychological challenges. Mental health struggles aren't signs of weakness or failure. They're part of being human in a complex world that sometimes overwhelms our evolved coping mechanisms.

Seeking help, learning skills, and working toward wellness demonstrates strength, not weakness. You've chosen growth over resignation, action over passivity, hope over despair. That choice matters.

Trust the Process

Some days you'll doubt whether I-CBT works. Some days you'll doubt whether you're doing it right. Some days you'll doubt whether you'll ever really recover.

In those moments, return to evidence. What does your tracking data show? Has there been improvement? Even modest improvement counts. Progress doesn't require perfection.

Trust that consistent application of these tools produces results. Research shows they work for the majority of people who genuinely engage with them. Tens of thousands of people have recovered using these principles.

The process works. It requires patience, persistence, and practice—but it works.

Your Life Awaits

Beyond obsessive doubt lies the life you want to live. Maybe that means career achievement. Maybe it means rich relationships. Maybe it means creative expression. Maybe it means simply enjoying ordinary days without constant mental interference.

Whatever life you envision, it's possible. OCD doesn't have to define your future. The time and energy currently consumed by obsessive doubt can be reclaimed for whatever matters to you.

This isn't magical thinking. It's realistic hope based on evidence. People recover. Not perfectly—no one lives perfectly. But sufficiently. Functionally. With manageable symptoms that don't prevent them from building meaningful lives.

You can be one of those people. In many ways, you already are—you've already made substantial progress just by learning these concepts and practicing these tools.

Keep Going

There will be hard days ahead. There will also be easier days. There will be setbacks and there will be breakthroughs. There will be moments of doubt and moments of confidence.

Through all of it, keep using your tools. Keep distinguishing imagination from reality. Keep building trust in your senses. Keep resisting compulsions even when the urge is strong.

Keep going.

Not because it's easy—it often isn't. Not because results are immediate—they rarely are. But because you deserve freedom from obsessive doubt. Because you deserve to live the life you want. Because recovery is possible, and you're worth the effort it requires.

You've got this.

The tools work. You can do this. Your future self—the one living with manageable symptoms, engaging fully in life, free from the prison of obsessive doubt—is waiting for you to take the next step.

Take it.

And then take the next one.

And the one after that.

That's how recovery happens. One step at a time. One tool application at a time. One resisted compulsion at a time.

You're on your way. Keep going.

Appendix A: Quick Reference Guide

The 5-Minute I-CBT Summary

The Core Problem: Obsessive doubt happens when you confuse imagination with reality. You infer that something is true without sensory evidence supporting it.

The Solution: Systematically distinguish between what your senses actually tell you (reality) versus what you imagine might be true (imagination). If a concern is 100% imagination-based, don't respond with compulsions.

The Five Tools:

1. Reality Sensing Check

- What do I see?
- What do I hear?
- What do I feel/touch?
- What do I smell?
- What do I taste?
- Conclusion: Sensory evidence vs. imagination

2. Inference Detective

- What exactly am I concluding?
- What sensory evidence supports this?
- What am I imagining/assuming?
- Which reasoning devices am I using?
- What are alternative explanations?

3. Spotting Reasoning Devices Identify which thinking tricks you're using:

- Categorical reasoning

- Imaginary sequences
- Selective attention
- Subjective probability escalation
- Inverse inference
- Distrust of normal perception
- Overimportance of thought
- Necessity for proof
- Thought-action fusion
- Absorption in personal narrative
- Self as central observer
- Excessive responsibility

4. Building Trust in Your Senses

- Pay full attention when doing things once
- Trust what your senses tell you
- Accept that sensory evidence is sufficient
- Practice delayed verification

5. The 100% Imagination Test "If I remove all imagination—all 'what if' thinking—is there any sensory evidence left supporting this concern?"

- If no → Don't perform compulsion
- If yes → Respond appropriately to actual evidence

Emergency Tools

When Anxiety Is Overwhelming:

Urge Surfing (for intense compulsion urges):

1. Notice the urge without acting on it
2. Rate intensity 0-10
3. Observe it like a wave—it will rise, peak, fall
4. Check intensity every 2-5 minutes
5. Usually peaks around 10-15 minutes
6. Ride it down without acting

Grounding Exercise (for disconnection from reality):

- 5 things you see
- 4 things you hear
- 3 things you physically feel
- 2 things you smell
- 1 thing you taste

The 30-Second Response:

1. Pause and name it (5 seconds): "Obsessive doubt appearing"
2. Apply tool (15 seconds): "100% Imagination Test—evidence or imagination?"
3. Decide and act (10 seconds): If imaginary, no compulsion; continue activity

Quick Checklists

Daily I-CBT Practice Checklist: ☐ Morning grounding (2-5 minutes) ☐ Used tools when obsessions arose ☐ Resisted at least one compulsion ☐ Evening tracking (2 minutes)

Weekly Review Checklist: ☐ Reviewed tracking data ☐ Identified wins and challenges ☐ Extracted lessons learned ☐ Adjusted plan if needed ☐ Set goals for next week

Warning Signs Checklist (Check if you notice these): ☐ Increased obsessive thought frequency ☐ Decreased tool usage ☐ Small increases in compulsions ☐ Avoidance creeping back ☐ Increased anxiety about triggers ☐ Difficulty dismissing thoughts ☐ Seeking reassurance more

If you checked 2+ warning signs: → Increase tracking immediately → Use tools 5+ times daily proactively → Review relevant chapters → If no improvement in 2-3 weeks, seek professional support

Appendix B: The 12 Reasoning Devices

1. Selective Attention and Focus

What it is: Focusing exclusively on information confirming your concern while ignoring contradictory evidence or broader context.

Example 1: Focusing only on the possibility of contamination on a surface while ignoring that it looks clean, smells normal, and you've touched similar surfaces thousands of times without illness.

Example 2: Focusing only on a person's neutral facial expression while ignoring their friendly tone, positive words, and engaged body language.

Example 3: Focusing only on one ambiguous physical sensation while ignoring overall normal body functioning.

Counter-strategy: Deliberately broaden attention. Ask: "What am I not noticing while focusing on this concern? What information contradicts my worry?"

2. Imaginary Sequences

What it is: Creating detailed narratives about how something bad happened or will happen, treating these stories as reality or likely reality.

Example 1: "Someone sick touched this handle yesterday → their germs are on it → I touched it → germs transferred to my hand → I'll get seriously ill → I might die."

Example 2: "I might have hit someone → they're injured on the road → police are looking for me → I'll be arrested → my life will be ruined."

Example 3: "My partner seemed distant tonight → they're losing interest → they're going to leave me → I'll be alone forever."

Counter-strategy: Label it as storytelling. Ask: "Am I observing events or narrating possibilities? What actually happened versus what I'm imagining might happen?"

3. Categorical Reasoning

What it is: Assuming that because something belongs to a category, it automatically has all the properties you attribute to that category, without checking the specific instance.

Example 1: "This is a public restroom → all public restrooms are dirty → therefore this restroom is dirty" (without looking at whether this specific restroom appears clean).

Example 2: "This is a doorknob → doorknobs have germs → this doorknob has dangerous germs" (without evidence this specific doorknob is contaminated).

Example 3: "This person is [group member] → [group members] are [quality] → this person must be [quality]" (prejudice/stereotyping operates through categorical reasoning).

Counter-strategy: Check the specific instance. Ask: "What do I actually observe about THIS specific thing, not about the category it belongs to?"

4. Subjective Probability Escalation

What it is: Treating something as likely or certain based on how it feels rather than on actual probability.

Example 1: A headache feels like it probably indicates a brain tumor, despite brain tumors being extremely rare and headaches being extremely common.

Example 2: It feels likely you hit someone while driving, despite seeing no impact, hearing no sound, feeling no bump, and seeing no one injured.

Example 3: It feels certain others are judging you harshly, despite lack of evidence in their actual behavior.

Counter-strategy: Check actual probability. Ask: "What are the realistic odds based on base rates and evidence, not based on how it feels?"

5. Inverse Inference

What it is: Reversing a logical relationship inappropriately.

Example 1: "I'm not 100% certain the door is locked → therefore it's probably unlocked" (uncertainty about perception doesn't change actual lock state).

Example 2: "Absence of evidence that it's safe → presence of evidence that it's dangerous" (not proving safety doesn't prove danger).

Example 3: "If I loved them, I'd feel certain → I don't feel certain → therefore I don't love them" (reversing the direction of inference).

Counter-strategy: Check the logic. Ask: "Am I reversing cause and effect? Does A → B actually mean not-B → not-A?"

6. Distrust of Normal Perception

What it is: Doubting your senses even though they're functioning normally and providing clear information.

Example 1: You saw the lock engage, heard the click, felt the key turn, but still doubt whether it's really locked.

Example 2: You see your hands are clean, but doubt whether they're really clean.

Example 3: You remember turning something off, but doubt whether you really did it.

Counter-strategy: Affirm sensory reliability. Ask: "Do I have actual reason to doubt this perception, or am I doubting normal sensory functioning?"

7. Overimportance of Thought

What it is: Treating the mere occurrence of a thought as meaningful or significant.

Example 1: "I had a thought about harming someone → this thought must mean something about my character or intentions."

Example 2: "I thought 'Do I love them?' → having this thought means there's probably a real problem with the relationship."

Example 3: "I imagined something going wrong → thinking this makes it more likely to happen."

Counter-strategy: Recognize thoughts as mental events. Ask: "Does having a thought make it important? Or is it just a random mental event?"

8. Necessity for Proof

What it is: Demanding absolute certainty or positive proof rather than accepting sensory evidence as sufficient.

Example 1: "I need absolute proof there are zero germs on my hands" (impossible without lab testing; sensory evidence of cleanliness should suffice).

Example 2: "I need proof that I definitely didn't hit anyone" (sensory evidence of no impact should suffice).

Example 3: "I need certainty that I love my partner" (feelings are inherently ambiguous; demanding certainty is unrealistic).

Counter-strategy: Accept sensory evidence as sufficient. Ask: "Is sensory information enough for this decision, or am I demanding impossible certainty?"

9. Thought-Action Fusion

What it is: Confusing thoughts with actions or intentions, or believing thoughts influence external events.

Example 1: "I thought about pushing someone off a platform → thinking this means I might actually do it."

Example 2: "I imagined something bad happening → imagining it makes it more likely to occur."

Example 3: "I had an aggressive thought → this thought is morally equivalent to actually being violent."

Counter-strategy: Separate thoughts from actions. Ask: "Do thoughts cause events? Do thoughts equal actions? Or are they completely different domains?"

10. Absorption in Personal Narrative

What it is: Maintaining a story about yourself that filters all information to fit the narrative, regardless of actual evidence.

Example 1: "I'm a contaminated person" → interpreting all situations through this lens, seeing contamination everywhere.

Example 2: "I'm someone who always fails" → interpreting successes as flukes and failures as confirmations.

Example 3: "I can't maintain relationships" → interpreting normal relationship challenges as evidence of this narrative.

Counter-strategy: Check evidence against narrative. Ask: "Does actual evidence support this self-story, or am I filtering reality to maintain a narrative?"

11. Self as Central Observer

What it is: Overestimating how much others notice, focus on, or think about you.

Example 1: "Everyone at the party noticed my awkward comment and is judging me" (most people were focused on themselves, not analyzing you).

Example 2: "Everyone can see my anxiety" (most people don't notice subtle signs others perceive as obvious).

Example 3: "They're all thinking about my [perceived flaw]" (others usually aren't thinking about you as much as you imagine).

Counter-strategy: Reality-check attention. Ask: "Do I have evidence others are focusing on me this much? How much do I typically focus on analyzing others?"

12. Excessive Responsibility

What it is: Feeling disproportionately responsible for preventing unlikely events or for things outside your control.

Example 1: "If I don't check perfectly, a fire might start and it will be my fault."

Example 2: "If I don't wash enough, I might spread germs and cause someone's death."

Example 3: "If something bad happens to anyone after they interacted with me, it's my responsibility."

Counter-strategy: Clarify actual responsibility. Ask: "What am I actually responsible for? What's within my control versus outside it?"

Appendix C: Worksheets and Logs

Reality Check Log

Date/Time	Situation	Concern	Visual	Auditory	Touch	Smell	Taste	Sensory Evidence?	Imaginary?	100% Imaginary?	Response
										Yes/No	

Instructions: Complete one row each time you apply the Reality Sensing Check. Use this to track patterns and build evidence that your concerns are typically imagination-based.

Inference Investigation Worksheet

Date: _____

1. What exactly am I concluding? (State the specific inference)

_____

2. What sensory evidence supports this inference?

Vision:
_____
_____

Hearing:
_____
_____

Touch:
_____
_____

Smell:

Taste:

3. What am I imagining or assuming?

4. Which reasoning devices am I using? ☐ Selective attention ☐ Imaginary sequences ☐ Categorical reasoning
☐ Subjective probability escalation ☐ Inverse inference ☐ Distrust of normal perception
☐ Overimportance of thought ☐ Necessity for proof ☐ Thought-action fusion
☐ Absorption in personal narrative ☐ Self as central observer ☐ Excessive responsibility

5. What are alternative explanations?

A.

B.

C.

6. Conclusions: ☐ Inference is primarily imagination-based ☐ Sensory evidence is minimal or absent
☐ Alternative explanations are more probable

7. Appropriate response:

_____

8. Did I follow through? ☐ Yes ☐ No

9. Results:

Progress Tracker

Week of: _____

Primary Metric: _____ (e.g., "Times checked door")

Day	Metric Number	Resisted Compulsions	Used Tools	Anxiety (1-10)	Notes
Mon					
Tue					
Wed					
Thu					
Fri					
Sat					
Sun					

Weekly Average: _____

Progress this week:

_____
_____

Challenges:
_____
_____

Adjustments needed:
_____
_____

Daily Practice Journal

Date: _____

Morning Practice (2-10 minutes): ☐ Completed ☐ Skipped
Notes:
_____
_____

Tool Usage Today: Reality Check: _____ times 100% Imagination Test: _____ times
Inference Detective: _____ times
Other: _____

Compulsions: Total: _____
Resisted: _____

Wins Today:

Challenges Today:

Lesson Learned:

Evening Practice (2-5 minutes): ☐ Completed ☐ Skipped
Notes:
_____
_____

Appendix D: Resources

Recommended Reading

I-CBT Specific:

- O'Connor, K. P., & Aardema, F. (2012). *Clinician's Handbook for Obsessive Compulsive Disorder: Inference-Based Therapy.* Wiley.
- O'Connor, K. P., Aardema, F., & Pélissier, M. C. (2005). *Beyond Reasonable Doubt: Reasoning Processes in Obsessive-Compulsive Disorder and Related Disorders.* Wiley.

General OCD:

- Hyman, B. M., & Pedrick, C. (2010). *The OCD Workbook: Your Guide to Breaking Free from Obsessive-Compulsive Disorder* (3rd ed.). New Harbinger.
- Grayson, J. (2014). *Freedom from Obsessive-Compulsive Disorder: A Personalized Recovery Program for Living with Uncertainty.* Penguin.

Acceptance-Based Approaches:

- Hershfield, J., & Corboy, T. (2013). *The Mindfulness Workbook for OCD.* New Harbinger.

For Family Members:

- Landsman, K. J., Rupertus, K. M., & Pedrick, C. (2005). *Loving Someone with OCD.* New Harbinger.

Websites and Organizations

International OCD Foundation (IOCDF)

- Website: iocdf.org
- Therapist directory, support groups, annual conference, extensive resources
- Highly recommended primary resource

Anxiety and Depression Association of America (ADAA)

- Website: adaa.org
- Resources on anxiety disorders including OCD

Association for Behavioral and Cognitive Therapies (ABCT)

- Website: abct.org
- Find a therapist directory

Beyond OCD

- Website: beyondocd.org
- Free therapy programs, educational resources

OCD-UK

- Website: ocduk.org
- UK-based charity with excellent international resources

Made of Millions

- Website: madeofmillions.com
- Peer support community for mental health

How to Find a Therapist

1. Search specialized directories:

- IOCDF therapist directory (iocdf.org/ocd-finding-help)

- Psychology Today directory (psychologytoday.com) - filter by OCD specialty
- ABCT therapist directory (abct.org)

2. Look for specific credentials:

- Licensed mental health professional (psychologist, social worker, counselor, psychiatrist)
- Specialization in OCD treatment
- Training in I-CBT or CBT/ERP
- Membership in professional organizations (IOCDF, ABCT)

3. Questions to ask potential therapists:

- Do you have specific training in I-CBT or inference-based approaches?
- How many people with OCD have you treated?
- What does your typical OCD treatment look like?
- What are your expectations for homework/practice between sessions?
- How do you measure progress?

4. Consider teletherapy:

- Many I-CBT specialists offer video sessions
- Expands access beyond your geographic location
- Check insurance coverage for out-of-state providers

5. University training clinics:

- Graduate students supervised by expert faculty
- Often reduced-cost services
- High-quality treatment

Support Groups

In-Person Groups:

- IOCDF Affiliate support groups (find via iocdf.org)
- Hospital-based programs
- Community mental health centers

Online Communities:

- IOCDF online support groups
- Reddit: r/OCD (use with caution - can be triggering)
- Facebook groups (search "OCD support")

Cautions for online communities:

- Can be helpful for connection and support
- Can also be triggering through symptom sharing
- Reassurance-seeking is common and unhelpful
- Quality of advice varies
- Use as supplement, not replacement for professional care

Appendix E: Frequently Asked Questions

Q: How long does I-CBT take to work?

A: Most people see initial improvement within 6-8 weeks of consistent practice. Significant improvement typically occurs over 12-20 weeks. Full recovery—reaching subclinical symptom levels—often takes 4-6 months. These timelines assume regular practice of tools and exercises, not just reading about them.

Q: Can I do I-CBT on my own, or do I need a therapist?

A: Research shows self-directed I-CBT can be effective, especially for people who consistently complete exercises and track progress. However, professional guidance generally produces better outcomes. Ideal approach: Use this book as primary educational resource while working with a therapist for personalized guidance and support. If therapists aren't accessible, self-directed work using this book can still produce meaningful improvement.

Q: Will obsessive thoughts ever go away completely?

A: Probably not entirely, and that's actually okay. Intrusive thoughts are universal—everyone has occasional weird, unwanted thoughts. Recovery doesn't mean thoughts disappear; it means you recognize them as meaningless mental events rather than important information requiring action. The thoughts become background noise rather than compelling concerns.

Q: What if my obsessions are different from the examples in the book?

A: The specific content of obsessions varies widely, but the underlying process—confusing imagination with reality through reasoning devices—remains consistent. Apply the same tools to your specific content. Reality Sensing Check, 100% Imagination Test, and identifying reasoning devices work across all obsessive themes.

Q: Can I use I-CBT if I'm on medication?

A: Yes. I-CBT and medication work well together. Medication often makes it easier to engage with I-CBT tools by reducing overall anxiety. I-CBT teaches skills that remain effective even after medication ends, potentially preventing relapse when you eventually discontinue medication.

Q: What's the difference between I-CBT and traditional CBT or ERP?

A: Traditional CBT challenges thought content and appraisals. ERP focuses on exposure to feared situations with response prevention. I-CBT addresses something more fundamental: the inference-making process that confuses imagination with reality. All approaches work well; I-CBT often works better for cognitive obsessions (pure O, mental contamination, relationship doubts) than traditional ERP. Many therapists now integrate approaches.

Q: How do I know if my concern is 100% imaginary or based on real evidence?

A: Apply the 100% Imagination Test systematically: "If I remove ALL imagination—all 'what if' thinking, all assumptions, all possibilities—is there any sensory evidence left?" Be strict: sensory means what you see, hear, touch, smell, or taste right now. If the answer is "no sensory evidence," the concern is 100% imaginary. If sensory evidence exists, respond appropriately to that actual evidence.

Q: What should I do when I feel stuck or not making progress?

A: First, check whether you're actually practicing tools consistently (not just reading about them). If yes, consider: Are you applying tools correctly? Are there obstacles (depression, life stress) interfering? Would professional guidance help? Has enough time passed (at least 6-8 weeks of consistent practice)? If genuinely stuck after 8+ weeks of consistent practice, seek professional support.

Q: Can I-CBT help with other conditions besides OCD?

A: The core principle—distinguishing reality from imagination—applies to various conditions involving cognitive distortions: GAD, social anxiety, health anxiety, body dysmorphic disorder, some aspects of depression. However, these conditions often require additional interventions. I-CBT principles can be one component of comprehensive treatment.

Q: What if my family doesn't understand or support my recovery work?

A: Educate them using chapter 22 resources. Provide specific guidance about helpful versus unhelpful behaviors. If they remain unsupportive, consider: Can you access support elsewhere (friends, support groups, therapist)? Can you pursue recovery despite lack of family support? Sometimes recovery requires setting boundaries with unsupportive people.

Q: How do I prevent relapse long-term?

A: Maintain at least minimal tool use even when doing well. Don't completely abandon I-CBT practices. Notice early warning signs (increased obsessive thoughts, decreased tool use, avoidance returning) and respond immediately by increasing practice. Stay connected to support systems. Address life stressors proactively. Review this book periodically as refresher.

Q: Is it normal to still have some symptoms after recovery?

A: Yes, completely normal. Recovery typically means symptoms are manageable and don't significantly interfere with functioning, not that symptoms are entirely absent. Most recovered individuals still have occasional obsessive thoughts—they just recognize them appropriately and don't respond with compulsions. Success is functional improvement, not perfection.

Q: What if I-CBT doesn't work for me?

A: I-CBT works for majority of people who genuinely engage with it, but not everyone. If it doesn't help after consistent practice: Try working with a therapist if you were self-directing. Consider combining with medication. Explore other evidence-based approaches (traditional ERP, ACT). Ensure depression, trauma, or other conditions aren't interfering with treatment response. Different people respond to different approaches—not responding to one doesn't mean you can't recover.

Glossary: Terms Made Simple

Accommodation: When family members or others participate in compulsions, modify their behavior to reduce your anxiety, or enable OCD symptoms. Generally maintains OCD rather than helping recovery.

Anchor: Grounding yourself in present sensory reality rather than getting lost in imaginary futures or ruminated pasts.

Anxiety: Emotional state involving apprehension, worry, and physical tension. Normal human emotion that becomes problematic when disproportionate to actual threats or when it significantly impairs functioning.

Behavioral experiment: Deliberately testing a prediction to gather evidence about what actually happens versus what you imagine will happen.

Categorical reasoning: Assuming something has properties based on category membership without checking the specific instance. (Reasoning device #3)

Checking compulsion: Repeatedly verifying something (door locked, stove off, email sent correctly) despite clear sensory evidence that it's done.

Cognitive-behavioral therapy (CBT): Family of psychotherapies focusing on relationships between thoughts, emotions, and behaviors. Includes traditional CBT, ERP, I-CBT, ACT, and other approaches.

Compulsion: Repetitive behavior or mental act performed in response to obsessive doubt, typically aimed at reducing anxiety or preventing feared outcomes. Common types: checking, washing, counting, seeking reassurance, mental reviewing.

Contamination obsession: Excessive fear of germs, dirt, bodily fluids, chemicals, or other contaminants leading to avoidance or washing/cleaning compulsions.

Distrust of normal perception: Doubting your senses even though they're functioning normally and providing clear information. (Reasoning device #6)

ERP (Exposure and Response Prevention): Traditional OCD treatment involving systematic exposure to feared situations while preventing compulsive responses.

Excessive responsibility: Feeling disproportionately responsible for preventing unlikely events or for things outside your control. (Reasoning device #12)

Exposure: Deliberately engaging with feared situations or triggers rather than avoiding them. Component of most CBT approaches for anxiety disorders.

Exposure hierarchy: Ranked list of feared situations ordered from least to most difficult, used for systematic gradual exposure.

Grounding: Practices that anchor you in present sensory reality, helping you feel more connected to your body and environment.

Harm obsessions: Intrusive thoughts about causing harm to yourself or others, or fear of having accidentally caused harm. Not desires or intentions—unwanted, disturbing thoughts that contradict your values.

I-CBT (Inference-Based Cognitive Behavioral Therapy): Treatment approach focusing on how obsessive doubt forms through confusion of imagination with reality. Addresses reasoning processes underlying obsessive inferences.

Imaginary sequences: Creating detailed narratives about how something bad happened or will happen, treating these stories as reality or likely reality. (Reasoning device #2)

Inference: Conclusion drawn about reality that goes beyond direct sensory observation. Obsessive inferences are conclusions drawn without sensory evidence supporting them.

Intrusive thought: Unwanted thought, image, or urge that pops into mind uninvited. Universal human experience. Becomes problematic when you attribute importance to the thought or believe it reflects your character or predicts behavior.

Inverse inference: Reversing a logical relationship inappropriately. (Reasoning device #5)

Necessity for proof: Demanding absolute certainty or positive proof rather than accepting sensory evidence as sufficient. (Reasoning device #8)

Obsession: Persistent, intrusive thought, image, or urge that causes anxiety or distress. In OCD, obsessions are typically about contamination, harm, symmetry, relationships, religion/morality, or other themes.

Obsessive inference: Specific conclusion drawn about reality without sensory evidence. The core problem in I-CBT's understanding of OCD.

OCD (Obsessive-Compulsive Disorder): Mental health condition characterized by obsessions (intrusive thoughts causing distress) and compulsions (repetitive behaviors or mental acts performed to reduce distress or prevent feared outcomes).

Overimportance of thought: Treating the mere occurrence of a thought as meaningful or significant. (Reasoning device #7)

Reassurance-seeking: Asking others to confirm that everything is okay, that nothing bad will happen, that you didn't cause harm, etc. Provides brief relief but maintains OCD by preventing you from building confidence in your own judgment.

Reality Sensing Check: I-CBT tool involving systematically examining what your five senses actually tell you about a situation, distinguishing sensory evidence from imagination.

Reasoning device: Cognitive process that substitutes imagination for reality, creating false inferences. I-CBT identifies 12 specific reasoning devices that drive obsessive doubt.

Relapse: Return to clinically significant symptom levels after a period of improvement or recovery.

Response prevention: Not performing compulsions even when the urge is strong. Central component of ERP and I-CBT.

Selective attention: Focusing exclusively on information confirming your concern while ignoring contradictory evidence or broader context. (Reasoning device #1)

Self as central observer: Overestimating how much others notice, focus on, or think about you. (Reasoning device #11)

Sensory evidence: Information directly provided by your five senses (sight, hearing, touch, smell, taste). I-CBT distinguishes this from imagination-based inferences.

Setback: Temporary increase in symptoms during recovery. Normal part of the process. Different from full relapse.

Subjective probability escalation: Treating something as likely or certain based on how it feels rather than on actual probability. (Reasoning device #4)

Thought-action fusion: Confusing thoughts with actions or intentions, or believing thoughts influence external events. (Reasoning device #9)

Trigger: Situation, object, thought, or sensation that activates obsessive doubt.

100% Imagination Test: Key I-CBT tool asking: "If I remove all imagination, is there any sensory evidence left supporting this concern?" If no, the concern is imagination-based and doesn't warrant compulsive response.

Urge surfing: Technique of observing compulsive urges without acting on them, recognizing they rise, peak, and fall like waves.

Y-BOCS (Yale-Brown Obsessive Compulsive Scale): Standard clinical measure of OCD symptom severity, scored 0-40. Used in research and clinical practice to assess symptoms and track treatment progress.

References

- **Aardema, F., & O'Connor, K. P. (2003).** Seeing white bears that are not there: Inference processes in obsessions. *Journal of Cognitive Psychotherapy*, 17(1), 23–37.

- **Aardema, F., & O'Connor, K. P. (2007).** The menace within: Obsessions and the self. *Journal of Cognitive Psychotherapy*, 21(3), 182–197.

- **Aardema, F., & O'Connor, K. P. (2012).** Dissolving the tenacity of obsessional doubt: Implications for treatment outcome. *Journal of Behavior Therapy and Experimental Psychiatry*, 43(2), 855–861.

- **Aardema, F., Emmelkamp, P. M., & O'Connor, K. P. (2005).** Inferential confusion, cognitive change and treatment outcome in obsessive–compulsive disorder. *Clinical Psychology & Psychotherapy*, 12(5), 337–345.

- **Aardema, F., Kleijer, T. A. M., Trihey, M., O'Connor, K. P., & Emmelkamp, P. M. G. (2006).** Processes of inference, schizotypal thinking, and obsessive–compulsive behaviour in a normal sample. *Psychological Reports*, 99(1), 213–220.

- **Aardema, F., Moulding, R., Melli, G., Radomsky, A. S., Doron, G., Audet, J.-S., & Purcell Lalonde, M. (2017).** The role of feared possible selves in obsessive–compulsive and related disorders: A comparative analysis. *Journal of Obsessive-Compulsive and Related Disorders*, 13, 12–18.

- **Aardema, F., O'Connor, K. P., Emmelkamp, P. M., Marchand, A., & Todorov, C. (2005).** Inference-based treatment of obsessive–compulsive disorder: A controlled trial. *Journal of Behavior Therapy and Experimental Psychiatry*, 36(2), 135–153.

- **Aardema, F., O'Connor, K. P., Emmelkamp, P. M., Marchand, A., & Todorov, C. (2005).** Inferential confusion in obsessive–compulsive disorder: The Inferential Confusion Questionnaire. *Behaviour Research and Therapy*, 43(3), 293–308.

- **Aardema, F., Radomsky, A. S., O'Connor, K. P., & Julien, D. (2009).** Inferential confusion, obsessive beliefs and obsessive–compulsive symptoms: A multidimensional investigation of cognitive domains. *Clinical Psychology & Psychotherapy*, 15(4), 227–238.

- **Aardema, F., Wu, K. D., Careau, Y., O'Connor, K. P., Julien, D., & Dennie, S. (2013).** The expanded version of the Inferential Confusion Scale: Further development and validation in clinical and non-clinical samples. *Journal of Psychopathology and Behavioral Assessment*, 35(3), 299–411.

- **Abramowitz, J. S., Franklin, M. E., Schwartz, S. A., & Furr, J. M. (2003).** Symptom presentation and outcome of cognitive–behavioral therapy for obsessive–compulsive disorder. *Journal of Consulting and Clinical Psychology*, 71(6), 1049–1057.

- **Abramowitz, J. S., Taylor, S., & McKay, D. (2009).** Obsessive–compulsive disorder. *The Lancet*, 374(9688), 491–499.

- **American Psychological Association. (2013).** Recognition of psychotherapy effectiveness. *Psychotherapy*, 50(1), 102–109.

- **Bowen, S., & Marlatt, A. (2009).** Surfing the urge: Brief mindfulness-based intervention for college student smokers. *Psychology of Addictive Behaviors*, 23(4), 666–671.

- **Cisler, J. M., & Koster, E. H. (2010).** Mechanisms of attentional biases towards threat in anxiety disorders: An integrative review. *Clinical Psychology Review*, 30(2), 203–216.

- **Clear, J. (2018).** *Atomic Habits: An easy and proven way to build good habits and break bad ones*. Penguin Random House.

- **Coles, M. E., Radomsky, A. S., & Horng, B. (2006).** Exploring the boundaries of memory distrust from repeated checking: Increasing external validity and examining thresholds. *Behaviour Research and Therapy*, 44(7), 995–1006.

- **Craske, M. G., Treanor, M., Conway, C. C., Zbozinek, T., & Vervliet, B. (2014).** Maximizing exposure therapy: An inhibitory learning approach. *Behaviour Research and Therapy*, 58, 10–23.

- **Cromer, K. R., Schmidt, N. B., & Murphy, D. L. (2007).** An investigation of traumatic life events and obsessive–compulsive disorder. *Behaviour Research and Therapy*, 45(7), 1683–1691.

- **Dugas, M. J., & Robichaud, M. (2007).** *Cognitive–behavioral treatment for generalized anxiety disorder: From science to practice*. Routledge.

- **Fairburn, C. G. (2008).** *Cognitive Behavior Therapy and Eating Disorders*. Guilford Press.

- **Foa, E. B., Liebowitz, M. R., Kozak, M. J., Davies, S., Campeas, R., Franklin, M. E., ... Tu, X. (2005).** Randomized, placebo-controlled trial of exposure and ritual prevention, clomipramine, and their combination in the treatment of obsessive–compulsive disorder. *American Journal of Psychiatry*, 162(1), 151–161.

- **Grant, J. E., & Chamberlain, S. R. (2016).** Trichotillomania. *American Journal of Psychiatry*, 173(9), 868–874.

- **Hedman, E., Axelsson, E., Görling, A., Ritzman, C., Ronnheden, M., El Alaoui, S., ... Ljótsson, B. (2014).** Internet-delivered exposure-based cognitive–behavioural therapy and behavioural stress management for severe health anxiety: Randomised controlled trial. *The British Journal of Psychiatry*, 205(4), 307–314.

- **Hiss, H., Foa, E. B., & Kozak, M. J. (1994).** Relapse prevention program for treatment of obsessive–compulsive disorder. *Journal of Consulting and Clinical Psychology*, 62(4), 801–808.

- **Hofmann, S. G., & Otto, M. W. (2008).** *Cognitive Behavioral Therapy for Social Anxiety Disorder: Evidence-Based and Disorder-Specific Treatment Techniques*. Routledge.

- **Hofmann, S. G., Asnaani, A., Vonk, I. J., Sawyer, A. T., & Fang, A. (2012).** The efficacy of cognitive behavioral therapy: A review of meta-analyses. *Cognitive Therapy and Research*, 36(5), 427–440.

- **Julien, D., O'Connor, K. P., & Aardema, F. (2019).** Effectiveness of inference-based therapy for obsessive–

compulsive disorder: A naturalistic study. *Journal of Obsessive-Compulsive and Related Disorders*, 21, 72–79.

- **Koran, L. M., & Simpson, H. B. (2013).** Guideline Watch (March 2013): *Practice Guideline for the Treatment of Patients with Obsessive–Compulsive Disorder*. American Psychiatric Association.

- **Korotitsch, W. J., & Nelson-Gray, R. O. (1999).** An overview of self-monitoring research in assessment and treatment. *Psychological Assessment*, 11(4), 415–425.

- **Lally, P., Van Jaarsveld, C. H., Potts, H. W., & Wardle, J. (2010).** How are habits formed: Modelling habit formation in the real world. *European Journal of Social Psychology*, 40(6), 998–1009.

- **MacDonald, C. B., & Davey, G. C. (2005).** A mood-as-input account of perseverative checking: The relationship between stop rules, mood and confidence in having checked successfully. *Behaviour Research and Therapy*, 43(1), 69–91.

- **Najavits, L. M. (2002).** *Seeking Safety: A treatment manual for PTSD and substance abuse*. Guilford Press.

- **National Safety Council. (2020).** Odds of dying. *Injury Facts* database.

- **O'Connor, K. P., & Aardema, F. (2012).** *Clinician's Handbook for Obsessive Compulsive Disorder: Inference-Based Therapy*. John Wiley & Sons.

- **O'Connor, K. P., Aardema, F., & Pélissier, M.-C. (2005).** *Beyond Reasonable Doubt: Reasoning Processes in Obsessive–Compulsive Disorder and Related Disorders*. John Wiley & Sons.

- O'Connor, K. P., Aardema, F., Bouthillier, D., Fournier, S., Guay, S., Robillard, S., ... Pitre, D. (2005). Evaluation of an inference-based approach to treating obsessive–compulsive disorder. *Cognitive Behaviour Therapy*, 34(3), 148–163.

- O'Connor, K. P., Aardema, F., Robillard, S., Guay, S., Pélissier, M.-C., Todorov, C., ... Pitre, D. (2012). Cognitive behaviour therapy and medication in the treatment of obsessive–compulsive disorder. *Acta Psychiatrica Scandinavica*, 113(5), 408–419.

- O'Connor, K., & Robillard, S. (2009). Inference-based therapy: A cognitive approach to treating obsessive–compulsive disorder. In M. M. Antony & M. B. Stein (Eds.), *Oxford Handbook of Anxiety and Related Disorders* (pp. 411–422). Oxford University Press.

- Öst, L.-G., Havnen, A., Hansen, B., & Kvale, G. (2015). Cognitive behavioral treatments of obsessive–compulsive disorder: A systematic review and meta-analysis of studies published 1993–2014. *Clinical Psychology Review*, 40, 156–169.

- Palmer, S. E. (1999). *Vision Science: Photons to Phenomenology*. MIT Press.

- Parrish, C. L., & Radomsky, A. S. (2010). Why do people seek reassurance and check repeatedly? An investigation of factors involved in compulsive behavior in OCD and depression. *Journal of Anxiety Disorders*, 24(2), 211–222.

- Pélissier, M.-C., Reyes, C. M., & O'Connor, K. P. (2016). Coping strategies and outcome in inference-based therapy for obsessive–compulsive disorder. *Journal of Anxiety Disorders*, 38, 28–34.

- **Rachman, S. (1997).** A cognitive theory of obsessions. *Behaviour Research and Therapy*, 35(9), 793–802.

- **Rachman, S. (2002).** A cognitive theory of compulsive checking. *Behaviour Research and Therapy*, 40(6), 625–639.

- **Rachman, S. (2003).** *The Treatment of Obsessions.* Oxford University Press.

- **Rachman, S. (2004).** Fear of contamination. *Behaviour Research and Therapy*, 42(11), 1227–1255.

- **Rachman, S., & De Silva, P. (1978).** Abnormal and normal obsessions. *Behaviour Research and Therapy*, 16(4), 233–248.

- **Radomsky, A. S., & Alcolado, G. M. (2010).** Don't even think about checking: Mental checking causes memory distrust. *Journal of Behavior Therapy and Experimental Psychiatry*, 41(4), 345–351.

- **Radomsky, A. S., Rachman, S., & Hammond, D. (2001).** Memory bias, confidence and responsibility in compulsive checking. *Behaviour Research and Therapy*, 39(7), 813–822.

- **Radomsky, A. S., Alcolado, G. M., Abramowitz, J. S., Alonso, P., Belloch, A., Bouvard, M., … Wong, W. (2014).** Part 1—You can run but you can't hide: Intrusive thoughts on six continents. *Journal of Obsessive-Compulsive and Related Disorders*, 3(3), 269–279.

- **Romanelli, R. J., Wu, F. M., Gamba, R., Mojtabai, R., & Segal, J. B. (2014).** Behavioral therapy and serotonin reuptake inhibitor pharmacotherapy in the treatment of obsessive–compulsive disorder: A systematic review and meta-analysis of head-to-head randomized controlled trials. *Depression and Anxiety*, 31(8), 641–652.

- Salkovskis, P. M., Wroe, A. L., Gledhill, A., Morrison, N., Forrester, E., Richards, C., ... Thorpe, S. (2000). Responsibility attitudes and interpretations are characteristic of obsessive–compulsive disorder. *Behaviour Research and Therapy*, 38(4), 347–372.

- Schuster, C., Hilfiker, R., Amft, O., Scheidhauer, A., Andrews, B., Butler, J., ... Ettlin, T. (2011). Best practice for motor imagery: A systematic literature review on motor imagery training elements in five different disciplines. *BMC Medicine*, 9, 75.

- Seligman, M. E. P., Steen, T. A., Park, N., & Peterson, C. (2005). Positive psychology progress: Empirical validation of interventions. *American Psychologist*, 60(5), 410–421.

- Simpson, H. B., Foa, E. B., Liebowitz, M. R., Ledley, D. R., Huppert, J. D., Cahill, S., ... Petkova, E. (2008). A randomized, controlled trial of cognitive–behavioral therapy for augmenting pharmacotherapy in obsessive–compulsive disorder. *American Journal of Psychiatry*, 165(5), 621–630.

- Steketee, G., & Frost, R. O. (2007). *Compulsive Hoarding and Acquiring: Therapist Guide*. Oxford University Press.

- Steketee, G., Frost, R. O., Tolin, D. F., Rasmussen, J., & Brown, T. A. (2010). Waitlist-controlled trial of cognitive behavior therapy for hoarding disorder. *Depression and Anxiety*, 27(5), 476–484.

- Steketee, G., & Shapiro, L. J. (2005). Predicting behavioral treatment outcome for agoraphobia and obsessive–compulsive disorder. *Clinical Psychology Review*, 15(4), 317–346.

- Stewart, S. E., Beresin, C., Haddad, S., Stack, D. E., Fama, J., & Jenike, M. (2008). Predictors of family accommodation in obsessive–compulsive disorder. *Annals of Clinical Psychiatry*, 20(2), 65–70.

- **Taillon, A., O'Connor, K. P., Dupuis, G., & Lavoie, M. (2010).** Comparison of inference-based therapy and cognitive therapy in the treatment of obsessive–compulsive disorder. *International Journal of Cognitive Therapy*, 3(2), 148–162.

- **Tolin, D. F., Abramowitz, J. S., & Diefenbach, G. J. (2005).** Defining response in clinical trials for obsessive–compulsive disorder: A signal detection analysis of the Yale–Brown Obsessive Compulsive Scale. *Journal of Clinical Psychiatry*, 66(12), 1549–1557.

- **Twohig, M. P., Hayes, S. C., Plumb, J. C., Pruitt, L. D., Collins, A. B., Hazlett-Stevens, H., & Woidneck, M. R. (2010).** A randomized clinical trial of acceptance and commitment therapy versus progressive relaxation training for obsessive–compulsive disorder. *Journal of Consulting and Clinical Psychology*, 78(5), 705–716.

- **van den Hout, M., & Kindt, M. (2003).** Repeated checking causes memory distrust. *Behaviour Research and Therapy*, 41(3), 301–316.

- **Veale, D., & Neziroglu, F. (2010).** *Body Dysmorphic Disorder: A Treatment Manual*. John Wiley & Sons.

- **Visser, H. A., van Minnen, A., van Megen, H., Eikelenboom, M., Hoogendoorn, A. W., Kaarsemaker, M., ... van Oppen, P. (2018).** The relationship between adverse childhood experiences and symptom severity, chronicity, and comorbidity in patients with obsessive–compulsive disorder. *Journal of Clinical Psychiatry*, 75(10), 1034–1039.

- Visser, H. A., van Oppen, P., van Megen, H. J., Eikelenboom, M., & van Balkom, A. J. (2015). Obsessive–compulsive disorder; chronic versus non-chronic symptoms. *Journal of Affective Disorders*, 152, 169–174.

- Watkins, E. R., Mullan, E., Wingrove, J., Rimes, K., Steiner, H., Bathurst, N., … Scott, J. (2011). Rumination-focused cognitive-behavioural therapy for residual depression: Phase II randomised controlled trial. *The British Journal of Psychiatry*, 199(4), 317–322.

- Wegner, D. M., Schneider, D. J., Carter, S. R., & White, T. L. (1987). Paradoxical effects of thought suppression. *Journal of Personality and Social Psychology*, 53(1), 5–13.

- Wheaton, M. G., Berman, N. C., Franklin, J. C., & Abramowitz, J. S. (2016). Health anxiety: Latent structure and associations with anxiety-related psychological processes in a student sample. *Journal of Psychopathology and Behavioral Assessment*, 38(3), 402–410.

- Wilhelm, S., Phillips, K. A., Didie, E., Buhlmann, U., Greenberg, J. L., Fama, J. M., Keshaviah, A., & Steketee, G. (2014). Modular cognitive-behavioral therapy for body dysmorphic disorder: A randomized controlled trial. *Behavior Therapy*, 45(3), 314–327.

- Wilhelm, S., & Steketee, G. S. (2006). *Cognitive Therapy for Obsessive Compulsive Disorder: A Guide for Professionals*. New Harbinger Publications.

- Wood, W., & Rünger, D. (2016). Psychology of habit. *Annual Review of Psychology*, 67, 289–314.

- Wong, S. F., & Tsai, C. F. (2015). Long-term outcome of obsessive–compulsive disorder in a naturalistic setting. *Psychiatry Research*, 225(3), 262–266.

www.ingramcontent.com/pod-product-compliance
Lightning Source LLC
Chambersburg PA
CBHW072000150426
43194CB00008B/944